Macmillan Modern Languages
Series editor: Robert Clarke

Entrada

Robert Clarke

Language consultant: Rafael Sala

MACMILLAN
EDUCATION

First published 1989
Reprinted 1991

Published by
MACMILLAN EDUCATION LTD
Houndmills, Basingstoke, Hampshire RG21 2XS
and London
Companies and representatives
throughout the world

Designed by Raynor Design

Cover illustration by Susan Alcantarilla

Printed in Hong Kong

British Library Cataloguing in Publication Data
Clarke, Robert P
Entrada — (Macmillan modern languages).
1. Spanish language — Spoken Spanish
2. Spanish language — Examinations, questions, etc.
I. Title
468.3'421   PC4112
ISBN 0–333–45770–6

Cassette ISBN 0–333–48243–3
Teacher's pack ISBN 0–333–48352–9

Contents

Introduction

This book, and the cassette which goes with it, will help you to begin to learn Spanish: to speak it, to understand people who speak to you, to read it and to write it.

Types of work

Sometimes you will work with your teacher, sometimes by yourself and sometimes with a partner. You will always have a job to do — but make sure you know exactly what that job is before you start.

Things to learn

Each lesson begins with a list of the things you should be able to do in Spanish once you've finished the lesson. You will also find at the beginning of each lesson a list of *Frases clave*: the key phrases for the particular situations found in the lesson. You should try to learn this list, and the 'Words to learn' at the end of the lesson, by heart.

Working together

A lot of the work in this book involves swapping information in pairs (*Cada oveja con su pareja*): you look at one page and your partner looks at a different page and you ask each other questions to get certain information. You will soon get used to this, and it is more fun than working with the teacher all the time.

Understanding and checking

When you listen to or read Spanish, try to get the general idea first and don't give up if you meet a word you don't know. But if you are really stuck, the 'Words to Learn' at the end of the lesson or the complete 'Vocabulary List' at the end of the book should help. If you are writing Spanish, the 'Grammar Reference' for each lesson (Gramática) and the full 'Grammar Reference' at the end of the book will be useful.

¡Suerte!

Bienvenida a España

► Aims ◄

1 Finding out about Spanish in the world
2 Looking at some similarities between Spanish and English
3 Saying 'Hello' and 'Goodbye'
4 Saying how you are and asking how someone is
5 Giving your name and asking someone else's name

Spanish: a useful language

Six and a half **million** British people go on holiday to Spain every year. Perhaps you and your family have already been there. Find out how many of the pupils in your class have been to Spain and where they went. Then trace the map of Spain on page 6 into your exercise book and mark on the map where the members of your class went. Put each person's name near the name of the place and find out which other parts of Spain tourists visit. (Your teacher will help you if you do not know where the places are.)

Ask those pupils who have been to Spain to bring their photos or postcards to school and put them on a big map of Spain near the places they visited. Ask them what they liked about Spain and make a list of the things they liked. Did they like the food? Or the weather? Or the discos? Or the Spanish people?

It is difficult to get to know people if you cannot speak to them or understand them when they speak to you. The Spaniards are very friendly and are always delighted when someone has made the effort to learn a few words of their language. Unfortunately, many English-speaking tourists do not make the effort and think the best way to deal with foreigners is to talk loudly to them in English! What these people do not know is that, when you can speak Spanish, people are friendlier to you, services improve and you have a much better holiday among the Spanish people. It is **not** true that everyone in Spain who works in the tourist areas speaks English. Ask any of your friends who have been there. But it **is** true that if you can speak Spanish, you can explore Spain much better, meet fascinating people and see far more of the country than someone who can only speak English.

Spanish: an important language

Even if Spanish were spoken only in Spain, it would still be worth learning it; but Spanish is an international language spoken in nineteen countries in Latin America. At the United Nations there are only five official languages: English, Spanish, Russian, Chinese and French. The table will show you where Spanish stands in the world league of languages and how many people speak it as their first language. The map below shows you where Spanish is spoken in Latin America and the numbers tell you how many million speakers of Spanish there are in each country.

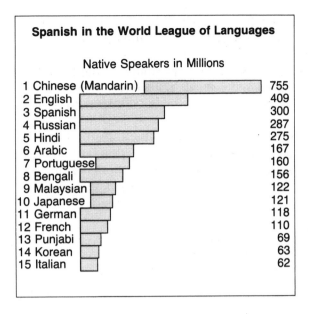

Spanish in the World League of Languages

Native Speakers in Millions

	Language	Native Speakers in Millions
1	Chinese (Mandarin)	755
2	English	409
3	Spanish	300
4	Russian	287
5	Hindi	275
6	Arabic	167
7	Portuguese	160
8	Bengali	156
9	Malaysian	122
10	Japanese	121
11	German	118
12	French	110
13	Punjabi	69
14	Korean	63
15	Italian	62

Cuba 10 000 000
Honduras 4 200 000
República Dominicana 6 300 000
México 77 700 000
Guatemala 8 000 000
Nicaragua 2 900 000
Puerto Rico 3 300 000
El Salvador 5 000 000
Venezuela 18 600 000
Costa Rica 2 500 000
Colombia 28 200 000
Panamá 2 100 000
Ecuador 9 100 000
Perú 19 200 000
Bolivia 6 000 000
Paraguay 3 600 000
Uruguay 3 000 000
Chile 11 900 000
Argentina 29 100 000
(España) 38 400 000

The United States of America has a lot of Spanish speakers and there are fifteen million Americans who speak Spanish. In the world there are more than 300 million people who speak Spanish and, by the year 2000, when you might be looking for work, there will be more than 400 million. With the Spanish you are going to learn and the English you speak already, you will be able to speak to more people in more countries than with any other two languages. That could be important to you in whatever career you intend to follow.

Spanish: an easy language

Spanish and Italian are the easiest languages for English-speaking people to learn. There are no sounds in Spanish that we do not already have somewhere in English, and once you have learned these sounds you say exactly what you see and you write exactly what you hear.

Here are four foreign languages. After you have listened to each person speaking, write down which language you think it is. The four languages are Russian, French, German and Spanish, though not necessarily in that order.

The answer is on page 12.

You already know quite a lot of Spanish words, because the Spaniards have borrowed words from English. What do you think these Spanish words are in English?

el fútbol	la radio
el rugby	la televisión
el críquet	el animal
el tenis	el jersey
el béisbol	el suéter

(El and la are just the words for 'The'.) Other Spanish words are quite similar to English words, and you can guess what they mean.

What do you think these Spanish words are in English?

la fotografía	la chaqueta
la bicicleta	la lección
la motocicleta	el dentista
la farmacia	la fruta
la clase	el accidente

Ask the pupils in the class who have been to Spain if they can remember any Spanish words they heard or saw. Your teacher will tell you how to say them correctly and will tell you what they mean if you cannot guess the meaning. Put a list of the important words you discover on the classroom wall and learn them.

Now we can begin

In each lesson you will find a list of important words and sentences which you must learn by heart. This list is called *Frases clave* (Key phrases).

Frases clave

¡Hola! Hello.
Hasta luego. See you soon.
Adiós. Good-bye.
¿Qué tal? How are you?
Muy bien, gracias. Very well, thank you.
¿Cómo te llamas? What's your name? (What are you called?)
Me llamo Juan. My name is John. (I'm called John)

 ### Conversaciones

1 ¡Hola!

Chico: ¡Hola!
Chica: ¡Hola!
Chico: ¿Qué tal?
Chica: Muy bien, gracias. ¿Y tú?

Chico: Muy bien. ¿Cómo te llamas?
Chica: Me llamo Ana. ¿Y tú?
Chico: Me llamo Juan.

2 ¿Qué tal?

Chica: ¡Hola! ¿Qué tal?
Chico: Muy bien, gracias. ¿Cómo te llamas?
Chica: Me llamo Marta. ¿Y tú? ¿Cómo te llamas?
Chico: Me llamo Paco.
Chica: Muy bien. Adiós, Paco.
Chico: Adiós, Marta. Hasta luego.

Work with your partner until you can say both conversations correctly. Then look at this list of Spanish names and find your own name. If it is not there, choose a name you like and practise the conversations further with three different people.

Chicos (Boys)	*Chicas* (Girls)
Agustín	Alicia
Alberto	Amelia
Alfonso	Anita
Andrés	Carmen
Antonio	Carolina
Arturo	Clara
Carlos	Cristina
Diego	Dolores
Emilio	Dora
Federico	Elena
Felipe	Francisca
Francisco	Gloria
Jaime	Isabel
Jorge	Juanita
José	Luisa
Juan	Margarita
Luis	María
Manuel	Mercedes
Pablo	Pepita
Paco	Pilar
Pedro	Rita
Rafael	Rosario
Ricardo	Rosita
Roberto	Susana
Tomás	Teresa

Remember that Spanish people shake hands when they greet each other. Move around the class, greet other pupils, ask how they are and what they are called in Spanish. Try to write down their names and then check them with the list.

When you speak to your teacher, you put *don* (for a man) or *doña* (for a woman) in front of the name:

¡Hola, don Luis!
¡Hola, doña María!

And when you say good-bye, you again put don or *doña* in front of the name:

Adiós, don Luis.
Hasta luego, doña María.

Spain: a fascinating country

If you have been to Spain, or have seen tourist brochures, you may think that the whole of Spain is like the photographs on page 5. Nothing could be further from the truth. Whatever interests you, Spain can offer it. If you like walking, what better place for a stroll than the Valle de Arán in the province of Lérida in the north of Spain? If you are interested in ancient buildings, you could not find a better example than the Roman aqueduct in Segovia, and if you like exploring old castles, you could spend several fascinating hours in the Alcázar, also in Segovia.

Perhaps you prefer modern cities with discotheques, shops and street markets. If you do, the Ramblas in Barcelona will provide you with all you want. You already know that Spain can offer magnificent beaches with a full range of water sports, but did you know that in the south of Spain, near Granada, you can go skiing in the morning and, after a short drive, swim in a warm sea in the afternoon?

You could spend a lifetime exploring Spain and its history and still not have time to see everything Spain has to offer.

Words to learn

You should learn these words by heart lesson by lesson. The Vocabulary List at the back of the book contains all the words used in the book and it can be used to look up words you have forgotten.

Ch and *ll* are separate letters in Spanish. Words which begin *ch* are found after words which begin *c*, and *ll* are found after those which begin *l*.

accidente(m)	accident	*¡hola!*	hello
adiós	goodbye	*jersey(m)*	jersey
animal(m)	animal	*lección(f)*	lesson
béisbol(m)	baseball	*llamarse*	to be called
bicicleta(f)	bicycle	*me llamo*	I'm called
bien	well	*te llamas*	you're called
clase(f)	class	*motocicleta(f)*	motorbicycle
¿cómo?	how? what?	*muy*	very
críquet(m)	cricket	*muy bien*	very well
chaqueta(f)	jacket	*¿qué?*	what? which?
dentista(m)	dentist	*¿qué tal?*	how are you?
farmacia(f)	chemist's	*radio(f)*	radio
fotografía(f)	photograph	*rugby(m)*	rugby
fruta(f)	fruit	*suéter(m)*	sweater
hasta	until	*televisión(f)*	television
hasta luego	see you later	*tenis(m)*	tennis

Answer to language quiz

The languages were: German, French, Spanish and Russian.

¿Quién eres tú?

► Aims ◄

1 Giving your full name
2 Saying how old you are
3 Giving your nationality
4 Saying where you are from

Frases clave

1 ¿Cómo te llamas?

¿Cómo te llamas?   What's your name?

Me llamo Nick Wood.   I'm called Nick Wood.

2 ¿Cuántos años tienes?

¿Cuántos años tienes?   How old are you?

Tengo doce años.   I'm twelve (years old).

Tengo once años.   I'm eleven.

Tengo trece años.   I'm thirteen.

3 ¿Eres inglés?

¿Eres inglés?   Are you English? (Boy)

Sí, soy inglés.   Yes, I'm English (Boy)

¿Eres inglesa?   Are you English? (Girl)

Sí, soy inglesa.   Yes, I'm English. (Girl)

¿Eres escocés/escocesa?   Are you Scottish? (Boy/Girl)

No, soy irlandés/irlandesa.   No, I'm Irish. (Boy/Girl)

¿Eres galés/galesa?   Are your Welsh? (Boy/Girl)

Sí, soy galés/galesa.   Yes, I'm Welsh. (Boy/Girl)

¿Eres australiano/a?   Are you Australian? (Boy/Girl)

Sí, soy australiano/a.   Yes, I'm Australian. (Boy/Girl)

¿Eres canadiense?   Are you Canadian? (Boy & Girl)

Sí, soy canadiense.   Yes, I'm Canadian. (Boy & Girl)

¿Eres neozelandés/neozelandesa?   Are you a New Zealander? (Boy/Girl)

No, no soy neozelandés/neozelandesa.   No, I'm not a New Zealander (Boy/Girl)

¿Eres español/española?   Are you Spanish? (Boy/Girl)

Sí, soy español/española.   Yes, I'm Spanish. (Boy/Girl)

4 ¿Eres de aquí?

¿Eres de aquí?   Are you from around here?

Sí, soy de aquí.   Yes, I'm from around here.

No, no soy de aquí.   No, I'm not from around here.

¿De dónde eres?   Where are you from?

Soy de Newcastle.   I'm from Newcastle.

 ## Conversaciones

1 Un grupo de chicos ingleses en un club de jóvenes en España

Chico: ¡Hola! Bienvenida al club.
Chica: Gracias. ¿Cómo te llamas?
Chico: Me llamo Manolo. ¿Y tú? ¿Cómo te llamas?
Chica: Me llamo Mary. María en español, ¿no?
Chico: Eso es. ¿De dónde eres, María?
Chica: Soy de Liverpool.

2 Otro chico y otra chica

Chica: ¡Hola! ¿Qué tal?
Chico: Muy bien, gracias. ¿Y tú?
Chica: Bien. Me llamo Ana. ¿Cómo te llamas tú?
Chico: Me llamo Pedro. Peter en inglés, ¿no?
Chica: Sí, eso es. ¿Eres de aquí?
Chico: Sí, soy de aquí, de Ávila.

3 Dos chicos más

Chico: ¡Hola! Te llamas Marta, ¿no?
Chica: Eso es. ¿Cómo te llamas tú?
Chico: Me llamo Rafael y tengo doce años. ¿Cuántos años tienes?
Chica: Tengo doce años. ¿Eres de Ávila?
Chico: Sí, soy de Ávila. ¿De dónde eres tú?
Chica: Soy de Bootle.
Chico: Eres escocesa, ¿no?
Chica: No, soy inglesa. Y tú eres español, ¿no?
Chico: Claro.

4 El director del club y un chico

Director: ¡Hola! ¿Cómo te llamas?
Chico: David. ¿Y tú?
Director: Alberto.

Chico: ¿Eres de Ávila?
Director: Eso es. ¿De dónde eres tú?
Chico: De Newcastle.
Director: ¿Eres inglés o australiano?
Chico: Soy australiano.

 ## ¿Comprendes?

Do you understand? Can you answer the following questions in English?

Primera conversación

1 What are the two young people called?
2 Where is the girl from?
3 What is her name in Spanish?

Segunda conversación

1 What is Pedro's name in English?
2 Where is he from?

Tercera conversación

1 What is the boy's name and where is he from?
2 What nationality does he think Marta is?
3 What nationality is she?

Cuarta conversación

1 What do you find out about the director of the club?
2 What do you find out about the boy?

 ## Vamos a hablar

Now work with your partner and practise the four conversations until you can say them as well as the Spanish speakers. Then change the conversations to fit yourself, putting your name, age and town in place of the ones found in the book.

 ## Cada oveja con su pareja (Pair-work)

Partner B: Turn to page 175 for your instructions.

Partner A: Your partner is going to ask you some questions. Reply to them as if you were the boy in the photograph, using the information given here. Then, when you have answered his/her questions, ask your partner the questions in the left-hand column. Make a note of his/her answers.

¿Cómo te llamas?   José Pérez.
¿Cuántos años tienes?   13.
¿De dónde eres?   Ávila.
¿Eres inglesa o española?   Español.

When you have finished, do the exercise again but this time give genuine answers.

Actividades

¿Cómo te llamas? ¿Cuántos años tienes?
¿De dónde eres? ¿Eres español (española) o
inglés (inglesa) o ¿qué?

You are each person in turn. Say who you
are, give your age, say where you are from
and what your nationality is. (Remember
that if you are a girl in some of them,
you must say: *inglesa, española, galesa,
escocesa, irlandesa*, etc.) For example:

*Me llamo Peter. Tengo doce años. Soy de
Londres. Soy inglés.*

Peter	12	Londres
María	8	Ávila
Manolo	13	Madrid
Alice	11	Glasgow
Paco	10	Sevilla
David	14	Cardiff
Carmen	7	Bilbao
Lucy	9	Belfast
Sharon	15	Auckland
Ana	6	Toledo

Sopa de letras – Letter soup

Start from the top left-hand corner and go
from letter to letter to find the message.
Some of the words are written backwards.
Copy the message into your writing book.
Do not write in the text book.

M	X	O	T	K	E	A	Z	I	L
E	L	J	N	M	C	Ñ	R	P	S
T	L	W	X	I	O	O	Y	Y	E
Z	A	B	C	D	D	S	F	O	S
G	M	O	I	G	O	S	L	S	P
A	T	Z	S	N	O	O	K	A	A
E	R	C	A	E	P	Y	D	L	Ñ
R	C	E	B	T	T	R	E	L	O
Z	L	F	E	L	V	W	S	I	L
M	D	G	B	W	O	H	E	V	A

Sopa de números – Number soup

Unscramble the following mixed-up
numbers. Write them out correctly and put
the number alongside. For example:

Nocic = cinco = 5

1 trucao   6 zeid
2 crete   7 code
3 sert   8 tiees
4 cretoca   9 nuo
5 noec   10 ceinqu

Ejercicios

Ejercicio número uno

¿Cuántos hay? (How many are there?)

Give a single Spanish number to say how many players there are in the following teams. For example:

¿Cuántos hay en un equipo de críquet?
  Once.

1 *¿Cuántos hay en un equipo de fútbol?*
2 *¿Cuántos hay en un equipo de rugby?*
3 *¿Cuántos hay en un equipo de béisbol?*
4 *¿Cuántos hay en un equipo de baloncesto (basketball)?*
5 *¿Cuántos hay en un equipo de críquet?*

Ejercicio número dos

¿Cuántos hay?

Give a single Spanish number in answer to each question. For example:

¿Cuántas personas hay en esta familia?
  Seis.

1 *¿Cuántos gatos hay en este árbol?*

2 *¿Cuántos perros hay en este campo?*

3 *¿Cuántas serpientes hay en este zoo?*

4 *¿Cuántos hámsters hay en esta jaula?*

5 *¿Cuántos peces hay en esta pecera?*

Ejercicio número tres

¿De dónde eres?

Say what nationality these people are. For example:

Me llamo Peter y soy de Londres. Eres inglés, ¿no?

1 Me llamo María y soy de Málaga.
2 Me llamo Irene y soy de Edimburgo.
3 Me llamo Paco y soy de Madrid.
4 Me llamo Anne y soy de Belfast.
5 Me llamo Martin y soy de Melbourne.

Ejercicio número cuatro

Ejercicio escrito

Copy out these sentences and fill in the gaps in the words. Each full stop = one missing letter.

1 ¡Hol.! Me ll... Pedro y soy d. Madrid.
2 Ten.. doce a... y soy ingl..
3 No so. galés; soy españ..
4 Me llamo Marta y tengo tr... años.
5 ¿Có.. te llam..? Me llam. Rafael.

My Personal Dossier

You can now begin to write your Personal Dossier in Spanish and, if possible, keep it in a folder, separate from your other written work. Decorate it with photographs, sketches, plans of your house and bedroom, etc. For the first section, try to say something about yourself in answer to the following questions:

¿Cómo te llamas? ¿Cuántos años tienes? ¿De dónde eres? ¿Eres inglés (inglesa), escocés (escocesa), galés (galesa), irlandés (irlandesa), australiano (australiana), canadiense o neozelandés (neozelandesa)?

Vamos a escuchar (Let's listen to some Spanish)

Same or different?

Listen to the Spanish speakers on the tape, each of whom says two words. If you think the two words are the same, put a tick next to the number of the taped item and, if you think they are different, put a cross.

Which is the odd one out?

On the tape, you will hear people saying three Spanish words each. Listen to these words carefully. Then write down 1, 2 or 3 for the word you think is different from the other two. For example, if you think the second word is different, you will write 2.

Who are they?

Now listen to the girl talking on the tape, and write down in English her name, her age, where she is from and what her nationality is.

Do the same with the boy talking on the tape.

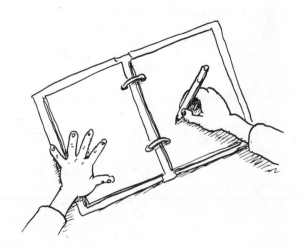

Lectura

Read carefully these openings to three
letters received from Spanish young people
and then write down in English what you
have learned about them.

Querida Ana: Málaga, 12 de enero

¡Hola! Me llamo Asunción y tengo trece años.
Soy de Málaga, una ciudad en el sur de
España. Hay cinco personas en mi familia: mi
madre, mi padre, yo y mis dos hermanos...

Querido Peter: Bilbao, 2 de mayo

¡Hola! ¿Qué tal? Me llamo Felipe y soy
de Bilbao, una ciudad industrial del
norte de España. Tengo doce años. En
casa somos seis: mi padre, mi madre,
yo y mis tres hermanas...

¡Hola, amigo!   Alicante, 23 de abril
Mi nombre es Bernardo y soy de Alicante, una
ciudad en la costa mediterránea de España. Tengo
quince años. En mi familia hay tres personas:
mi padre, mi madre y yo. Soy hijo único...

Explanations

Greeting people

Remember that Spanish people shake hands when they meet even if they know each other very well. Girls and women kiss each other on both cheeks. *Hola* or 'Hello' is now a very common greeting among young people, and you will learn how to greet older people later in the book.

Gramática (Grammar)

Giving your name

In Spanish you say:

Me llamo Peter.   I'm called Peter. (I call myself Peter)

when someone asks your name with the question:

¿Cómo te llamas?   What's your name. (What do you call yourself?)

Giving your age

You say:

Tengo doce años.   I'm twelve. (I have twelve years)

when you are asked your age with the question:

¿Cuántos años tienes?   How old are you? (How many years do you have?)

Giving your nationality

You say:

Soy inglés.   I'm English. (If you are a boy)

Soy inglesa.   I'm English. (If you are a girl)

Soy canadiense.   I'm Canadian. (Used for both boys and girls)

That is how you answer the questions:

¿Eres inglés?
¿Eres inglesa?

Saying where you are from

You say:

Soy de Birmingham.   I'm from Birmingham.

This is the answer to the question:

¿De dónde eres?   Where are you from? (From where are you?)

Important things to notice

1 **Saying 'I' and 'you'**
There is a Spanish word for 'I', but you do not normally use it.
The simple Spanish word   *Soy* = I am...

Soy inglesa   I'm English. (A girl is speaking)

Soy de Leeds.   I'm from Leeds.

Eres = you are...
Eres español, ¿no?   You are Spanish, aren't you?

Eres de Toledo.   You are from Toledo.

It is difficult to mix up *soy* and *eres* and so the separate words for 'I' (*yo*) and 'you' (*tú*) are not usually spoken.

In the same way: *Tengo* = I have
Tengo doce años.   I'm twelve (I have twelve years)

Tengo dos hermanas.   I've got two sisters.

In the same way: *Tienes* = you have
Tienes once años.   You're eleven. (You have eleven years)

Tienes tres hermanos.   You have three brothers.

2 **Questions and exclamations**
In Spanish a question begins with a question mark upside down ¿ and finishes with one the right way up ? You must learn to begin all your questions with the upside down question mark. For example:

¿Cómo te llamas?

Exclamations start and end with exclamation marks in the same way. For example:

¡Hola!

3 **Stress marks**
Some words in Spanish have stress marks on certain letters. They are there to show you where

to put the stress on that word. For example:

Soy inglés. (You stress the last part of the word.)

You will also find stress marks on question words so that you will not mix them up with other words which are spelt the same. For example:

¿Cómo te llamas? ¿Cuántos años tienes? ¿De dónde eres?

How to say 'no' or 'not'

This is very simple in Spanish and you use the word no.

¿Eres inglés?	Are you English?
No.	No.

¿Tienes doce años?	Are you twelve years old?
No tengo doce años.	I'm not twelve years old.

The numbers 1–15

These you must learn!

uno	one	nueve	nine
dos	two	diez	ten
tres	three	once	eleven
cuatro	four	doce	twelve
cinco	five	trece	thirteen
seis	six	catorce	fourteen
siete	seven	quince	fifteen
ocho	eight		

Words to learn

año(m)	year	grupo(m)	group
aquí	here	hámster(m)	hamster
por aquí	around here	hermana(f)	sister
árbol(m)	tree	hermano(m)	brother
australiano	Australian	industrial	industrial
baloncesto(m)	basketball	inglés	English
campo(m)	field	jaula(f)	cage
canadiense	Canadian	madre(f)	mother
capital(f)	capital	mediterráneo	Mediterranean
casa(f)	house	naturalmente	naturally
ciudad(f)	city, town	neozelandés	New Zealander
claro	of course	norte(m)	north
club(m)	club	otro	other, another
club de		padre(m)	father
jóvenes	youth club	pecera(f)	fishbowl
costa(f)	coast	perro(m)	dog
chico(m)	boy	persona(f)	person
¿de dónde?	where from	pez(m)	fish
director(m)	leader, headmaster	¿quién?	who?
equipo(m)	team	ser	to be
escocés	Scottish	soy	I am
eso es	that's so	eres	you are
España(f)	Spain	serpiente(f)	snake
español	Spanish	sur(m)	south
familia(f)	family	tener	to have
galés	Welsh	tengo	I have
gato(m)	cat	tienes	you have
gracias (f.pl.)	thank you	zoo(m)	zoo

Mi familia y yo

▶ Aims ◀

1 Talking about your family
2 Giving names and ages of your family
3 Describing people

Frases clave

1 Mi familia

¿Cuántas personas hay en tu familia?   How many people are there in your family?

Hay cinco.   There are five.

¿Quiénes son?   Who are they?

Mi padre, mi madre, mis dos hermanos y yo.   My father, my mother, my two brothers and me.

¿Hay muchas personas en tu familia?   Are there many people in your family?

No, sólo hay tres.   No, there are only three.

¿Quiénes son?   Who are they?

Mi madre, mi hermana y yo.   My mother, my sister and me.

¿Tienes hermanos?   Have you any brothers or sisters?

Sí, tengo un hermano y una hermana.   Yes, I have one brother and one sister.

¿No tienes hermanos?   Don't you have any brothers or sisters?

No, soy hijo único.   No, I'm an only child.

2 ¿Cómo se llaman?

¿Cómo se llama tu hermana mayor?   What's your elder sister called?

Se llama Isabel.   She's called Elizabeth.

Y, ¿cómo se llama tu hermano menor?   And what's your younger brother called?

Se llama Pedro.   He's called Peter.

¿Cómo se llaman tus padres?   What are your parents called?

Mi padre se llama Juan, y mi madre se llama María.   My father is called John, and my mother is called Mary.

3 ¿Cuántos años tienen, y cómo son?

¿Cuántos años tiene tu hermana mayor?   How old is your elder sister?

Tiene veintitrés años.   She's twenty-three.

¿Cómo es tu hermana mayor?   What's your elder sister like?

Es alta y delgada.   She's tall and slim.

Y, ¿cuántos años tienen tus padres?   And, how old are your parents?

Mi padre tiene cuarenta años y mi madre tiene treinta y ocho años.   My father is forty and my mother is thirty-eight.

¿Cómo son tus padres?   What are your parents like?

Mi padre es bajo y gordo, y mi madre es alta y muy guapa.   My father is short and fat and my mother is tall and very beautiful.

¿Cuántos años tiene tu hermano menor?   How old is your younger brother?

Tiene trece años.   He's thirteen.

¿Cómo es?   What's he like?

Es bastante bajo y muy feo.   He's fairly short and very ugly.

Conversaciones

1 Mi hermana menor

Manolo:	¡Hola, Isabel! ¿Qué tal?
Isabel:	¡Hola, Manolo! Muy bien, gracias. ¿Y tú?
Manolo:	Regular. ¿Quién es esta chica?
Isabel:	Es mi hermana menor. Tiene once años, y se llama Mari-Carmen.
Manolo:	¡Hola, Mari-Carmen! ¿Cómo estás?
Mari-Carmen:	Bastante bien, gracias.
Manolo:	¿Eres inteligente como tu hermana, Mari-Carmen?
Mari-Carmen:	¡Claro que sí! Soy muy inteligente.

2 Una foto de mi familia

Juan:	¡Mira! Esta es una foto de mi familia.
Carmen:	Éste es tu padre, ¿verdad?

Juan:	Sí, es mi padre. Se llama Manuel, tiene cuarenta y dos años y es bajo y bastante gordo.
Carmen:	¿Es simpático?
Juan:	Sí, es muy simpático y también es bastante inteligente.
Carmen:	Y, ¿quién es este niño? ¿Es tu hermano menor?
Juan:	Sí, es el bebé de la familia. Sólo tiene tres años.
Carmen:	¿Cómo se llama?
Juan:	Paco.
Carmen:	¿Cómo es Paco?
Juan:	Francamente, es horrible. Es muy estúpido y también bastante feo.
Carmen:	Tu madre es muy guapa, ¿no?
Juan:	Sí, es muy guapa. Es muy cariñosa también.
Carmen:	Pero, ¿dónde estás tú en la foto?
Juan:	Yo soy el fotógrafo, tonta.
Carmen:	Ah, sí. Ahora comprendo.

3 No tengo hermanos

Pepe:	¿Tienes hermanos, Alonso?
Alonso:	No, no tengo hermanos. Soy hijo único. ¿Y tú? ¿Tienes hermanos, Pepe?
Pepe:	Sí, tengo una hermana y un hermano.

Alonso: ¿Cómo se llama tu hermana?
Pepe: Se llama Maruja.
Alonso: ¿Es menor que tú?
Pepe: No, es mayor. Yo tengo trece años y Maruja tiene diecisiete.
Alonso: Y, ¿cómo se llama tu hermano?
Pepe: Se llama Rafael, y tiene doce años.
Alonso: ¿Es menor que tú, entonces?
Pepe: Eso es.
Alonso: ¿Cómo son tus hermanos?
Pepe: Pues, Maruja es alta y delgada, y Rafael es bastante bajo y también bastante gordo.
Alonso: ¿Son simpáticos?
Pepe: Rafa es muy simpático, pero Maruja es antipática a veces.

 ## Comprendes?

Do you understand? Can you answer the following questions in English?

Mi hermana menor

1 How old is the younger sister?
2 What is she called?
3 Is she intelligent or stupid?

Una foto de mi familia

¿Verdad o mentira? (True or false?) Copy out and correct the ones you think are false.

1 The father is forty-three years old.
2 He is short and fairly fat.
3 The baby is called Paco.
4 He is eight years old.
5 He is very intelligent.
6 Juan is not in the photo because he took it.

No tengo hermanos

¿Comprendes? Can you answer the following questions in Spanish?

1 ¿Cuántos hermanos tiene Alonso?
2 ¿Cómo se llaman los hermanos de Pepe?
3 ¿Cuántos años tiene Maruja?
4 ¿Maruja es mayor o menor que Pepe?

5 ¿Cómo se llama el hermano de Pepe?
6 ¿Es mayor o menor que Pepe?
7 ¿Cómo es Maruja?
8 ¿Cómo es Rafa?

 ## Vamos a hablar

¿Cuántos hermanos tienen? ¿Cómo se llaman? ¿Cuántos años tienen?

Follow the lines, and then say how many brothers or sisters each person has, what they are called and how old they are.

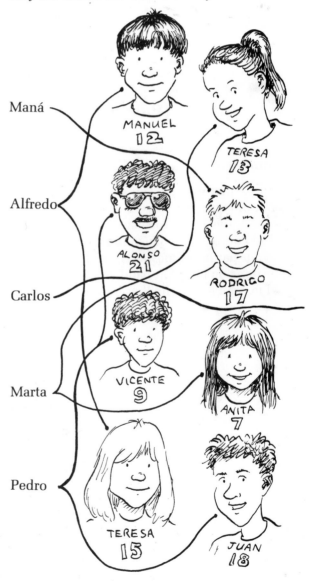

Cada oveja con su pareja (Pair-work) (1)

Mi familia

Partner B: Turn to page 175.

Partner A: You start first

Your partner is going to ask you some questions about your family. Use the information given in the right hand column to answer the questions. Then, when you have answered his/her questions, ask your partner the questions in the left-hand column, and make a note of his/her replies.

¿Tienes hermanos?	2
¿Son chicos o chicas?	1 hermana, 1 hermano
¿Cómo se llaman?	Pedro y Marta
¿Cuántos años tiene tu hermano?	15
¿Y cuántos años tienen tus hermanas?	17

When you have finished, do the exercise again but this time give answers for your own situation, ignoring any questions which do not apply.

Cada oveja con su pareja (Pair-Work) (2)

¿Cómo es?

Your partner will ask you some questions about the members of your 'family'. Use the pictures given here to answer the questions put to you. Then, when you have answered all your partner's questions, ask him/her the questions on the right-hand side of the page, and make a note of his/her replies.

¿Cómo es tu padre?
¿Cómo es tu madre?
Y tu hermano, ¿cómo es?
Y, ¿cómo es el bebé de la familia?

When you have finished, do the exercise again, but this time give answers for your own family and do not answer any questions which do not apply to you. For example, there may not be a baby in your family.

Ejercicios

Ejercicio número uno

¿Cómo es? ¿Cómo son?

Ejemplo:

¿Cómo es tu hermana?
Es alta y delgada.

¿Cómo son tus padres?
Son bajos y gordos.

1 ¿Cómo es tu padre?

2 ¿Cómo son tus hermanas?

3 ¿Cómo es tu hermano menor?

4 ¿Cómo son tus hermanos?

5 ¿Cómo es tu madre?

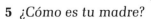

Ejercicio número dos

¿Cómo se llama tu madre? ¿Cuántos años tiene?

Ejemplo:

¿Cómo se llama tu madre?
Se llama María.
¿Cuántos años tiene?
Tiene cuarenta años.

1 ¿Cómo se llama tu hermano menor? ¿Cuántos años tiene?

2 ¿Cómo se llama tu padre? ¿Cuántos años tiene?

3 ¿Cómo se llama tu hermana mayor? ¿Cuántos años tiene?

4 ¿Cómo se llama el bebé? ¿Cuántos años tiene?

5 *¿Cómo se llama tu profesor/profesora de español? ¿Cuántos años tiene?*

6 *¿Cómo se llama tu amigo/amiga favorito/favorita? ¿Cuántos años tiene?*

Ejercicio número tres

Copy out these sentences into your writing book and choose the correct word from the three which are given. For example:

Mi madre es...   bajo/baja/bajos
Mi madre es baja.

1 *Mi profesor de*   feo/fea/feos
    inglés es...
2 *Mis hermanos son...*   gordo/gorda/
                                gordos
3 *Mi padre es...*   alto/alta/altos
4 *Mi hermana es...*   guapo/guapa/
                                guapos
5 *Mi amigo*   bajo/baja/bajos
    favorito es...

 ## My Personal Dossier

Write the next section to your Personal Dossier by talking about the members of your family, putting photos or sketches in where needed. Give the name, age and size of each member of your family. For example:

Mi hermano menor se llama Peter. Tiene ocho años. Es alto y delgado y muy inteligente.

 ## Vamos a escuchar

Listen carefully to this recording of a Spanish girl talking about herself and her family. Take notes and then write down what you have found out about their names, ages, height, etc.

 ## Lectura

¿Comprendes el español escrito?

Read the letter opposite carefully and then answer the questions in English.

1 How many people are there in the family?
2 What is the father like?
3 What is his name and how old is he?
4 What is his job?
5 What do you learn about the mother?
6 How does Carolina describe her brother?

Gramática

Adjectives

In this lesson you have learned about adjectives. Adjectives are used to describe people or things. Words like 'tall', 'short', 'fat', 'thin' are adjectives in English. In Spanish, adjectives change when they are used with different nouns. For example:

Gordo (Fat)
Mi padre es gordo   My father is fat.
Mi madre es gorda   My mother is fat.
Mis hermanos son gordos   My brothers are fat.
Mis hermanas son gordas   My sisters are fat.

All adjectives which end in o follow the same pattern as *gordo*.

Adjectives which end in anything else work differently. For example:

Mi padre es fuerte.   My father is strong.
Mi madre es fuerte.   My mother is strong.
Mis hermanos son fuertes.   My brothers are strong.
Mis hermanas son fuertes.   My sisters are strong.

You can see that 'fuerte' does not change when a single person or thing is being described, and it adds an 's' when two or more persons or things are being described.

Ávila, 23 de febrero

Querido Manuel:

Con esta segunda carta hay una foto de mi familia. El hombre muy alto y muy guapo es mi padre. Se llama Francisco y tiene cuarenta y dos años. Es profesor de inglés en el Instituto Santa Teresa de Ávila. Mi madre está cerca de mi padre. Se llama Dolores y tiene treinta y cinco años. Es secretaria en la oficina del Instituto. Yo soy la chica baja y bastante gorda y estoy al lado de mi madre. Como ya sabes, me llamo Carolina y tengo doce años. El chico muy feo y alto es mi hermano. Se llama Pepe. Tiene dieciséis años y es ¡horrible!

Escríbeme pronto con una foto de tu familia.

un abrazo muy fuerte

Carolina

'My' = mi

To say 'my' mother, sister, etc. you use *mi*, and, if you are talking about more than one person or thing, you say *mis*.

Mi padre es profesor.	My father is a teacher.
Mis hermanas son secretarias.	My sisters are secretaries.

Some more numbers

You must now learn the numbers 15–50. Here they are:

15	quince		26	veintiséis
16	dieciséis		27	veintisiete
17	diecisiete		28	veintiocho
18	dieciocho		29	veintinueve
19	diecinueve			
20	veinte		30	treinta
21	veintiuno		34	treinta y cuatro
22	veintidós		40	cuarenta
23	veintitrés		41	cuarenta y uno
24	veinticuatro		50	cincuenta
25	veinticinco		57	cincuenta y siete

You can see that numbers 1–29 are written as one word, and numbers 30–57, etc. are written as three words. For example:
45 = *cuarenta y cinco*.

Words to learn

abrazo(m)	embrace, hug		*hay*	there is, there are
alto	tall		*hermoso*	beautiful
amiga(f)	friend		*horrible*	horrible
amigo(m)	friend		*Instituto(m)*	secondary school
antipático	unpleasant		*inteligente*	intelligent
bajo	small, short		*lado(m)*	side
bastante	fairly, rather		*al lado de*	at the side of, beside
bebé(m)	baby		*mayor*	elder, bigger
cariñoso	affectionate		*menor*	younger, smaller
carta(f)	letter		*mi*	my
cerca(de)	near (to)		*mirar*	to look (at)
como	as, how, like		*mira*	look
comprender	to understand		*niño(m)*	boy
comprendo	I understand		*oficina(f)*	office
comprendes	you understand		*padres (m.pl.)*	parents
¿dónde?	where?		*profesor(m)*	teacher
ésta	this one		*regular*	O.K., average
estar	to be (position)		*saber*	to know, know how to
estás	you are		*sabes*	you know
éste	this one		*secretaria(f)*	secretary
estúpido	stupid		*segundo*	second
favorito	favourite		*simpático*	nice, pleasant (of people)
fotógrafo (m)	photographer		*sólo*	only
francamente	frankly		*tonto*	foolish, stupid
fuerte	strong		*tu*	your
gordo	fat		*único*	only
guapo	pretty, handsome		*ya*	already, now

Mi casa y mi ciudad

► Aims ◄

1 Saying where you live
2 Saying where your house is
3 Describing your house and town
4 Asking about your friend's house

Frases clave

1 ¿Dónde vives?

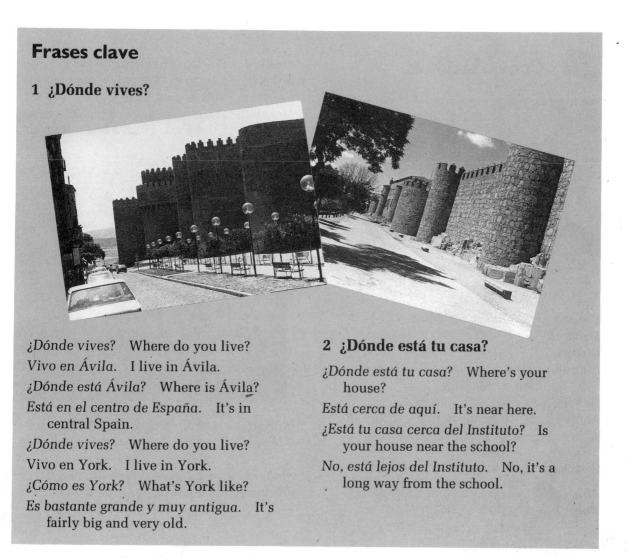

¿Dónde vives?   Where do you live?

Vivo en Ávila.   I live in Ávila.

¿Dónde está Ávila?   Where is Ávila?

Está en el centro de España.   It's in central Spain.

¿Dónde vives?   Where do you live?

Vivo en York.   I live in York.

¿Cómo es York?   What's York like?

Es bastante grande y muy antigua.   It's fairly big and very old.

2 ¿Dónde está tu casa?

¿Dónde está tu casa?   Where's your house?

Está cerca de aquí.   It's near here.

¿Está tu casa cerca del Instituto?   Is your house near the school?

No, está lejos del Instituto.   No, it's a long way from the school.

3 ¿Cómo es tu casa?

¿Cómo es tu casa?   What's your house like?

Es bastante grande.   It's fairly big.

¿Es grande tu casa?   Is your house big?

No, es muy pequeña.   No, it's very small.

¿Es moderna o vieja?   Is it modern or old?

Es moderna.   It's modern.

4 Y tu casa, ¿cómo es?

¿Cuántas habitaciones hay en tu casa?   How many rooms are there in your house?

Hay once.   There are eleven.

¿Es bonita tu casa?   Is your house nice?

Sí, es muy bonita.   Yes, it's very nice.

¿Está tu casa en el centro de la ciudad?   Is your house in the centre of the town?

Sí, está en el centro, cerca del Instituto.   Yes it's in the centre, near the school.

Conversaciones

1 ¿Dónde vives?

Robert: ¿Dónde vives, Manuel?
Manuel: Vivo en Toledo.
Robert: ¿Dónde está Toledo?
Manuel: Está en el centro de España, al sur de Madrid.
Robert: ¿Cómo es Toledo?
Manuel: Es bastante grande y muy antigua.

2 Tú vives en Londres, ¿verdad?

Manuel: Tú vives en Londres, ¿verdad?
Robert: No. Vivo en Basingstoke, una ciudad bastante cerca de Londres.

Manuel: ¿Es una ciudad antigua?
Robert: No, no es antigua. Es una ciudad muy moderna.
Manuel: ¿Es bonita?
Robert: No. Es una ciudad bastante fea.

3 ¿Dónde está tu casa?

Robert: ¿Dónde está tu casa en Toledo?
Manuel: Está en el centro de la ciudad en la Calle del Pozo.
Robert: ¿Está cerca del Instituto?
Manuel: No, está bastante lejos del Instituto. El Instituto está en la Avenida de América a un kilómetro de mi casa.

Robert: ¿Qué hay de interés en Toledo?

Manuel: ¡Huy, mucho! Hay la catedral, muchas iglesias muy antiguas y la Casa del Greco. Es una ciudad muy antigua y muy interesante.

4 ¿Cómo es Basingstoke?

Manuel: ¿Dónde está tu casa en Basingstoke?

Robert: Está en el centro, muy cerca del Instituto.

Manuel: ¿Qué hay de interés para los jóvenes en Basingstoke?

Robert: No hay mucho. Hay dos cines, tres discotecas y una piscina, pero es una ciudad bastante aburrida.

5 ¿Es grande tu casa?

Robert: ¿Es grande tu casa?

Manuel: No, es bastante pequeña. No hay muchas casas grandes en Toledo.

Robert: ¿Cuántas habitaciones tiene?

Manuel: Hay siete; la cocina, el comedor, un salón pequeño, un cuarto de baño y tres dormitorios.

Robert: ¿Tienes tu propio dormitorio?

Manuel: Sí, pero es muy pequeño.

6 ¿Cómo es tu casa en Basingstoke?

Manuel: ¿Es moderna o antigua tu casa?

Robert: Es muy moderna. Toda la ciudad es moderna.

Manuel: ¿Es grande o pequeña?

Robert: Es bastante grande. Hay nueve habitaciones; la cocina, el comedor, un salón bastante grande, dos cuartos de baño y cuatro dormitorios.

Manuel: ¿Tienes tu propio dormitorio?

Robert: Sí, tengo un dormitorio bastante grande.

 ¿Comprendes?

Do you understand? Can you answer the following questions?

Primera conversación

¿Verdad o mentira? (True or false?) Correct the ones which are false.

1 Toledo is in central Spain to the north of Madrid.
2 It is fairly big.
3 It is very old.

Segunda conversación

1 Basingstoke is quite near to London.
2 It is a very old town.
3 It is a fairly ugly town.

Tercera conversación

Answer in English.

1 Where is Manuel's house in Toledo?
2 Is his house near his school?
3 How far away is his school from his house?
4 What is there of interest in Toledo?

Cuarta conversación

Answer in English.

1 Where is Robert's house?
2 What is there of interest for young people in Basingstoke?
3 What sort of a town is Basingstoke?

Quinta conversación

Draw and label a plan of Manuel's house in Toledo.

Sexta conversación

¿Verdad o mentira?

1 All of Basingstoke is new.
2 The house described is quite small.
3 It has four bedrooms.
4 Robert shares a bedroom.

Vamos a hablar

Work with your partner on three of the six conversations until you can say them as well as the Spanish speakers. Then change the three you have chosen and make them fit the town and house you live in.

Cada oveja con su pareja

Partner B: Turn to page 176.

Partner A: Before you begin, copy the map on page 35 into your writing book, writing down all the information it contains.

Your partner will ask you where various towns and cities in Spain are. Use the information found on the map to answer the questions put to you. Then, ask your partner where the towns and cities mentioned below are, and write them onto your copy of the map.

¿Dónde está San Sebastián?
¿Dónde está Málaga?
¿Dónde está Alicante?
¿Dónde está Cáceres?
¿Dónde está Madrid?

¿Está cerca o lejos?

Check with your partner that your two maps are accurate, and then use them to ask each other these questions, taking turns to ask and answer.

¿Está Toledo cerca de Madrid?
¿Está Valencia cerca de San Sebastián?
¿Está Bilbao lejos de Málaga?
¿Está San Sebastián lejos de Bilbao?
¿Está Madrid lejos de Alicante?
¿Está Sevilla cerca o lejos de Cáceres?

¿Qué se dice? (What do you say?)

Work with your partner. One of you is A and the other B. Take turns to be A or B.

¿Dónde vives?

A: (Ask your partner where he/she lives.)
B: *Vivo en Toledo.*
A: (Ask him/her what Toledo is like.)
B: *Es bastante grande y muy antigua.*
A: (Ask what there is of interest in Toledo.)
B: *Pues, hay la catedral, muchas iglesias muy antiguas y la Casa del Greco.*

¿Cómo es tu casa?

A: (Ask your partner what his/her house is like.)
B: *Pues, es bastante grande.*
A: (Ask him/her whether it is a new or old house.)
B: *Es antigua.*
A: (Ask him/her how many rooms there are in the house.)
B: *Hay diez.*

¿Dónde está tu casa?

A: (Ask your partner where his/her house is.)

B: *Está en el centro de la ciudad.*

A: (Ask if it is near the school.)

B: *Está bastante lejos del Instituto.*

A: (Ask whether the school is old or modern.)

B: *Es muy antiguo.*

¿Cuántas habitaciones hay en tu casa?

A: (Ask your partner how many rooms there are in his/her house.)

B: *Hay siete; la cocina, el comedor, un salón, un cuarto de baño y tres dormitorios.*

A: (Ask if he/she has his/her own bedroom.)

B: *Sí, pero es muy pequeño.*

A: (Ask if it is a nice bedroom.)

B: *Sí, es bastante bonito.*

Actividades

¡Ataque! (Battleships)

Rule a piece of paper into thirty-six squares and number them 1–36. In five of the squares sketch the following animals, making sure your partner does not see them.

un *perro* (a dog) = 10 points
un *gato* (a cat) = 8 points
un *hámster* (a hamster) = 6 points
una *serpiente* (a snake) = 4 points
un *pez* (a fish) = 2 points

Take it in turns to shoot at your partner's squares with the question:

¿Qué hay en el número...?

The answers are:

Nada (Nothing)   i.e. a miss
En el número...hay... (In number...there is...)   i.e. a hit

The winner is the one who finds all the animals and wins 30 points. (By crossing out your first choice of squares and choosing others, you can play the game several times on the same piece of paper.)

 ## ¿Qué se dice?

Take it in turns with your partner to ask and answer the following questions.

1 *¡Hola! ¿Cómo te llamas?*
2 *¡Hola! ¿Qué hay?*
3 *¿Cuántos años tienes?*
4 *¿Es grande tu dormitorio?*
5 *¿Tienes hermanos?*
6 *¿Cuántos años tiene tu madre?*
7 *¿Cómo es tu ciudad?*
8 *¿Dónde vives?*
9 *¿Está tu ciudad cerca de Londres?*
10 *¿Cuántos son doce y seis?*

Ejercicios

Ejercicio número uno

Dibujos (Sketches)

Draw the following and display them on the classroom wall.

1 *Es alto, muy viejo y muy delgado.*
2 *En mi familia hay cuatro personas: mi padre, mi madre, mi hermano menor y yo.*
3 *Tengo un gato en mi dormitorio.*
4 *Mi hermana mayor es muy alta y delgada.*
5 *Hay tres gatos en la cocina.*

Ejercicio número dos

¿Verdad o mentira?

Read each of the following sentences carefully. If it is correct, write down the number of the sentence and mark it with a **v**. If it is incorrect, copy it out and correct it.

1 *Madrid es una ciudad muy grande en la costa del norte de España.*
2 *Toledo está al sur de Madrid.*
3 *Valencia está en el oeste de España.*
4 *Bilbao es una ciudad industrial en el norte de España.*
5 *Sevilla está en el este de España cerca de Valencia.*

Ejercicio número tres

¿Y la pregunta?

The following are answers. Can you write down the questions? For example:

Tengo doce años.   ¿Cuántos años tienes?

1 *Soy de Toledo.*
2 *Me llamo Manuel.*
3 *Muy bien, gracias.*
4 *Mi casa es bastante grande.*
5 *Mi Instituto está en el centro de la ciudad.*
6 *Mi padre se llama Federico.*
7 *No tengo mi propio dormitorio.*
8 *Hay seis personas en mi familia.*

9 *Barcelona está en la costa.*
10 *Vivo en Ávila.*

Ejercicio número cuatro

¡Búscalo!

Start with the circled letter and find the question and answer in each 'grid'. You can go in any direction you choose.

```
1  V  I  V  S        2  Ⓔ  N  O        B
   O  N  O  E           R  E  S  O  E  A
   É  D  Ⓓ  V           S  D  Y  D  R
   N  E  V  I           E  A     C
   L  E  O  N           Q  U     E
                           I     L
                                 O
                                 N
                                 A
```

My Personal Dossier

Continue writing your Personal Dossier by answering the following questions. You could add a labelled plan of your house or flat to the Dossier, together with any photographs you may have.

¿Dónde vives? ¿Está tu ciudad (pueblo) en el norte de Inglaterra (de Australia, del Canadá, de Nueva Zelanda)? ¿Es grande o pequeña tu ciudad (o pequeño tu pueblo)? ¿Cómo es tu casa? ¿Está tu casa cerca de tu Instituto? ¿Es grande o pequeña tu casa? ¿Cuántas habitaciones hay en tu casa? ¿Qué son? ¿Tienes tu propio dormitorio?

 ## Vamos a escuchar

Listen to the people on the tape, each of whom says a pair of sentences. If the second sentence is the same as the first, repeat it. If the second sentence is different, do not repeat it.

 ## La casa de una chica española

Listen carefully to the recording of a Spanish girl, and then select the correct answer from the ones given below.

1 The girl is called:
 a Isabel;
 b Inés;
 c Elisa;
 d Luisa.

2 She is from Barcelona which is a city:
 a in the south of Spain;
 b in the west of Spain;
 c in the north of Spain;
 d in the east of Spain.

3 Her house is:
 a in Las Ramblas;
 b in the city centre;
 c near to France;
 d near her school.

4 In her house there are:
 a ten rooms;
 b seven rooms;
 c eight rooms;
 d nine rooms.

5 The kitchen is:
 a very big;
 b very nice;
 c very small;
 d near the bathroom.

6 In the house there are:
 a two bedrooms;
 b four bedrooms;
 c three bedrooms;
 d five bedrooms.

7 In her room Isabel has:
  a a hamster;
  b a cat;
  c many posters;
  d a dog.

8 From home to school, Isabel has a journey of:
  a one kilometre;
  b two kilometres;
  c three kilometres;
  d four kilometres.

 ## Lectura

Read this letter from a Spanish penfriend carefully and then answer the questions in English.

> Málaga, 23 de abril
>
> Querido amigo:
>
> ¡Hola! ¿Qué tal? En esta carta hay una descripción de Málaga. Málaga es una ciudad bastante grande en el sur de España. Está en la costa y hay muchos turistas ingleses en la ciudad durante el verano. De interés para los turistas hay la Catedral y también las iglesias históricas de Santiago y del Sagrario. Hay también las ruinas del antiguo teatro romano en un parque de la ciudad. Mi casa está cerca del parque en el centro de Málaga. Es una casa bastante grande y muy bonita con una cocina pequeña, un cuarto de baño, un salón, un comedor y tres dormitorios. Mi dormitorio es pequeño pero es muy bonito con muchos pósters de mi grupo favorito en las paredes. Mi grupo favorito se llama Los Diablos y es muy popular en España ¿Cómo se llama tu grupo favorito? ¿Cómo es tu ciudad? Escríbeme pronto.
>
> Un abrazo de tu amigo,
>
> Paco Pérez.

1 List five things you have found out about Málaga from the letter.
2 List four things you have found out about your friend's house.
3 What do you learn about his room?
4 What does he ask you in his last two questions?

Explanations

Spanish houses

Most Spanish people live in flats because they live in big cities where houses are not easily affordable. The flats and houses are often larger than in other countries because Spanish families tend to be larger than families in many other parts of the world. The houses are generally more simply furnished than in other countries because the Spanish spend much of their time out of doors enjoying their good climate and entertain friends in cafés and restaurants rather than at home.

Gramática

Saying where you live

You use the verb *vivir* to say where you live.

Vivo en Londres.	I live in London.
¿Dónde vives?	Where do you live?
Manuel vive en un piso.	Manuel lives in a flat.

You will notice that the ending of the verb changes according to whether you wish to say 'I', 'you' or 'he'. If you learn this simple pattern, it will help you with other verbs later on. The pattern is:

viv**o**
viv**es**
viv**e**

and all verbs which end like *vivir* with the letters -ir follow the pattern.

How to ask questions

The easiest way is to use your voice to make the sentence into a question, and question marks when you write it down.

Eres inglés.	You are English.
¿Eres inglés?	Are you English?
Es española.	She's Spanish.
¿Es española?	Is she Spanish?

Another way is to put ¿no? at the end of the sentence.

Eres galés.	You are Welsh.
Eres galés, ¿no?	You are Welsh, aren't you?

Or you can use the word ¿verdad? to ask a similar question.

Es canadiense	He's Canadian
Es canadiense, ¿verdad?	He's Canadian, isn't he?

For other questions, you use question words at the beginning.

¿Qué? (What?)
¿Qué es?   What is it?

¿Dónde (Where?)
¿Dónde vives?   Where do you live?

¿De dónde? (Where from?)
¿De dónde eres?   Where are you from?

¿Cómo? [How, what?]
¿Cómo es tu casa?   What's your house like?

¿Cuántos/Cuántas? (How many?)

¿Cuántos dormitorios hay en la casa?	How many bedrooms are there in the house?
¿Cuántas habitaciones hay?	How many rooms are there?

How to change the meaning of adjectives slightly

You use words like *muy* or *bastante*:

Es tonto.	He's stupid.
Es muy tonto.	He's very stupid.
Es bastante tonto.	He's rather stupid. (He's fairly stupid.)

Saying where someone or something is

You use the verb *estar*.

Estoy en Madrid.	I am in Madrid.
¿Dónde estás?	Where are you?
Sevilla está en el sur.	Seville is in the south.

You already know another verb to say 'I am, you are, he is, etc.' but *estar* is a special verb to show **where** someone or something is. It is used to show the **position** of someone or something.

Masculine and Feminine

It sounds strange but everything in Spanish is either Masculine or Feminine. It is not just people that are Masculine or Feminine but everything — tables, chairs, houses — **everything**.

How do you know whether a word is Masculine or Feminine? Here are a few simple rules.

1 All male people are Masculine.

El profesor es alto.   The teacher is tall.
El chico es bajo.   The boy is short.

2 Nearly all words which end with the letter *-o* are Masculine.

El dormitorio es grande.   The bedroom is large.
El libro es pequeño.   The book is small.

3 All female people are Feminine.

La profesora es   The teacher is
  inteligente.   intelligent. (A female
                          teacher.)
La chica es delgada.   The girl is slim.

4 Nearly all words which end with the letter *-a* are Feminine.

La casa es vieja.   The house is old.
La discoteca es bonita.   The discotheque is nice.

5 In dictionaries and vocabulary lists you are told whether the word is Masculine or Feminine. For example:

director (m)   The small *m* tells you
                          that *director* is
                          Masculine.
persona (f)   The small *f* tells you
                          that *persona* is
                          Feminine.

6 The word for 'The' also tells you whether the word is Masculine or Feminine.

El director   The headmaster.
                        El tells you that *director*
                          is Masculine.
La directora   The headmistress.
                        La tells you that
                          directora is Feminine.

You also get help from the word for 'a' or 'an'.

Un profesor   A teacher.
                        Un tells you that
                          profesor is Masculine.
Una profesora   A teacher.
                        Una tells you that this is
                          a female teacher and
                          that the word is
                          Feminine.

Singular and Plural (Just one or more than one?)

To change a noun from the Singular to the Plural, follow these two rules.

1 Add the letter *-s* to any noun which ends with a vowel *-a*, *-e*, *-i*, *-o*, *-u*.

El chico es tonto.   The boy is stupid. (Just
                          one boy)
Los chicos son tontos.   The boys are stupid.
                          (More than one)

Notice that the word for 'the' has changed also from *el* to *los*.

La chica es tonta.   The girl is stupid. (Just
                          one girl)
Las chicas son tontas.   The girls are stupid.
                          (More than one)

Notice that the word for 'the' has changed also from *la* to *las*.

2 Add the two letters *-es* to nouns which end in anything else.

El profesor es aburrido.   The teacher is boring.
                          (Just one teacher)
Los profesores son   The teachers are boring.
  aburridos.   (More than one)
La habitación es   The room is small. (Just
  pequeña.   one room)
Las habitaciones son   The rooms are small.
  pequeñas.   (More than one room)

This means that you can **hear** the difference when someone is talking to you, and **see** the difference when you are reading.

Words to learn

aburrido	boring	interés(m)	interest
antiguo	old, ancient	interesante	interesting
avenida(f)	avenue	joven(m/f)	young person
bonito	nice, pleasant	kilómetro(m)	kilometre
calle(f)	street	lejos (de)	far (from)
catedral(f)	cathedral	moderno	modern
centro(m)	centre	oeste(m)	west
cine(m)	cinema	pared(f)	wall
cocina(f)	kitchen	piscina(f)	swimming pool
comedor(m)	dining-room	póster(m)	poster
¿cuánto?	how much?	pozo(m)	well (for water)
¿cuántos?	how many?	propio	own
cuarto de baño(m)	bathroom	romano	Roman
descripción(f)	description	ruina(f)	ruin
discoteca(f)	discotheque	salón(m)	sitting room
dormitorio(m)	bedroom	también	also
este(m)	east	teatro(m)	theatre
Francia(f)	France	turista(m/f)	tourist
grande	big, large	verano(m)	summer
habitación(f)	room	viejo	old
histórico	historical	vivir	to live
iglesia(f)	church	vivo	I live
importante	important	vives	you live

Mi dormitorio y mis cosas

▶ Aims ◀

1 Describing your bedroom at home
2 Talking about your pets
3 Talking about bicycles, computers, etc.

Frases clave

1 ¿Cómo es tu dormitorio?

¿Qué hay en tu dormitorio? What is there in your bedroom?

Pues, hay una cama, un armario, una mesa y una silla. Well, there's a bed, a wardrobe, a table and a chair.

¿Tienes pósters en las paredes? Have you got posters on the walls?

Sí, tengo muchos pósters. Yes, I've got lots of posters.

¿De qué son? What's on them?

Son de mis cantantes favoritos. They're of my favourite singers.

2 ¿Tienes algún animal en casa?

¿Tienes algún animal en casa? Have you got a pet at home?

Sí, tengo un perro. Yes, I've got a dog.

¿Cómo se llama? What's it called?

Se llama Tigre. It's called Tiger.

¿De qué color es? What colour is it?

Es marrón y negro. It's brown and black.

¿Es grande o pequeño? Is it big or small?

Es bastante grande. It's fairly big.

¿Qué come? What does it eat?

Come carne. It eats meat.

Tú tienes un gato, ¿verdad? You've got a cat, haven't you?

No, tengo una serpiente. No, I've got a snake.

¿De qué color es? What colour is it?

Es verde y amarilla. It's green and yellow.

¿Es larga o corta? Is it long or short?

Es larga; tiene un metro de largo. It's long; it's a metre long.

Y, ¿vive en la casa? And it lives in the house?

Sí, vive en una jaula en mi dormitorio. Yes, it lives in a tank in my bedroom.

3 ¿Tienes una bicicleta?

¿Tienes una bicicleta? Have you got a bike?

Sí, tengo una bicicleta. Yes, I've got a bike.

¿De qué color es? What colour is it?

Es roja y azul. It's red and blue.

¿Va deprisa? Does it go fast?

Sí, va muy deprisa. Yes, it goes very fast.

¿Vas al Instituto en bicicleta? Do you go to school on your bike?

Sí, voy en bicicleta todos los días. Yes, I go on my bike every day.

¿Tienes un ordenador? Have you got a computer?

Sí, tengo un ordenador. Yes, I've got a computer.

¿Qué haces con tu ordenador? What do you do on your computer?

Hago mis deberes y juego. I do my homework and I play games.

Conversaciones

1 ¿Cómo es tu dormitorio?

Carlos: ¿Tienes tu propio dormitorio, Elena?

Elena: Sí, tengo mi propio dormitorio. Es muy bonito.

Carlos: ¿Qué hay en tu dormitorio?

Elena: Pues, hay una cama, un armario, una mesa y una silla. También hay un tocadiscos y mi colección de discos.

Carlos: ¿Tienes pósters en las paredes?

Elena: Sí, tengo muchos pósters de mi grupo favorito.

Carlos: ¿Cuál es tu grupo favorito?

Elena: Se llama Los Diablos. Es fenomenal.

2 ¿Tienes animales en casa?

Andrés: ¿Tienes algún animal en casa, Anita?

Anita: Sí, tengo un gato.

Andrés: ¿Cómo se llama?

Anita: Se llama Fifi.

Andrés: ¿De qué color es?

Anita: Es blanco y gris.

Andrés: ¿Qué come?

Anita: Come pescado. ¿Tienes tú algún animal en casa, Andrés?

Andrés: No. Vivo en un piso muy pequeño y no hay sitio para animales.

Anita: ¡Qué lástima!

3 ¿Tienes una bicicleta?

Anita: Tú tienes una bicicleta, ¿verdad, Andrés?

Andrés: Sí, tengo una bicicleta. Es roja y amarilla.

Anita: ¿Adónde vas en tu bicicleta?

Andrés: Pues, voy al Instituto por la mañana y luego, por la tarde, voy a casa de mis amigos.

Anita: ¿No vas al campo?

Andrés: Claro que sí. Cuando hace buen tiempo, voy al campo con mis amigos.

Elena: ¿Tienes un tocadiscos en tu dormitorio, Carlos?

Carlos: No, no tengo un tocadiscos, pero tengo un ordenador.

Elena: ¡Un ordenador! ¡Qué suerte! ¿Qué haces con tu ordenador?

Carlos: Pues, hago mis deberes de matemáticas, y juego.

Elena: ¿Es difícil trabajar con un ordenador?

Carlos: No, no es difícil. Es muy fácil con un poco de práctica.

5 ¡Tienes una serpiente!

Felipe: ¡No me digas! ¿Tienes una serpiente en casa?

Ignacio: Eso es. Es negra y verde y tiene tres metros de largo.

Felipe: ¡Tres metros de largo! Pero, ¿dónde vive?

Ignacio: Vive debajo de mi cama en una jaula.

Felipe: ¿Qué come?

Ignacio: Come gatos, perros pequeños y queso.

Felipe: ¡Eso no es verdad! Las serpientes no comen queso.

Ignacio: Claro que no es verdad, tonto. No hablo en serio. Sólo tengo un ratón blanco muy pequeño que se llama Ronrón. Tiene ocho centímetros de largo y come queso.

Felipe: ¡No me digas! ¡Hombre! ¡Qué mentiroso eres!

 ## ¿Comprendes?

Do you understand? Can you answer the following questions?

Primera conversación

Can you make a plan of Elena's bedroom and label all the furniture and the other things she mentions?

Segunda conversación

Can you write down four things about Anita's pet?

Tercera conversación

1 What colour is Andrés's bike?
2 Where does he go on his bike?
3 When does he go into the countryside on his bike?

Cuarta conversación

1 Does Carlos have a record-player?
2 What does he have?
3 What does he do with it?
4 What is Carlos's opinion of working with computers?

Quinta conversación

1 Write down four things about the pet Ignacio does not have.
2 Write down four things about the pet he does have.

 ## Vamos a hablar

Rewrite the first conversation to fit your own bedroom and practise the result with your partner.

Practise the second conversation with your partner until you can say it as well as the native speakers. Then rewrite it to fit your own pet. (If you do not have a pet, imagine one.)

If you have a bike, rewrite the third conversation to fit your own bike. If you have a computer, choose the fourth conversation. If you have neither, choose the one you would like to have and rewrite one of the conversations to fit. Practise the result with your partner.

Work with your partner on the fifth conversation and produce a conversation as unlikely as the one that describes a three-metre cheese-eating snake. Some of the

following names of animals may help you:

un *elefante*   an elephant
un *león*   a lion
una *jirafa*   a giraffe
un *hipopótamo*   a hippopotamus
un *tigre*   a tiger
una *tarántula*   a tarantula spider

 ## Cada oveja con su pareja (I)

¿Cómo es tu dormitorio?

Partner B: Turn to page 176.

Partner A: Your partner will ask you questions about the bedroom in the picture below. Answer the questions, as if it were your bedroom, using the information in the picture. Then, ask your partner questions about his/her bedroom, and make a note of his/her answers: the questions are given below the picture.

¿Es grande tu dormitorio?
¿Cuántas camas hay en tu dormitorio?
¿Tienes un armario?
¿Hay sillas en tu dormitorio?
¿Tienes un tocadiscos?
¿Tienes algún animal en tu dormitorio?
¿Qué hay en la pared?

Cada oveja con su pareja (2)

¿Tienes algún animal en casa?

Partner B: turn to page 178.

Partner A: Your partner will ask you questions about your pet animal. Use the information in the picture to answer the questions. Then, ask your partner the questions about his/her pet animal which are given below the picture: make a note of his/her answers.

¿Tienes algún animal en casa?
¿Cómo se llama?
¿Es grande o pequeño?
¿De qué color es?
¿Qué come?

When you have finished, work through the questions again but answer them about your own pet, if you have one. If you do not have a pet, invent one.

Actividades

Odd one out

Find which word does not go with the others and say why.

1 Gato, gris, perro, hámster.
2 Queso, azul, blanco, negro.
3 Cama, casa, armario, mesa.
4 Grande, pequeño, largo, rojo.
5 Madre, padre, hermano, director.
6 Galés, irlandés, interés, español.
7 Salón, cocina, dormitorio, costa.
8 Críquet, clase, fútbol, rugby.
9 Catedral, cine, discoteca, habitación.
10 Otro, oeste, este, norte.

¿Qué quiere decir?

What do you say if you want to know her name, age, where she's from and if she has a pet animal?

¿De quién son estas cosas?

Trace the lines to find out which things belong to which people and write down all you find out about them. Start with a person's name in each case. For example:

Paco tiene un perro. El perro se llama Moreno. Tiene dos años y es marrón. Come carne.

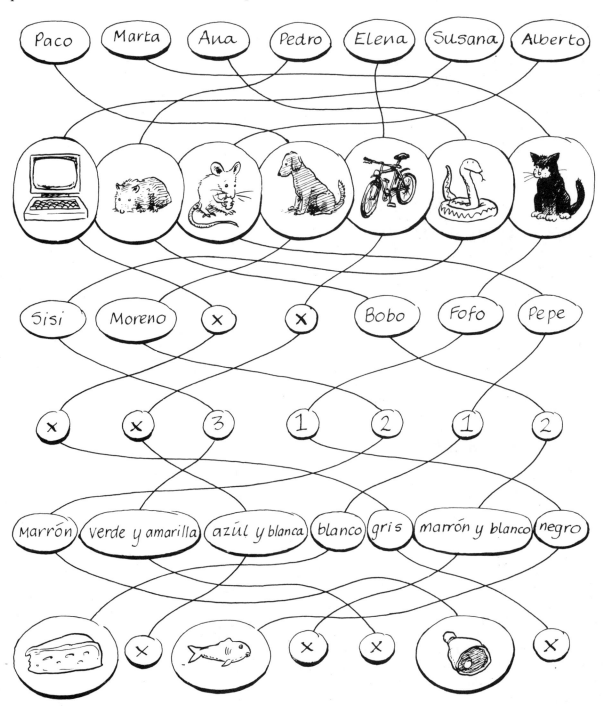

Busca las palabras

Five animals, five colours and five sizes are hidden in the square. When you have found them, write a sentence with one or more of the words in it, to show you know what they mean. For example, if you find *alta*, *jirafa*, *grande*, you could write: *La jirafa es grande y alta*. (Only one of these words is in the square.) All the words go across or down, and some of the letters are used twice. **Do not write in the textbook**.

K	L	Z	G	A	T	O	V
B	A	J	O	D	L	N	E
H	R	R	O	J	O	P	R
A	G	R	A	N	D	E	D
M	O	A	L	G	R	Q	E
S	P	E	R	R	O	U	A
T	Z	F	A	I	P	E	Z
E	J	N	T	S	Q	Ñ	U
R	A	C	O	R	T	O	L
T	W	X	N	E	G	R	O

 ## ¿Qué se dice?

Work with your partner. One of you is A and the other B. Take it in turns to be A or B.

¿Cómo es tu dormitorio?

A: *¿Cómo es tu dormitorio?*
B: (Tell him/her that it is small but very nice.)
A: *¿Qué hay en tu dormitorio?*
B: (Tell him/her you have a bed, a wardrobe, a large table and two chairs.)
A: *¿Tienes un tocadiscos?*
B: (Tell him/her that you don't, but you do have a computer.)

A: *¿Es difícil trabajar con ordenadores?*
B: (Tell him/her that it's quite easy with a little practice.)

¿Tienes algún animal en casa?

A: (Ask your partner if he/she has a pet animal at home.)
B: *Sí, tengo un hámster.*
A: (Ask what it is called.)
B: *Se llama Macho.*
A: (Ask what colour it is.)
B: *Es marrón y blanco.*
A: (Ask if it is big or small.)
B: *Es pequeño, tonto. Todos los hámsters son pequeños.*

¿Tienes una bicicleta?

A: *¿Tienes una bicicleta?*
B: (Say you do.)
A: *¿De qué color es?*
B: (Tell him/her it is blue and white.)
A: *¿Va deprisa?*
B: (Tell him/her that it goes fairly fast.)
A: *¿Adónde vas en tu bicicleta?*
B: (Tell him/her that you go to school in the morning and to the youth club in the evening.)

¡No me digas!

A: *¿Tienes una serpiente en casa?*
B: (Tell him/her that you do.)
A: *¿Cómo es?*
B: (Tell him/her that it is very big. It is four metres long.)
A: *¿De qué color es?*
B: (Tell him/her that it is yellow, red and black.)
A: *¿Dónde vive?*
B: (Tell him/her that it lives in a large tank in the bathroom.)
A: *¿Qué come?*
B: (Tell him/her that it eats fish, meat and fruit.)
A: *Eso no es verdad. Las serpientes no comen fruta.*

B: (Tell him/her that you are not talking seriously and that you do not have a snake. You have a small cat called Moto.)

A: ¡Qué mentiroso eres!

Ejercicios

Ejercicio número uno

Números flotantes

Match the floating numbers to the words, but be careful! There are more numbers than words.

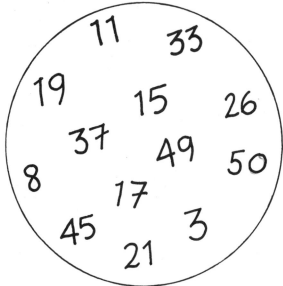

veintiséis
cuarenta y cinco
diecinueve
treinta y siete
quince

once
cincuenta
treinta y tres
veintiuno
cuarenta y nueve

Ejercicio número dos

¿Qué animal es?

Draw a quick sketch of the animal described. Write the Spanish name underneath.

1 *Vive en África o la India. Es gris, muy grande y muy fuerte. Tiene una trompa muy larga.*
2 *Se llama 'el amigo del hombre'. Hace 'guau' y come carne.*
3 *Es marrón y blanco y vive en una jaula. Su nombre español es muy similar al nombre inglés.*
4 *Es gris o negro o marrón o blanco. Hace 'miau' y come pescado.*
5 *Es verde y negra. Es muy larga. No hay muchas en Inglaterra.*

Ejercicio número tres

Write four sentences about each of the following:

1 *Mi amigo favorito/mi amiga favorita.*
2 *Mi profesor favorito/mi profesora favorita.*
3 *Mi animal favorito.*
4 *Mi clase favorita.*

For example, for **1** you could write:

Mi amigo favorito se llama Alan. Tiene doce años. Es alto y delgado. Tiene un perro negro en casa.

Ejercicio número cuatro

Draw the following and display them on the classroom wall. Take care, because some of them are rather odd!

1 *Tengo un gato que se llama Miriam. Es verde y rojo. Come fruta.*
2 *Mi profesor de matemáticas es muy alto y muy delgado. Tiene el pelo blanco.*
3 *En casa tengo una serpiente muy larga. Es roja y amarilla y come queso.*
4 *En mi habitación hay una jaula muy grande. En la jaula hay un cocodrilo muy grande que se llama Monstruo. Come profesores.*

My Personal Dossier

Continue writing your Personal Dossier by drawing a plan of your bedroom with labels on all the furniture and other objects. Add a photo or a sketch of your pet if you have one, or your bike or personal computer and write a few sentences about them.

 ## Vamos a escuchar

¡Hola a todos!

Your teacher has received a cassette from a Spanish school which is meant for all of you. Listen carefully and then answer the following questions in English.

1 Where is Paca from?
2 Where is that city?
3 Is it large or small?
4 Where is her house in the city?
5 What is her house like?
6 Where does she do her homework?
7 Who is her favourite singer?
8 Which is her favourite football team?
9 What is her pet's full name, and what do they call it?
10 How old is the pet?

 ## Lectura

Match the descriptions to the pictures. There is one description too many.

1

2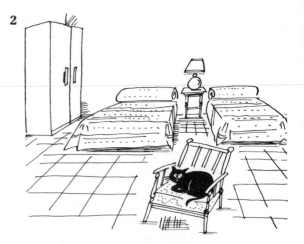

a En mi dormitorio hay una cama, una mesa grande y tres sillas. Tengo pósters en la pared.
b Mi dormitorio es grande y muy bonito. Mi hámster vive en una jaula pequeña en una mesa debajo de la ventana. En la pared hay pósters de mis cantantes favoritos.
c Mi serpiente vive en una jaula grande en una mesa debajo de la ventana en mi dormitorio. En el dormitorio también hay una cama, un armario, una mesa y dos sillas. En la pared tengo pósters de mi equipo de fútbol favorito.
d Mi gato es grande y negro. Su sitio favorito en toda la casa es una silla en mi dormitorio. En mi dormitorio también tengo dos camas, un armario y una lámpara en una mesa al lado de la cama.

Explanations

Pets in Spain

Pets are not as popular in Spain as they are in Britain. For example, there are certainly fewer dogs because most Spaniards live in flats where there is not enough room for dogs to play. However, cats are popular and many Spanish people have a pet cat. The most popular pet in Spain is probably a bird in a cage kept on the balcony of the flat where it can enjoy the fresh air and sunshine and sing as much as it wants.

In Madrid on Sunday mornings there is an enormous market called the Rastro, and one complete street of this market is given over to the sale of pets. There are puppies, kittens and hundreds of birds in tiny cages.

Some caged birds in Spain are used for hunting. A partridge is kept partly as a pet but also as a decoy. When the caged partridge is placed in a field, it calls out and other partridges come down to investigate. The hunter can then shoot them for food.

Pets in Spain are fed mainly from scraps and leftovers and so you will not see rows of tinned pet food in Spanish shops and supermarkets.

Gramática

Saying 'There is' or 'There are'

You use *hay* for both expressions.

Hay una serpiente en la cocina.	There is a snake in the kitchen.
Hay dos gatos en el salón.	There are two cats in the sitting-room.

More ways of asking questions

¿De qué color? (What colour?)

¿De qué color es tu bicicleta?	What colour is your bike?

¿De quién? (Whose?)

¿De quién es?	Whose is it?
Es de Paco.	It's Paco's.

¿Dónde? (Where?)

¿Dónde está el gato?	Where is the cat?
En la cocina.	In the kitchen.

¿De dónde? (Where from?)

¿De dónde es Marta?	Where is Marta from?
Es de Ávila.	She's from Ávila.

¿Adónde? (Where...to?)

¿Adónde vas?	Where are you going to?
Voy al Instituto.	I'm going to school.

Saying you have 'a lot' or 'much'

You use *mucho* which agrees with the noun.

Tengo muchos amigos.	I've got a lot of friends. (Male friends)
Tengo muchas amigas.	I've got a lot of friends. (Female friends)
No tengo mucho dinero.	I haven't got a lot of money.
Tengo mucha fruta.	I've got a lot of fruit.

An adjective to be careful with

Largo means 'long' so do not mix it up with *grande* which means 'big' or 'large'.

La serpiente es larga.	The snake is long.
El elefante es grande.	The elephant is big.

Where do you put adjectives?

In English, adjectives come in front of the noun, for example:
  'a blue bike'
but in Spanish they normally come after the noun, for example:
  una bicicleta azul.

Important regular verbs

Verbs are regular when they follow a pattern. *Comer* (to eat) is a regular verb and, in the singular, follows the same pattern as *vivir* (to live), seen in Lesson 4.

vivo	I live
vives	you live
vive	he/she/it lives

comer has the same pattern:

como	I eat
comes	you eat
come	he/she/it eats

For example:

Como mucha fruta.	I eat a lot of fruit.
¿Comes mucho?	Do you eat a lot?
Juan no come en casa.	John does not eat at home.

Important irregular verbs

Verbs are called 'irregular' when they do not follow a pattern, and with these ones you will have to learn each verb as it comes along. Many common verbs are irregular in Spanish, as they are in English.

Ir (to go)

voy	I go
vas	you go
va	he/she/it goes

For example:

Voy al Instituto.	I go to school.
Vas al campo.	You go to the countryside.
Marta va a la discoteca.	Martha goes to the discotheque.

Hacer (to do, to make)

Only the First Person Singular ('I') is irregular, the rest is regular.

hago	I do, make	These follow the
haces	you do, make	same pattern as
hace	he/she/it does, makes	*comer* or *vivir*

For example:

Hago mis deberes.	I do my homework.
Haces café.	You make coffee.
Pedro hace la cama.	Peter makes the bed.

Jugar (to play)

This verb changes the u for ue in the Singular forms (and in the Third Person Plural).

juego	I play
juegas	you play
juega	he/she/it plays

For example:

Juego al críquet.	I play cricket.
Juegas al golf.	You play golf.
María juega al squash.	Mary plays squash.

Saying 'your' in Spanish

You use the word *tu* for the singular and change it to *tus* for the plural.

Tu padre es inglés.	Your father is English.
Tus amigos son españoles.	Your friends are Spanish.

Talking about the weather

You use part of the verb *hacer* seen earlier with other words.

¿Qué tiempo hace?	What's the weather like?
Hace buen tiempo.	The weather is fine.

Saying how long something is

For length you use the word *largo* (long)

Tiene cinco metros de largo.	It is five metres long.

Exclamations

In English, exclamations end with an exclamation mark, for example:
How interesting!

In Spanish, they start and end with an exclamation mark, the first one upside down, for example:

¡Qué interesante!	How interesting!
¡Qué aburrido!	How boring!

For nouns, you use the same expression.

¡Qué chico!	What a boy!
¡Qué chicas!	What girls!

Adding emphasis to what you say

You use the word *claro* in the following ways:

¿Comprendes?	Do you understand?
Claro.	Of course.
Claro que sí.	Of course I do.
Claro que comprendo.	Of course I understand.
Claro que no.	Of course I don't.
Claro que no comprendo.	Of course I don't understand.

Words to learn

¿adónde?	where...to?	*gris*	grey
África(f)	Africa	*guau*	woof-woof
alguno	some	*hablar*	to speak, talk
amarillo	yellow	*hablo*	I speak, talk
armario(m)	wardrobe, cupboard	*hacer*	to do, make
azul	blue	*hago*	I do, make
blanco	white	*haces*	you do, make
cama(f)	bed	*hombre(m)*	man
cantante(m/f)	singer	*India(f)*	India
centímetro(m)	centimetre	*ir*	to go
cocodrilo(m)	crocodile	*voy*	I go
colección(f)	collection	*vas*	you go
color(m)	colour	*va*	he/she/it goes
comer	to eat	*jugar*	to play
come	he/she/it eats	*juego*	I play
con	with	*lámpara(f)*	lamp
corto	short	*largo*	long
¿cuál?	which, which one	*lástima(f)*	pity, shame
debajo [de]	underneath	*mañana(f)*	morning
deber(m)	duty	*por la mañana*	in the morning
deberes(m.pl.)	homework	*marrón*	brown
decir	to say	*matemáticas(f.pl.)*	mathematics
¡no me digas!	you don't say!	*mentiroso*	lying, liar
deprisa	fast, quickly	*mesa(f)*	table
día(m)	day	*metro(m)*	metre
todos los días (m.pl.)	every day	*miau*	miaow
difícil	difficult	*mucho*	much, a lot
disco(m)	record	*negro*	black
fácil	easy	*ordenador(m)*	computer
fenomenal	phenomenal, super	*para*	for, destined for
		pelo(m)	hair

pequeño	small, little	silla(f)	chair
pescado(m)	fish	suerte(f)	luck, good luck
poco	little, a little	tarde(f)	afternoon, evening
práctica(f)	practice	por la tarde	in the afternoon, evening
pues	then, well	tiempo(m)	weather
queso(m)	cheese	tocadiscos(m)	record-player
ratón(m)	mouse	trompa(f)	trunk (of elephant)
rojo	red	ventana(f)	window
ropa(f)	clothes	verdad(f)	truth, true
serio	serious		
en serio	seriously		

Un buen repaso

 Primera parte: Vamos a escuchar

Cinco españoles

Listen to these five Spanish people describing themselves on the tape, and then write down in English their full name, age, nationality and where they are from.

1

2

3

4

5

Escuchamos otra vez

Now listen to the same five people telling
you something about their families and
choose the correct answers from the ones
given below.

1 In this family, including the speaker,
  there are:
  a five people;
  b six people;
  c seven people;
  d eight people.

2 His father is:
  a 45 years old;
  b 35 years old;
  c 40 years old;
  d 45 years old.

3 His father is:
  a short and fat;
  b tall and fat;
  c tall and slim;
  d short and slim.

4 We know his father is very intelligent
  because he is:
  a an English teacher;
  b an architect;
  c a bank director;
  d a maths teacher.

5 His mother is:
  a rather fat and ugly;
  b rather fat but very pretty; ✓
  c very thin;
  d very fat.

6 The elder brother is called:
  a Pepe; ✓
  b Paco;
  c Pedro;
  d Juan.

7 He is:
  a thin;
  b short and fat;
  c tall and fat;
  d tall and slim like this father. ✓

8 The younger brother is:
  a very slim;
  b very stupid; ✓
  c rather fat;
  d quite intelligent.

Choose the correct description of this girl's
family and give your reasons for rejecting
the other two.

a Her family is small — she only has one sister. Her mother is thirty-five years old and her father is thirty-seven. She herself is rather short but quite pretty.

b In this family there are only three people: her parents and herself. Her mother is thirty-three years old and her father is thirty-eight. Her mother is quite tall and very intelligent and her father is short and fairly fat. She is very tall and, according to her friends, quite pretty.

c She is an only child and so there are three people in the family. Her mother is called Matilde and is thirty years old and her father is called Basilio and is thirty-eight. She is quite short but very intelligent.

Which is correct and which are incorrect?

a This man has a wife and two daughters.
b He is not married.
c He has a wife and three daughters.

1 In this girl's family there are:
  a seven people;
  b six people;
  c five people;
  d four people.

2 She has:
  a one elder brother;
  b one elder brother and one elder sister;
  c two younger brothers;
  d two elder brothers and one younger sister.

3 Arturo is:
  a 20 years old and a student;
  b 22 years old and a student;
  c 25 years old and a dentist;
  d 20 years old and unemployed.

4 Her younger sister is:
  a very pretty;
  b quite tall;
  c short and fat;
  d tall and pretty.

5 Both the speaker and her sister are:
  a working in an office;
  b pupils at a secondary school;
  c very tall;
  d very pretty.

Which of the pictures below best represents this person's family?

La casa de Andrés

Now listen to Andrés describing his house and choose the house plan from the three given below which best fits the description.

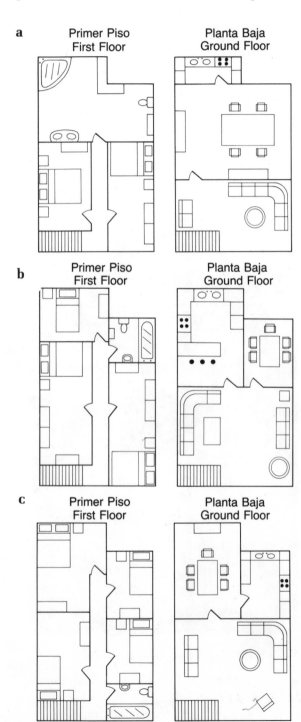

Mis animales

Now listen to these five people describing their pets and match up their names to their animals.

1 *Andrés*
2 *Gloria*
3 *Alberto*
4 *Pepita*
5 *Juan*

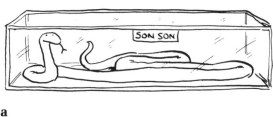

a

b

c

d

e

Segunda parte: Vamos a hablar

¿Qué se dice?

Work with your partner and practise the following role-plays. Use your Spanish name in the first one. Then take a new name, age, nationality, etc. and do it again. Take it in turns to play the part of A and B.

¿Cómo te llamas?

A: *¿Cómo te llamas?*
B: (Give your name.)
A: *¿Cuántos años tienes?*
B: (Give your age.)
A: *¿Eres español (española)?*
B: (Give your nationality.)
A: *¿De dónde eres?*
B: (Say where you are from.)

¿De dónde eres?

A: *¿De dónde eres?*
B: (Give the name of your town or village.)
A: *¿Es grande o pequeño (pequeña)?*
B: (Say what size it is.)
A: *¿Dónde está exactamente?*
B: (Say where your town/village is in the country.)
A: *¿Es una ciudad/un pueblo industrial?*
B: (Say whether your town/village is industrial.)

¿Cómo es tu familia?

A: *¿Cuántas personas hay en tu familia?*
B (Give the number of people.)
A: *¿Quiénes son?*
B: (Give details of parents, brothers and sisters.)
A: *¿Cómo se llaman tus hermanos/hermanas?*
¿Cómo se llama tu hermano/hermana?
B: (Give details of names.)
A: *¿Cuántos años tienen?*
¿Cuántos años tiene?
B: (Give details of age.)

¿Cómo es tu casa?

A: *¿Es grande tu casa?*
B: (Say whether your house is big or small.)
A: *¿Cuántos dormitorios hay?*
B: (Give the number of bedrooms.)
A: *¿Tienes tu propio dormitorio?*
B: (Say whether you have your own room or not.)
A: *¿Qué hay en tu dormitorio?*
B: (Describe the furniture, etc. in your bedroom.)
A: *¿Tienes pósters en las paredes?*
B: (Say whether your room is decorated with posters.)

Cada oveja con su pareja (1)

Make a sketch of the pet you would like to have. Give it a name, decide what colour it is, where it lives and what it eats, putting all these details onto the sketch.

Work with a partner; decide who will ask the questions first. Do not let your partner see the sketch, but use it to answer the questions put to you. Your partner will make a sketch of your pet from your description: compare this with your original.

When it is your turn to ask the questions, make a sketch of the pet your partner describes and compare it with your partner's sketch.

Here are the questions to ask:

¿Tienes algún animal en casa?
¿Cómo es, grande o pequeño/pequeña?
¿De qué color es?
¿Cómo se llama?
¿Dónde vive?
¿Qué come?

Cada oveja con su pareja (2)

Make a sketch of your bedroom with all the furniture and other things in it. Write on the sketch the colours of the things in your bedroom, or colour these in.

Work with a partner; decide who will ask the questions first. Do not let your partner see the sketch, but use it to answer the questions put to you. Your partner will make a sketch of your bedroom from your description, and indicate the colours: compare this with your original.

When it is your turn to ask the questions, make a sketch of your partner's bedroom, writing the colours on it or colouring the items in: compare the result with your partner's sketch.

Here are the questions to ask:

¿Es grande o pequeño tu dormitorio?
¿Qué hay en tu dormitorio?
¿Tienes televisión en tu dormitorio?
¿Tienes pósters en las paredes?
¿De qué son?
¿De qué color son las paredes?
¿Tienes un tocadiscos en tu dormitorio?
¿Tienes un ordenador?

Tercera parte: Vamos a leer

Una carta de Lola

Read this page from a letter written by a Spanish girl and answer the questions in English.

1. Where is Lola's house?
2. How many rooms are there?
3. Where is the bathroom?
4. What is there at the side of the house?
5. What is there behind the house?
6. Where is Lola's bedroom?
7. What does she use the table for?
8. Who is her favourite singer?
9. Is her English record collection up to date?

2

Mi casa está en el centro de la ciudad cerca del Instituto. Es una casa bastante grande con ocho habitaciones: una cocina, un comedor y un salón bastante grande en la planta baja y cuatro dormitorios y un cuarto de baño en el primer piso. Al lado de la casa hay un garaje donde guardamos el coche y detrás de la casa hay un jardín bastante grande y muy bonito con árboles y flores. Mi dormitorio está al lado del cuarto de baño y es bastante pequeño. En el dormitorio tengo una cama grande y muy cómoda, un armario para mi ropa, una mesa pequeña donde hago mis deberes y dos sillas. También tengo mi tocadiscos y mi colección de discos. Mi cantante favorito se llama Julio Iglesias y, naturalmente, es español, pero tengo también muchos discos de cantantes ingleses como los Beatles y los Rolling Stones.

Por la mañana voy al Instituto con mi hermana, Isabel, y estudio muchas asignaturas. Para mí el inglés es muy difícil. ¿Es fácil o difícil el español para ti? No como en el instituto porque la comida es muy mala. Por la tarde hago mis deberes en casa y luego veo la televisión. Hay muchos programas ingleses y norteamericanos en la televisión española como Barrio Sésamo, MASH y Mundo Disney. No hay programas españoles en la televisión inglesa, ¿verdad? Escríbeme pronto y mándame una foto de ti y de tu familia.

Un abrazo de tu amiga,

Lola

mandar - send
guardar - keep.

10 What does she say about English in school?
11 Why does she not have lunch at school?
12 What does she do in the evening?
13 What does she tell you about Spanish television?
14 What does she want you to do soon?
15 What does she ask you to send her?

Have a guess

These are signs and notices you might see when travelling in Spain. Can you guess what they mean? Write the meaning down in English.

Cuarta parte: Vamos a escribir

1

Read again the page of the letter on page 61. Then write a similar page giving roughly the same information about yourself and your house, etc. that Lola gives in her letter.

2

Write a letter to a Spanish penfriend — your first to that particular penfriend — in which you give the following information about yourself:

a name, age and where you are from;

b size of town or village where you are from and which part of the country it is in;

c size and type of house or flat; number of rooms, etc;

d your own bedroom and its contents;

e any pets or other possessions you have.

(You will find your Personal Dossier will be very helpful in writing such a letter.)

Remember to begin your letter:

Querido Juan: If you are writing to a boy called Juan, for example

Querida Lola: If you are writing to a girl called Lola, for example

and end it:

Un abrazo de tu amigo/tu amiga,
    before signing your name.

Quinta parte: Vamos a jugar

Hear-Say

Play this game in groups of four. Each of you takes a board, number **1**, **2**, **3** or **4**. The person with board **1** starts by saying **Uno**.

When you hear the number in Column A on your board say the number opposite in Column B. You should end up with *Veinte*.

1

Column A (Hear)	Column B (Say)
	uno
cuatro	cinco
seis	siete
diecinueve	veinte
once	doce

2

Column A (Hear)	Column B (Say)
doce	trece
ocho	nueve
dos	tres
catorce	quince
diecisiete	dieciocho

3

Column A (Hear)	Column B (Say)
cinco	seis
dieciséis	diecisiete
tres	cuatro
trece	catorce
nueve	diez

4

Column A (Hear)	Column B (Say)
dieciocho	diecinueve
siete	ocho
uno	dos
diez	once
quince	dieciséis

Crucigrama de animales

All the answers are the names of animals. Copy the crossword into your exercise book and complete the puzzle.
Do not write in the book.

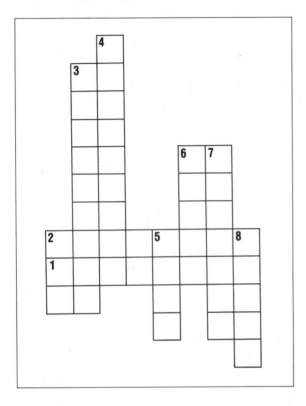

Horizontal

1 Este animal es gris y es muy grande. Vive en África y en la India.

Vertical

2 Vive en agua.
3 En Europa este animal vive sólo en un zoo. Vive en agua, pero no es un pez.
4 Es un animal muy largo. Es verde o negro o amarillo.
5 Este animal hace 'miau' y come pescado.
6 Es un animal muy pequeño que come queso.
7 Este animal es también pequeño. Es marrón y vive en una jaula.
8 Este animal es el 'amigo del hombre'. Come carne.

When you have completed the crossword puzzle, write out the sentences below filling in the gaps with the appropriate words from the crossword.

a La . . . . que tengo tiene dos metros de largo y es verde y amarilla.
b El salmón es un . . . .
c El . . . es un animal muy fuerte de la India.
d El . . . que tengo es negro y blanco. Hace 'miau' y bebe leche.
e Mi . . . . marrón vive en una jaula pequeña en la cocina.
f El enemigo de mi . . . . . es mi gato.
g El . . . . vive en un zoo cerca de mi casa. Tiene dos o tres metros de largo y es verde.
h Mi . . . . se llama Monstruo. Es marrón y blanco y hace 'guau'.

Juego de colores

Sketch the following, using coloured pens or pencils or writing the colours onto your sketch. Some are rather odd!

1 Tengo un ratón verde en mi dormitorio. Está cerca de la cama.
2 Hay una serpiente azul en mi cocina. Está en la mesa.
3 El perro de mi amigo tiene cinco metros de largo. Es amarillo y gris.
4 Hay un elefante rojo en el jardín. Está al lado del coche.
5 El pez negro está en un tanque de agua en el salón.

Sopa de habitaciones

Can you sort out these mixed up rooms of the house? Copy out the sentence with the name of the room spelled correctly.

1 Hay una mesa pequeña en la **nacioc**.
2 En mi **mitrodooir** tengo un tocadiscos y mi colección de discos.
3 Hay una mesa grande y cinco sillas en el **dromoce**.
4 El **lonas** de mi casa es bastante bonito.
5 El **ñotocadebaur** está en el primer piso.

Checklist I

Keep a page of your Personal Dossier for charting your progress. Write out the checklist below, with the boxes to tick and cross.

By now you should be able to do the following things in Spanish. Can you?
- give your name, age, nationality and say where you are from ☐
- talk about your family, giving their names, ages and descriptions ☐

- say where you live with descriptions of your town or village and house ☐
- talk about your bedroom and its contents, any pets you have and things like bicycles, record-players, computers, etc. ☐

Check against the other pages in your Dossier that you can carry out all of these tasks. If you can, put a tick in the box and, if you cannot do so, ask your teacher to revise the things you are not sure of.

Words to learn

agua(f)	water	hija(f)	daughter
argentino	Argentinian	internacional	international
arquitecto(m)	architect	jardín (m)	garden
arriba	up, upstairs	leche(f)	milk
asignatura(f)	school subject	malo	bad
atletismo(m)	athletics	mandar	to send
autobús(m)	bus	museo(m)	museum
beber	to drink	ninguno	none, not any
calor(m)	heat	norteamericano	North American
hace calor	it is hot	piso(m)	floor, storey, flat
comercial	commercial	planta(f)	floor, storey
comida(f)	meal, food, lunch	planta baja	ground floor
cómodo	comfortable	plata(f)	silver
comprar	to buy	programa(m)	programme
detrás [de]	behind	prohibido	prohibited, forbidden
enemigo(m)	enemy	pueblo(m)	village, small town
entrada(f)	entrance, ticket	río(m)	river
escribir	to write	salmón(m)	salmon
estación(f)	station, season	sitio(m)	room, place
estudiante(m/f)	student	todo	all
estudiar	to study	todos	everybody
Europa	Europe	turismo(m)	tourism
exactamente	exactly	valenciano	from Valencia
flor(f)	flower	ver	to see, watch
garaje(m)	garage	visitar	to visit
guardar	to keep, store	yo	I

Mi vida en el colegio

Frases clave

1 ¿Cómo es tu vida diaria?

¿A qué hora te levantas por la mañana? What time do you get up in the morning?

Me levanto a las siete. I get up at seven o'clock.

¿Qué tomas para el desayuno? What do you have for breakfast?

Tomo pan con mermelada. I have bread and jam.

¿Qué bebes? What do you drink?

Bebo té o zumo de fruta. I drink tea or fruit-juice.

¿A qué hora sales de casa? What time do you leave the house?

Salgo de casa a las ocho y media. I leave the house at half-past eight.

¿Cómo vas al Instituto? How do you get to school?

Si hace buen tiempo, voy en bicicleta, y si hace mal tiempo, cojo el autobús. If the weather is fine, I go on my bike, and if the weather is bad, I catch the bus.

¿A qué hora llegas al Instituto? What time do you arrive at school?

Llego a las nueve menos cuarto. I arrive at a quarter to nine.

¿A qué hora empiezan las clases? At what time do classes begin?

Empiezan a las nueve y diez. They begin at ten past nine.

2 ¿Qué hora es?

¿Qué hora es? What's the time?

Es la una. It's one o'clock.

Son las dos. It's two o'clock.

Son las tres y cuarto. It's a quarter past three.

Son las cuatro y media. It's half-past four.

Son las cinco y veinte. It's twenty past five.

Son las seis menos veinticinco. It's twenty-five to six.

Son las siete menos cuarto. It's a quarter to seven.

3 ¿Cómo es tu vida en el Instituto?

¿Cuánto tiempo duran las clases? How long do classes last?

Duran una hora. They last for one hour.

¿Cuántas asignaturas estudias? How many subjects do you study?

Estudio seis asignaturas. I study six subjects.

¿Cuáles son? Which ones are they?

Son el inglés, el español, las ciencias, las matemáticas, el arte y la informática. They're English, Spanish, Science, Maths, Art and Computer Studies.

No comprendo. ¿Qué es la informática? I don't understand. What is *informática*?

Es el trabajo con ordenadores y cosas así. It's working with computers and things like that.

¿En qué clase trabajas mucho? In which class do you work hard?

Trabajo mucho en la clase de física. I work hard in the Physics class.

¿Por qué? Why?

Porque es muy interesante y también porque es una asignatura muy importante. Because it's very interesting and also because it's a very important subject.

Yo no comprendo la física. Creo que es muy aburrida. I can't understand Physics. I think it's very boring.

¡Qué va! Es muy fácil. Not at all! It's very easy.

 Conversaciones

1 En casa

Robert, un chico inglés, está en casa de su amigo español, Manuel.

Manuel: ¿A qué hora te levantas por la mañana, Robert?

Robert: En casa me levanto a las ocho.

Manuel: Y, ¿qué tomas para el desayuno?

Robert: Tomo . . . ¿cómo se dice 'cornflakes' en español?

Manuel: ¿'Cornflakes'? No comprendo eso.

Robert: Un momento. ¿Dónde está el diccionario? Sí, aquí está. Mira...'cornflakes' son copos de maíz en español.

Manuel: Pues no hay copos de maíz en esta casa. Yo tomo pan con mermelada de fresa. ¿Qué bebes?

Robert: Pues en casa bebo leche o té.

Manuel: Pues aquí la leche no es muy buena. Hay café o zumo de fruta. ¿Vale?

Robert: Claro que vale. Estoy en España, ¿no?, y tomo lo que toman los españoles.

Manuel: Muy bien.

2 Robert y Manuel en casa

Robert: ¿A qué hora sales de casa por la mañana?

Manuel: Salgo a las ocho y cuarto.

Robert: ¿Cómo vas al Instituto?

Manuel: Voy en bicicleta pero, si hace mal tiempo, cojo el autobús. Pero vamos a ir los dos a pie porque el Instituto no está lejos.

Robert: ¿A qué hora llegas al Instituto por lo general?

Manuel: Cuando voy en bicicleta, llego a las nueve menos veinte.

Robert: Y las clases empiezan, ¿a qué hora?

Manuel: Empiezan a las nueve en punto.

Robert: Creo que va a ser muy interesante pasar un día contigo en el Instituto.

Manuel: Claro que sí.

3 Camino del Instituto

Karen, una chica inglesa, está en España con su amiga española, Elena.

Karen: ¿Cuántas asignaturas estudias en el colegio, Elena?

Elena: Pues yo estudio siete asignaturas.

Karen: ¿Cuáles son? Por ejemplo, ¿qué tienes mañana?

Elena: Mañana es jueves, ¿verdad?

Karen: Creo que sí.

Elena: Pues entonces por la mañana tengo inglés, matemáticas y español y, por la tarde tengo informática y corte.

Karen: No comprendo eso. ¿Qué es 'corte'?

Elena: Es la clase en que hago ropa: vestidos, faldas y cosas así. ¿No haces corte en tu Instituto?

Karen: Ah sí, ahora comprendo. Claro que hago corte en mi Instituto. Es mi asignatura favorita.

4 En el Instituto

En el Instituto, Elena presenta a Karen al director.

Elena: Buenos días, don Martín. Ésta es mi amiga inglesa, Karen.

Director: Bienvenida a España, Karen. Mucho gusto.

Karen: El gusto es mío, señor director. ¿Cómo está usted?

Director: Muy bien, gracias. ¿Y tú?

Karen: Estoy muy bien, gracias.

Director: ¡Qué bien hablas el español, Karen! ¿Aprendes el español en tu Instituto?

Karen: Sí, señor director. Tengo tres clases de español por semana. ¿Habla usted inglés, señor director?

Director: Lo siento mucho, Karen, pero no hablo inglés. No hablo más que español y un poco de francés. Bueno, es la hora de la primera clase, ¿verdad, Elena?

Elena: Sí. Creo que sí, don Martín. Son las nueve en punto.

Director: ¿De qué es tu primera clase hoy, Elena?

Elena: Hoy la primera clase es de inglés, don Martín.

Director: Una clase bastante fácil para ti, ¿verdad, Karen?

Karen: Espero que sí, señor director.

Director: Bueno. A clase las dos, y hasta pronto.

Karen: Adiós, señor director.

Elena: Hasta luego, don Martín.

Robert y Manuel camino de casa

Manuel: ¿Qué haces por la tarde cuando estás en casa, Robert?

Robert: Pues, primero hago los deberes y luego, si hace buen tiempo, juego al golf. Si hace mal tiempo, veo la televisión.

Manuel: ¿Juegas al golf?

Robert: Claro que sí. El golf es un deporte muy popular entre los jóvenes ingleses.

Manuel: ¿Cuál es tu programa favorito en la televisión?

Robert: Se llama 'Top of the Pops'.

Manuel: No comprendo eso. ¿Qué es 'Top of the Pops'?

Robert: Es un programa de discos de música 'pop'.

Manuel: Ah, sí, ahora comprendo. Hay programas como ése aquí en España.

Robert: ¿Tú practicas algún deporte, Manuel?

Manuel: Sí, en invierno practico el fútbol y, en verano, voy a la piscina.

 ## ¿Comprendes?

Answer the following in English.

Primera conversación

Make a list of what Robert does each morning.

Segunda conversación

True or false?

1 Manuel leaves home at half-past eight.
2 If the weather is fine, he goes to school on his bike.
3 Today Manuel and Robert will catch the bus.
4 He usually arrives at school at twenty to nine.
5 Classes begin at nine o'clock sharp.

Tercera conversación

1 How many subjects does Elena study at school?
2 Which classes does she have on Thursday mornings?
3 And on Thursday afternoons?
4 Which word does Karen not understand — and what does it mean?
5 What does Elena do in that class?

Cuarta conversación

Choose the correct answer from the three given.

1 The headteacher:
   a welcomes Karen to Spain;
   b asks her if she likes Spain;
   c speaks in English.

2 At home, Karen has:
   a two Spanish classes a week;
   b four Spanish classes a week;
   c three Spanish classes a week.

3 The headteacher speaks:
   a Spanish and English;
   b only Spanish;
   c Spanish and a little French.

4 Today Elena's first class is:
   a English;
   b Spanish;
   c Geography.

5 The headteacher:
   a sends the girls off to the class;
   b says he will see them at two o'clock;
   c hopes they enjoy their day.

Quinta conversación

1 Describe what Robert normally does in the evening, when he arrives home from school.
2 List Manuel's sporting activities.

 ## Vamos a hablar

Rewrite the first conversation to fit what you do, and practise the result with your partner.

Practise the second conversation with your partner as it is, and then rewrite it to fit what you do. Practise the result with your partner.

Rewrite the third conversation to fit what you do, and pretend not to understand what one of the subjects is. Practise the result with your partner.

Practise the fourth conversation in groups of three, with one of you being the headteacher.

Rewrite the fifth conversation to fit what you do and practise the result with your partner.

 ## Cada oveja con su pareja (1)

¿Cómo se dice?

Partner B: Turn to page 178.

Partner A: Your partner will ask you how to say in Spanish the five words in the left-hand column, for which you have a Spanish translation. Tell him/her how to say these.

Then, ask your partner how to say the five English words in the right-hand column, in Spanish.

For example: *¿Cómo se dice sugar en español?*

1	knife	*el cuchillo*	1	sugar
2	spoon	*la cuchara*	2	marmalade
3	milk	*la leche*	3	butter
4	plate	*el plato*	4	cup
5	bread	*el pan*	5	black coffee

Cada oveja con su pareja (2)

¿A qué hora?

Partner B: Turn to page 179.

Partner A: Your partner will ask you at what time you do various things: the times are given in the left-hand column. Give short answers, for example:

A las diez.

Then, find out at what time your partner does various things by asking the questions in the right-hand column; make a note of the answers you receive.

When you have finished, do the activity again, but this time give genuine answers as they apply to you.

 ¿A qué hora te levantas?

 ¿A qué hora llegas al Instituto?

 ¿A qué hora comes?

 ¿A qué hora haces los deberes?

 ¿A qué hora te vas a la cama?

 ## Cada oveja con su pareja (3)

¿En qué clase estás?

Partner B: Turn to page 179.

Partner A: Copy the timetable into your writing book. Your partner will have a similar timetable, but with different gaps. He/she will fill in the gaps by asking you:

¿En qué clase estás el (day of week) a las (time)?

Your answer will be: *Estoy en la clase de...*

When you have given this information, ask your partner the same questions in order to fill in the gaps on your timetable.

Hora	Lunes	Martes	Miércoles	Jueves	Viernes
9·00	Inglés		Matemáticas	Trabajos manuales	Matemáticas
10·00		Ciencias	Geografía	Matemáticas	Ciencias
11·00	Español	Corte	Ciencias	Francés	
2·00	Arte	Historia	Inglés		Deportes
3·00	Matemáticas	Inglés		Historia	Deportes

Cada oveja con su pareja (4)

Mi horario favorito

Draw a blank timetable and fill it in to make
your perfect timetable. You must include all
the subjects you study at the moment, but
you can have them as much or as little as
you like. Do not let your partner see your
timetable. He/she will then ask questions
about your timetable until he/she knows
how many classes you have for each subject
and why. When you have conveyed all this
information, ask your partner questions to
find out the same information about his/her
timetable. For example:

¿Cuántas clases de... tienes por semana?
Tengo... clases de...
¿Por qué?
Porque creo que
el/la,...es
⎧ *muy interesante.*
⎨ *muy fácil.*
⎪ *muy importante.*
⎩ *muy útil en la vida.*

Porque creo que
los/las... son
⎧ *muy interesantes.*
⎨ *muy fáciles.*
⎪ *muy importantes.*
⎩ *muy útiles en la vida.*

 ## ¿Qué se dice?

Work with your partner. One of you is A
and other B. Take it in turns to be A or B.

¿Cómo es tu vida diaria?

A: *¿A qué hora te levantas por la mañana?*
B: (Tell him/her you get up at 7.15.)
A: *¿Qué tomas para el desayuno?*
B: (Say you have bread and jam.)
A: *¿Qué bebes?*
B: (Say you drink milk or tea.)
A: *¿A qué hora sales de casa?*
B: (Tell him/her you leave home at 8.45.)

Now do the exercise again, but give genuine
answers.

¿Cómo vas al Instituto?

A: *¿Cómo vas al Instituto?*
B: (Say you go on your bike.)
A: *¿A qué hora llegas al Instituto?*
B: (Say you arrive at 8.50.)
A: *¿A qué hora empiezan las clases?*
B: (Say they start at 9.15.)

¿Qué estudias en el Instituto?

A: *¿Cuántas asignaturas estudias en el
Instituto?*
B: (Say you study six subjects.)
A: *¿Cuáles son?*
B: (Say you study English, Spanish,
Geography, History, Mathematics and
Sciences.)
A: *¿Cuál es tu asignatura favorita?*
B: (Say it is Spanish.)
A: *¿Por qué?*
B: (Say because it is very interesting and
important in life.)

Mucho gusto

A: (Greet the headteacher and introduce
your English friend.)
B: *Bienvenido a España. Mucho gusto.*
A: (Say the pleasure is yours, and ask how
the headteacher is.)
B: *Muy bien gracias. ¿Y tú?*
A: (Say you are fine. Ask if the
headteacher speaks English.)
B: *Lo siento mucho, pero no hablo inglés.
Tú hablas muy bien el español.*
A: (Say thank you very much and explain
that you study Spanish at school.)

Ejercicios

Ejercicio número uno

¿Qué hora es en otras
partes del mundo?

Ejemplo:

En Londres, Inglaterra, son las dos y cuarto
de la tarde.

14:15	Londres, Inglaterra

1 *¿Y en Santiago, Chile?*

10:15	Santiago, Chile

2 *¿Y en Anchorage, Alaska?*

4:15	Anchorage, Alaska

3 *¿Y en Nueva York, Estados Unidos?*

9:15	Nueva York, Estados Unidos

4 *¿Y en Madrid, España?*

15:15	Madrid, España

Ejercicio número dos

¿Cómo es tu vida diaria?

1 *¿A qué hora te levantas?*
2 *¿A qué hora tomas el desayuno?*
3 *¿A qué hora sales de casa?*
4 *¿A qué hora llegas al Instituto?*
5 *¿A qué hora empiezan las clases?*
6 *¿A qué hora comes?*
7 *¿A qué hora sales del Instituto por la tarde?*
8 *¿A qué hora haces los deberes?*
9 *¿A qué hora ves la televisión?*
10 *¿A qué hora te vas a la cama?*

Ejercicio número tres

¿Qué opinas?

Begin your sentence *Creo que*... to give your
opinion of the following school subjects. For
example:

¿Es aburrido el español?

Creo que es muy interesante.
1 *¿Es aburrido el español?*
2 *¿Es difícil el francés?*
3 *¿Es importante la informática?*
4 *¿Es fácil el inglés?*
5 *¿Es útil la física?*
6 *¿Es interesante la geografía?*
7 *¿Es útil el arte?*
8 *¿Son importantes las matemáticas?*
9 *¿Son divertidos los deportes?*
10 *¿Estás tú fuerte en español?*

Qué quiere decir?

When is this shop open? Is this in winter or
in summer?

**HORARIO DE VERANO
LUNES A VIERNES
MAÑANAS DE 9½ A 1½
TARDES DE 4 A 7**

Ejercicio número cuatro

Match the first part of the sentences from Column A to the correct second part from Column B. Be sure that your answers make sense!

A	B
1 Me llamo	a en bicicleta.
2 Me levanto	b en la clase de español.
3 Voy al Instituto	c el autobús.
4 Para el desayuno tomo	d los deberes.
5 Bebo	e la televisión.
6 No comprendo	f el golf.
7 Trabajo mucho	g a las ocho de la mañana.
8 Si hace mal tiempo cojo	h doce años.
9 En la clase de corte hago	i muy bien, gracias.
10 Hablo bastante bien	j Manuel.
11 Por la tarde hago	k té.
12 Veo	l pan con mermelada.
13 En el verano practico	m ropa.
14 Tengo	n la física.
15 Estoy	o el español.

My Personal Dossier

Add another section to your Personal Dossier, giving your timetable in Spanish, and saying at what time things happen in your daily life. For example:

Me levanto a las siete y media. Tomo el desayuno a las ocho y salgo de casa a las ocho y veinticinco, etc.

 Vamos a escuchar

1 ¿A qué hora?

Listen carefully to the short pieces of Spanish you will hear on the tape and write down the time that is found in each.

2 ¿Cómo es tu vida diaria?

Listen to the Spanish boy on the tape describing his daily routine; then answer the questions in English.

1. At what time does he get up?
2. Where does he have breakfast?
3. How does he get to school?
4. What does he do when he arrives at school?
5. How many classes does he have in the afternoon?
6. Which is his favourite subject?
7. Why?
8. Where does he have a coffee when he gets home from school?
9. What does he do in the park if the weather is fine?
10. At what time does he go to bed?

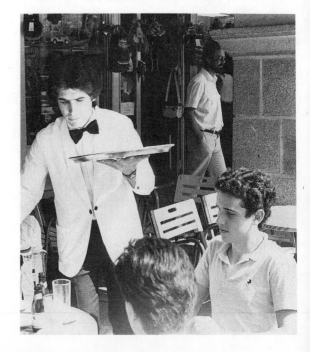

Lectura

Read the following letter and then write
down in English six things that the writer is
telling you.

Querido amigo;   Sevilla, 16 de marzo

En esta carta te voy a hablar de mi vida en el colegio. Como

ya sabes, soy alumno del Instituto Isabel Segunda de

Sevilla en el sur de España. Por la mañana salgo de casa a

las ocho y cuarto y voy al colegio en autobús con mis amigos.

Tengo cuatro clases por la mañana y tres por la tarde. No

trabajo mucho en el colegio porque las asignaturas son

aburridas y difíciles. Mi asignatura favorita es la

(educación física) porque es interesante y muy fácil. No

como en el colegio porque la comida es fatal. Salgo del

Colegio a las cuatro y voy a casa. En casa hago los

deberes y luego juego con mis amigos en el parque

cerca de mi casa. No veo mucho la televisión porque

la televisión aquí en España es aburrida. ¿Cómo es tu

vida en el colegio? ¿Tienes una asignatura favorita? Escríbeme

pronto y cuéntame lo que haces en el colegio.

Un abrazo muy fuerte de tu amigo,

                    Marcos

Now try to write a similar letter giving
roughly the same information as Marcos
gave you.

Explanations

Schools

Schools are much the same all over Europe, but in Spain the pupils do not wear uniform and most do not do homework: homework is not set in most schools. School hours are similar to yours, but the subject groups are changing so that pupils study slightly different things. A typical week in a Spanish school would include the following:

Spanish language and literature	3 hours per week
Mathematics	2 hours per week
Modern language (English or French)	3 hours per week
Physical education	2 hours per week
Religious studies	1 hour per week
Experimental sciences (Physics, Chemistry, Biology)	3 hours per week
Social sciences	2 hours per week
Technical studies (including Computer Studies)	3 hours per week
Art and Design	3 hours per week

Does a Spanish school week differ much from yours?

Gramática

Reflexive verbs

You know one of these verbs already and use it to give your name.

¿Cómo te llamas?	What's your name? (What do you call **yourself**)
Me llamo Pedro.	I'm called Peter. (I call **myself** Peter)

The words *me* and *te* placed before the verb tell you this is a Reflexive Verb. There is another one in this lesson:

¿A qué hora te levantas?	At what time do you get up?
Me levanto a las ocho.	I get up at eight o'clock.
Mi padre se levanta a las siete.	My father gets up at seven o'clock.

These words *me, te, se* are called Reflexive Pronouns and you must learn them as you learn the verbs. You can recognise Reflexive Verbs in word lists or dictionaries because they have *se* on the end.

llamarse	to be called
levantarse	to get up

Telling the time

You need to be able to tell the time in two ways.

1 ¿Qué hora es?   **What's the time?**
   Son las dos.   **It's two o'clock.**

You add on minutes, 'quarter past' and 'half past' by using the word *y*:

Son las dos y diez.	It's ten past two.
Son las dos y cuarto.	It's a quarter past two.
Son las dos y media.	It's half-past two.

From the minutes after 'half past', you use the next hour and take bits off, using the word *menos* which actually means 'less':

Son las tres menos veinticinco.	It's twenty-five to three. (It's three minus twenty-five minutes.)
Son las tres menos cuarto.	It's a quarter to three. (It's three minus a quarter.)
Son las tres menos cinco.	It's five to three. (It's three minus five.)

Remember that 'one' is singular and you use *Es la una...*

¿Qué hora es?	What's the time?
Es la una y diez.	It's ten past one.

2 ¿A qué hora?   At what time?

¿A qué hora llegas al colegio?	At what time do you arrive at school?
A las nueve y diez.	At ten past nine.

A has replaced *son* or *es* because *a* means at.

Three more verbs which need extra care

These verbs are irregular in the first person singular 'I' only.

Salir (to go out, leave)

Salgo de casa a las ocho.	I leave the house at eight o'clock.

Coger (to catch, pick up)

Cojo el autobús.	I catch the bus.

Estar (to be)

This describes position and is used for saying how you are at the moment.

Estoy en Madrid.	I'm in Madrid.
Estoy bien, gracias.	I'm well, thank you.

Verbs which change both the ending and the first part of the verb

One of these verbs you already know:

Jugar (to play)

The u of the first part changes to ue in the singular forms and the third person plural.

Juego al críquet.	I play cricket.
Juegas al golf.	You play golf.
Juega al rugby.	He plays rugby.
Juegan al tenis.	They play tennis.

(Other persons do not have this change, as you will see later.)

Another of these verbs is as follows:

Empezar (to begin)

The e of the first part changes to ie.

Empiezo a las cinco.	I begin at five.
Empiezas a las nueve.	You begin at nine.
Manuel empieza a las diez.	Manuel begins at ten.
Las clases empiezan a las dos.	The classes begin at two.

Saying 'why?' and 'because'

You need to take care with these two words because they are easy to mix up.

why?	*¿por qué?*
because	*porque*
¿Por qué estudias el español?	Why do you study Spanish?
Porque es muy interesante.	Because it is very interesting.

The days of the week

You must learn these.

el lunes	Monday
el martes	Tuesday
el miércoles	Wednesday
el jueves	Thursday
el viernes	Friday
el sábado	Saturday
el domingo	Sunday

To say 'on Monday' you simple say *el lunes*.

El lunes estudio en casa.	On Monday I study at home.

Notice that the days of the week start with a small letter.

Talking to adults and strangers

When you talk to members of your family, to friends or to animals you use the second singular to the verb, which ends in -s.

¿Hablas español?	Do you speak Spanish?
¿Juegas al golf?	Do you play golf?

When you talk to an adult or a stranger you have another form of the verb and another word for 'you'. This word is *usted* and is followed by the third singular of the verb.

Usted habla español.	You speak Spanish.
Usted juega al golf.	You play golf.

To ask a question you turn the verb and pronoun round.

¿Habla usted español?	Do you speak Spanish?
¿Juega usted al golf?	Do you play golf?

It is important to include the word *usted*, because the verb is the same form as for 'he' and 'she'. Therefore:

Habla español.	(He speaks Spanish.)
***Usted** habla español.*	(You speak Spanish.)

How to say you are sorry

You use the phrase:

Lo siento.	I'm sorry.

If you are very sorry, you add *mucho*.

Lo siento mucho.	I'm very sorry.

How to say you only speak English

To say 'only' you put *no* before the verb and *más que* after the verb.

Hablo inglés.   I speak English.
No hablo más que inglés.   I only speak English.

Words to learn

alumno(m)	pupil	*llegar*	to arrive
aprender	to learn	*mantequilla(f)*	butter
así	thus, so	*medio*	half
azúcar(m)	sugar	*menos*	less, minus
bienvenido	welcome	*mermelada(f)*	jam
bueno	good	*mío*	mine
café(m)	coffee, café	*momento(m)*	moment
café solo	black coffee	*música(f)*	music
cerrar [ie]	to close, shut	*naranja(f)*	orange
ciencia(f)	science	*nuestro*	our
coger	to catch, pick up	*olvidar*	to forget
colegio(m)	school	*pan(m)*	bread
contigo	with you	*parque(m)*	park
cortar	to cut	*pasar*	to pass, spend (of time)
corte(m)	dressmaking, sewing	*pie(m)*	foot
cosa(f)	thing	*a pie*	on foot
creer	to think, believe	*plato(m)*	plate, dish, course (meal)
cuchara(f)	spoon	*popular*	popular
cuchillo(m)	knife	*porque*	because
deporte(m)	sport	*¿por qué?*	why?
desayuno(m)	breakfast	*practicar*	to practise
diario	daily	*presentar*	to introduce
diccionario(m)	dictionary	*punto(m)*	point
durar	to last	*en punto*	sharp (of time)
empezar	to begin	*salir*	to leave, go out
entre	between, among	*semana(f)*	week
esperar	to wait	*sentir [ie]*	to feel
Estados Unidos (m.pl.)	United States	*lo siento*	I'm sorry
falda(f)	skirt	*taza(f)*	cup
fatal	fatal, horrible	*té(m)*	tea
francés	French	*ti*	you
fresa(f)	strawberry	*tomar*	to take, have (food & drink)
general	general	*trabajar*	to work
por lo general	generally	*trabajo(m)*	work
geografía(f)	geography	*trabajos manuales (m.pl.)*	craft and design
gusto(m)	pleasure		
mucho gusto	great pleasure	*tren(m)*	train
historia(f)	history	*útil*	useful
hora(f)	hour, time	*valer*	to be worth
informática(f)	computer studies	*vale*	O.K.
Inglaterra(f)	England	*vestido(m)*	dress
invierno(m)	winter	*vida(f)*	life
levantarse	to get up	*zumo(m)*	juice

Mi tiempo libre

Frases clave

1 ¿Qué haces cuando hace sol?

¿Qué haces cuando hace calor? What do you do when it's hot?

Tomo el sol en la playa. I sunbathe on the beach.

¿Qué haces cuando hace frío? What do you do when it's cold?

Me quedo en casa y veo la televisión. I stay in and watch television.

¿Sales si hace mal tiempo? Do you go out if the weather's bad?

No. Escucho mis discos en mi dormitorio. No. I listen to my records in my bedroom.

¿Qué deporte practicas cuando hace sol? Which sport do you play when it's sunny?

Practico el tenis. I play tennis.

¿Hace buen tiempo en España en el verano? Is the weather fine in Spain in the summer?

Sí, hace muy buen tiempo. Yes, the weather is very fine.

¿Llueve mucho en Inglaterra? Does it rain a lot in England?

Sí, llueve bastante, sobre todo en el invierno. Yes, it rains quite a lot, especially in the winter.

¿Vas a esquiar cuando nieva? Do you go skiing when it snows?

No, no voy a esquiar. No me gusta. No, I don't go skiing. I don't like it.

2 ¿Te gusta?

¿Te gusta el chocolate?   Do you like chocolate?

Sí, me gusta mucho.   Yes, I like it a lot.

¿Comes mucho queso?   Do you eat a lot of cheese?

No, no me gusta.   No, I don't like it.

¿Te gustan los mejillones?   Do you like mussels?

No, no me gustan.   No, I don't like them.

¿Te gusta jugar al tenis?   Do you like to play tennis?

Sí, me gusta bastante.   Yes, I like it quite a lot.

¿Te gusta bailar?   Do you like dancing?

No, no me gusta nada.   No, I don't like it at all.

 ## Conversaciones

1 Tú estás en España con tu amiga española

Tu amiga: Llueve muchísimo en Inglaterra, ¿verdad?

Tú: No. Llueve bastante en el invierno, pero en los meses de junio, julio y agosto, hace buen tiempo.

Tu amiga: ¿De veras? ¿Qué haces cuando hace buen tiempo?

Tú: Todo depende. En el verano juego al tenis o doy un paseo por el campo con mi perro.

Tu amiga: Y en el invierno cuando hace mucho frío y llueve, ¿qué haces?

Tú: Pues claro que no practico deportes. Me quedo en casa donde veo la televisión o voy a la discoteca.

Tu amiga: ¿Te gusta bailar entonces?

Tú: Sí, me gusta mucho, y bailo bastante bien. Pero, oye, ¿no llueve nunca aquí en España?

Tu amiga: Sí, llueve en el otoño en los meses de octubre y noviembre y hace bastante frío en los meses de diciembre y enero. Pero siempre tenemos un verano estupendo y hace mucho, mucho calor.

Tú: ¿Qué haces en el verano?
Tu amiga: Pues, tomo el sol en el jardín o voy a la piscina con mis amigas.
Tú: ¿Sabes nadar?
Tu amiga: Claro que sé nadar. Mis amigas dicen que nado muy bien.

Tu amiga quiere saber lo que te gusta comer y beber.

Tu amiga: Esta noche para la cena tenemos pescado. Creo que es merluza. ¿Te gusta la merluza?
Tú: Sí, me gusta mucho.
Tu amiga: Y con la merluza hay patatas fritas. Te gustan las patatas fritas, ¿no?
Tú: Sí, me gustan muchísimo. En casa como muchas patatas fritas.
Tu amiga: Y, ¿para beber? ¿Te gusta el vino?
Tú: No, no me gusta mucho. No bebo nunca vino en casa. Me gusta más el zumo de fruta.
Tu amiga: No sé si hay. Voy a preguntarlo a mamá más tarde. Y de postre creo que hay fruta. ¿Qué fruta te gusta?
Tú: Me gustan mucho las fresas. ¿Tienes fresas?
Tu amiga: Creo que sí.

Tú: ¿A qué hora es la cena?
Tu amiga: Más tarde que en Inglaterra. Sobre las nueve. ¿Tienes hambre ahora?
Tú: Sí.
Tu amiga: Pues hay tarta de manzana en la nevera. ¿Quieres un poco de tarta de manzana y una coca cola?
Tú: Sí, por favor.

3 Cenando con la familia

La madre: ¿Qué tal la merluza? ¿Te gusta?
Tú: Sí, me gusta mucho. Es muy buena.
La madre: Es una receta de mi abuela. Merluza en salsa verde. ¿Quieres un poco más?
Tú: No, gracias. Tengo bastante.
Tu amiga: ¿Quieres más patatas fritas? Te gustan mucho las patatas fritas, ¿no?
Tú: Sí, ya sabes que me gustan mucho, pero no quiero más.
La madre: ¿Quieres probar un poco de vino con gaseosa?
Tú: Pues, no bebo vino en casa. ¿Es muy fuerte? Me gusta más el zumo de fruta.

La madre:	Lo siento, pero no tengo zumo de fruta. Vamos. Estás en España y nosotros siempre tomamos vino con la comida.
Tú:	Bueno, voy a probarlo a ver si me gusta.
Tu amiga:	¿Traigo el postre, mamá?
La madre:	Sí. Está en la nevera. Hay fresas con nata, plátanos y manzanas. ¿Qué te gusta más?
Tú:	Me gustan más las fresas.
La madre:	Muy bien. Para ti fresas con nata y para mí un plátano. ¿Qué quieres, hija?
Tu amiga:	Voy a tomar fresas con nata.

4 Haciendo planes

El padre:	¿Qué vais a hacer mañana?
Tu amiga:	¿Quieres ir a la playa?
Tú:	¿Está lejos?
Tu amiga:	No. Está bastante cerca, a unos doce kilómetros. Cogemos el autobús que sale de aquí a las nueve de la mañana y llegamos a la playa a las diez menos cuarto.
El padre:	¿Queréis merienda?

Tu amiga:	No. Hay un mercado en un pueblo de la costa y me gusta ir de compras al mercado. Vamos a comprar pan, jamón y algo para beber en el mercado y comeremos en la playa. Luego podemos bañarnos y tomar el sol. Lo vamos a pasar 'bomba', ya verás.
Tú:	Espero que sí. ¿Puedo hacer la compra para la merienda? Me gusta hablar español, y necesito la práctica.
Tu amiga:	Claro que vas a comprar las cosas. Tienes que practicar mucho tu español.

 ¿Comprendes?

Answer the following.

Primera conversación

Complete the following:

1 In England it rains quite a bit...
2 In the summer, when the weather is good, the visitor...
3 When the weather is bad, the visitor...
4 In Spain it rains...
5 The weather in the summer in Spain is...
6 The Spanish friend knows how to...

Segunda conversación

1 List the things the visitor likes.
2 List the things the visitor dislikes.
3 Describe the snack offered by the Spanish person.

Tercera conversación

Write down the Spanish phrases for the following:

1 What's the hake like?
2 Do you want a bit more?
3 I've got enough.
4 I prefer fruit juice.
5 I'm going to have strawberries and cream.

Cuarta conversación

Answer in English.

1 Where are the two friends going tomorrow?
2 How far is it?
3 How will they get there?
4 Who will get a picnic?
5 Who will do the shopping in the market?

 # Vamos a hablar

Practise the first conversation with your partner.

Rewrite the second conversation with your partner, changing it so that it is what you would want to say. Practise the result with your partner. Practise the third and fourth conversations in groups of three with one of the group being the mother or the father respectively.

 ## Cada oveja con su pareja (1)

¿Qué tiempo hace en España?

Partner B: Turn to page 180.

Partner A: Copy this map of Spain into your writing book. Mark on it the towns and places given here, but *not* the symbols for the weather.

Your partner will ask you what the weather is like in Spain. Use the information from the map given here to answer the questions.

Then, ask your partner what the weather is like at all the places named on the map. Make a note of the weather, using symbols, on the map you have copied into your writing book.

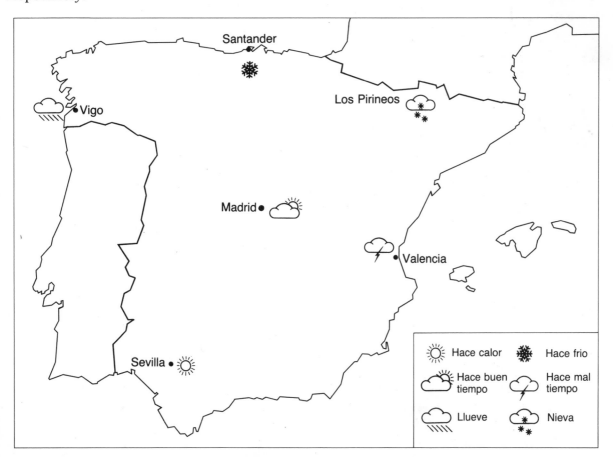

Cada oveja con su pareja (2)

¿Te gusta o no?

✓ = me gusta (remember gustan for plurals)
✓✓ = me gusta mucho
✗ = no me gusta
✗✗ = no me gusta nada

Partner B: Turn to page 181.

Partner A: Copy out the numbers 1–10 so you can record your partner's answers. He/she will ask you whether you like a number of different things. Give answers according to the ticks and crosses given after each question below. Then, ask your partner whether he/she likes these things, and record the answers, using the symbols above.

When you have finished, check that you have got the correct results. Then do the exercise again, but give genuine answers.

1 ¿Te gusta la historia?	✗
2 ¿Te gustan las fresas?	✓
3 ¿Te gusta tomar el sol?	✓
4 ¿Te gustan los chicos estúpidos?	✗✗
5 ¿Te gusta el español?	✓✓
6 ¿Te gusta estudiar?	✓✓
7 ¿Te gustan las patatas fritas?	✓
8 ¿Te gusta trabajar en el jardín?	✗
9 ¿Te gusta la informática?	✓
10 ¿Te gustan los discos de música clásica?	✓✓

Cada oveja con su pareja (3)

¿Te gusta el colegio?

Partner B: Turn to page 181.

Partner A: Choose the school subject that you like best from the following list and answer you partner's questions until he/she discovers the subject. Then try to find out which subject your partner has chosen. Remember to use the correct question, for example:

Los deportes = ¿Te gustan los deportes?
La música = ¿Te gusta la música?

1 El español.
2 El inglés.
3 Las matemáticas.
4 Las ciencias.
5 El arte.
6 La educación física.

Actividades

Mensaje secreto

Work with your partner to find the message hidden in the square. Start with the ringed letter and move in any direction. One letter is used twice. Then make up a similar message, conceal it in a square and give it to your partner to be worked out.

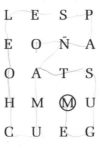

L   E   S   P

E   O   Ñ   A

O   A   T   S

H   M   Ⓜ   U

C   U   E   G

¿Qué se dice?

Work with your partner. One of you is A and the other B. Take it in turns to be A or B.

¿Qué te gusta?

A: ¿Te gusta el inglés?
B: (Say you like it a lot.)
A: ¿Por qué?
B: (Say it is very interesting.)
A: Pero el profesor es muy aburrido, ¿no?
B: (Say he is not boring and you like him a lot.)

¿Qué te gusta hacer?

A: *¿Qué te gusta hacer cuando hace sol?*
B: (Say you like swimming.)
A: *¿Adónde vas para nadar?*
B: (Say you go to the swimming pool near the school.)
A: *¿Con quién vas?*
B: (Say you go with your brother and your friends.)

Tu amigo español

A: *¿Llueve mucho en Inglaterra?*
B: (Say it rains quite a lot.)
A: *Y nieva mucho en el invierno, ¿verdad?*
B: (Say it snows quite a lot in the north of England. Ask your Spanish friend if it is never cold in Spain.)
A: *Sí, hace frío en el invierno sobre todo en el centro de España.*

Y, ¿si hace mal tiempo?

A: *¿Sales de casa si hace mal tiempo?*
B: (Say that you stay at home.)
A: *¿Qué te gusta hacer en casa?*
B: (Say you like listening to your records.)
A: *¿Qué clase de música te gusta?*
B: (Say you like pop music.)
A: *¿Tienes muchos discos?*
B: (Say you have got about 50.)

Ejercicios

Ejercicio número uno

Create sentences using the school subjects and adjectives given at the end of the exercise. Give your genuine opinions about the school subjects.

1 *Me gusta . . . porque es . . . .*
2 *No me gusta . . . porque no es . . . .*
3 *Me gusta mucho . . . porque es . . . .*
4 *No me gusta nada . . . porque es . . . .*
5 *Me gustan . . . porque son . . . .*
6 *No me gustan mucho . . . porque son . . . .*
7 *Me gustan muchísimo . . . porque son . . . .*
8 *Me gusta bastante . . . porque es . . . .*
9 *Me gusta . . . porque es . . . .*
10 *No me gusta mucho . . . porque es . . . .*

Las asignaturas

el inglés	*la informática*
el francés	*el arte*
el español	*las matemáticas*
el corte	*los deportes*
la educación física	*las ciencias*

Los adjetivos

(Remember to make them agree!)

interesante	*divertido*
útil	*fácil*
importante en la vida	*difícil*
aburrido	

Ejercicio número dos

Make up sensible sentences saying what you
do. Take one part from column A and one
from Column B.

COLUMNA A	COLUMNA B
Cuando hace buen tiempo	tomo el sol en el jardín.
Si hace mal tiempo	no salgo de casa.
Cuando hace mucho calor	voy a esquiar en la montaña.
Si hace frío	me quedo en casa y veo la televisión.
Cuando llueve	cojo el autobús y voy a la discoteca.
Si nieva	voy a la playa y nado en el mar.
Si hace sol	practico el golf con mis amigos.
Cuando hace muy mal tiempo	voy al cine con mis amigos.
Si hace mucho frío	no salgo porque no me gusta el calor.
Cuando hace buen tiempo en la costa	me quedo en casa y escucho mis discos.

Ejercicio número tres

¿Cuál es el verbo correcto?

Complete the sentences with a verb chosen
from those found at the end of the exercise.
Be careful! There are more verbs than you
need and some will not be used.

1 Por la mañana...a las ocho y cuarto.
2 En la clase de español...mucho porque
es muy interesante.
3 Con la cena siempre...leche o zumo de
fruta.
4 Por la tarde...el autobús y voy a la
discoteca.
5 ...mis deberes en el salón a las cinco de
la tarde.
6 Cuando hace buen tiempo...al tenis en
el parque.
7 Por la mañana...al Instituto a las nueve
menos cuarto.
8 Me gusta...cartas a mis amigos
españoles.
9 La primera clase en el Instituto...a las
nueve y veinte.
10 ...muy bien gracias. ¿Y usted?
11 ...doce años.
12 En casa por la tarde...la televisión.
13 No...el golf porque es muy aburrido.

14 No...en el Instituto porque la comida es
horrible.
15 ...inglés, francés y español.

Verbos

veo	juego	compro
tengo	me levanto	trabajo
como	llego	me llamo
escribir	cojo	soy
empieza	estoy	creo
bebo	hago	comprendo
olvido	practico	

Ejercicio número cuatro

¿Qué tiempo hace?

Write sentences about the weather taking
your information from the map found
on page 87. For example:

En Madrid hace sol.

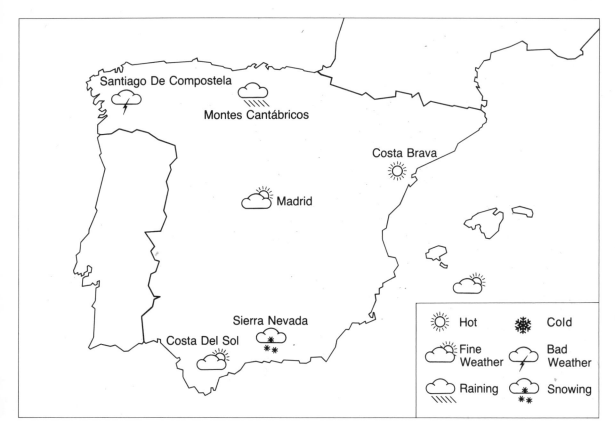

My Personal Dossier

Write the next section of your Personal Dossier saying what you like and dislike at school, what you like doing, given certain weather conditions, and what your favourite foods and drinks are. For example:

No me gustan las ciencias en el Instituto porque son muy difíciles.

Vamos a escuchar

Dos jóvenes españoles

Make a grid like the one below. Listen to the two interviews on the tape and write down in English the likes and dislikes of the two young people.

	likes at school	dislikes at school	likes as a pastime	dislikes as a pastime
María				
Pedro				

Lectura

Read the following letter, answer the
questions in English and then write a
similar letter giving roughly the same
information as that found in the letter.

Ávila. 20 de abril.

Querida amiga:

En esta carta te voy a hablar de lo que me gusta en el Instituto y de
lo que hago en mi tiempo libre. En el Instituto me gustan casi todas las
asignaturas sobre todo el inglés. Hablo bastante bien el inglés porque mi
madre es profesora de inglés y practico mi inglés en casa con ella por la tarde.
También me gustan mucho las ciencias. En mi Instituto que se llama el
Instituto Santa Teresa de Ávila, estudio la física, la química y la
biología y las tres asignaturas son muy interesantes y bastante fáciles
porque las profesoras son muy buenas. Por la tarde, cuando no tengo que
trabajar, me gusta mucho salir en mi bicicleta. Voy a casa de mi
amiga y vamos los dos al campo. En el campo tomamos el sol y,
a veces, nadamos en un río que hay cerca de mi casa.
No practico ningún deporte como el tenis o el baloncesto porque
los deportes no me gustan nada ¿Qué te gusta a ti estudiar en
el colegio? ¿Te gusta el español? Espero que sí. ¿Qué te gusta
hacer en tu tiempo libre? ¿Practicas algún deporte? Escríbeme
pronto y cuéntame lo que te gusta hacer en tu vida diaria.

Un abrazo muy fuerte de tu amiga,

Elena

---

1 What is your friend going to tell you
   about?
2 Which is your friend's favourite subject at
   school?
3 Why is it fairly easy for your friend?
4 Which science subjects are studied at

the Santa Teresa Secondary School?
5 How does your friend spend her free
   time?
6 Which sports does she play?
7 What does your friend want you to write
   about?

Explanations

The weather

If you have been to Spain, or seen holiday programmes about Spain on the television, you probably think that it is always sunny and hot throughout the year. This is not really true: the weather in Spain can be quite wintry at certain times of the year. The climate is what is called 'continental' and this means that, in the centre of the country, there are two or three months of tremendous heat in the summer and two or three months of extreme cold in the winter. The Spaniards describe their climate as *nueve meses de invierno y tres de infierno*. What do you think this means?

Differences in altitude can also bring about dramatic changes in the weather. In the Picos de Europa in the north of Spain tourists stroll around in the valleys dressed in shorts and summer dresses. If they take the cable-car to the top of the mountains, they find themselves shivering in their light clothing among snow which lasts all the year.

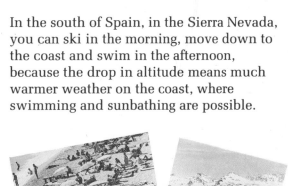

In the south of Spain, in the Sierra Nevada, you can ski in the morning, move down to the coast and swim in the afternoon, because the drop in altitude means much warmer weather on the coast, where swimming and sunbathing are possible.

Gramática

Talking about the weather

For many expressions of weather you use *hace* with a noun.

Hace buen tiempo.	The weather's fine.
Hace mal tiempo.	The weather's bad.
Hace sol.	It's sunny.
Hace calor.	It's hot.
Hace frío.	It's cold.
Hace viento.	It's windy.

Since you have a noun, you can change the meaning with *mucho*
Hace mucho sol.   It's very sunny.

Some weather expressions are from verbs other than *hacer.*

Llover (to rain)
Llueve mucho en el norte.   It rains a lot in the north.

To say what is happening now, you say:
Está lloviendo.   It's raining.

Nevar (to snow)
Nieva bastante en los Pirineos.   It snows quite a lot in the Pyrenees.

To say what is happening now, you say:
Está nevando.   It's snowing.

With one weather expression you usually use *hay*:
Hay niebla.   It's foggy.

And for one other you use *está*:
Está nublado.   It's cloudy.

Saying what you like, dislike and prefer

You use the verb *gustar*, but this verb means 'to please' and the Spanish sentence is rather different from the English one. For example:

I like **wine.**
becomes:
Wine pleases **me.**
Therefore you say:
El vino me gusta.
Or: *Me gusta el vino.*

This means that for all singular nouns you will use *gusta* and change the word in front of *gusta*:

Me gusta el vino.   I like wine.
Te gusta el vino.   You like wine.

If what pleases you is plural, *gusta* changes to *gustan*

I like **sweets.**
becomes:
Sweets please **me.**
Therefore you say:
Los caramelos me gustan.
Or: *Me gustan los caramelos.*

This means that for all plural nouns you will use *gustan* and change the word in front of *gustan*, according to **who** is liking the thing in question.

Me gustan las   I like apples.
  manzanas.
Te gustan las fresas. You like strawberries.

If what you like is an activity such as dancing, swimming, etc. you use *gusta*.
Me gusta bailar.   I like to dance.

If you dislike something, you simply put *no* in front of the verb.
No me gusta el tenis.   I don't like tennis.

To say slightly different things, you can use *mucho, bastante, nada*

Me gusta bastante.   I like it quite a lot.
Me gusta mucho.   I like it a lot.
No me gusta.   I don't like it.
No me gusta nada.   I don't like it at all.

To say you prefer something, you simply add *más*.
Me gusta la leche.   I like milk.
Me gusta más la leche. I prefer milk. (Milk pleases me more.)

Saying something is the greatest, most expensive, etc.

You add -*ísimo* to the adjective and make it agree with the noun.

Ese chico es tontísimo.   That boy is very, very stupid.
Esta casa es grandísima. This house is very, very big.

Los meses del año (The months of the year)

These you must learn. Normally they start with a small letter.

enero	January
febrero	February
marzo	March
abril	April
mayo	May
junio	June
julio	July
agosto	August
setiembre	September
octubre	October
noviembre	November
diciembre	December

Dates are then written as follows:

Mi cumpleaños es el   My birthday is the 9th
  nueve de febrero.   of February.

More verbs with an irregular first person singular ('I')

Dar (to give)
Doy un libro a mi   I give a book to my
  amigo.   friend.

Saber (to know, to know facts, to know how to)
Sé la hora.   I know what time it is.
Sé bailar.   I know how to dance.

Traer (to bring)
Traigo el postre a la   I bring the dessert to the
  mesa.   table.

Verbs which change both the ending and the first part of the verb

Some of these you saw in Lesson 7. Here are some more. Remember they change *o* or *u* for *ue*, and *e* for *ie* in the singular forms and third person plural.

Poder (to be able, can)

Puedo salir a las ocho.	I can leave at eight o'clock.
Puedes ver la televisión.	You can watch television.
Paco puede jugar al tenis.	Paco can play tennis.
Los chicos pueden comer ahora.	The boys can eat now.

Contar (to tell, relate) is a similar type of verb.

Querer (to wish, want, love)

Quiero dos kilos de peras.	I want two kilos of pears.
Quieres una manzana.	You want an apple.
Marta quiere bailar.	Martha wants to dance.
Las chicas quieren tomar el sol.	The girls want to sunbathe.

Saying 'we' and 'you' (the first and second persons plural)

The form of the verb for 'we' is very simple. Every single verb in Spanish ends -mos when it means 'we'.

Tomamos vino con la comida.	We have wine with food.
Tenemos dos clases por semana.	We have two classes a week.
Vivimos en Madrid.	We live in Madrid.

Each verb in Spanish ends in -is when it means 'you', referring to more than one person.

Tomáis vino con la comida.	You have wine with food.
Tenéis dos clases por semana.	You have two classes a week.
Vivís en Madrid.	You live in Madrid.

(Remember you use this form for talking to friends, members of your family, children and animals when you are talking to **more than one**.)

Saying you never do something

The key word is *nunca* (never) which you put in front of the verb:

Nunca tomo vino.	I never have wine.

or after the verb with *no* in front:

No tomo nunca vino.	I never have wine.

Comparing one thing with another

You put *más* in front of the adjective and *que* after it.

Soy inteligente.	I'm intelligent.
Soy más inteligente que tú.	I'm more intelligent than you.
Madrid es grande.	Madrid is big.
Madrid es más grande que Sevilla.	Madrid is bigger than Sevilla.

Saying what you are going to do

You use *ir* plus *a* plus a second verb in the Infinitive:

Voy a visitar Madrid.	I'm going to visit Madrid.
¿Qué vas a tomar?	What are you going to have?
Pedro va a llegar más tarde.	Peter is going to arrive later.

Saying what you have to do

You use *tener que* plus a second verb in the Infinitive:

Tengo que visitar Toledo.	I have to visit Toledo.
¿Qué tienes que hacer?	What do you have to do?
Manuel tiene que aprender el ruso.	Manuel has to learn Russian.

Words to learn

abuela(f)	grandmother	más	more
bailar	to dance	mejillón(m)	mussel
bañarse	to bathe	mercado(m)	market
bebida(f)	drink	merienda(f)	picnic, snack
bomba(f)	bomb	merluza(f)	hake
pasarlo 'bomba'	to have a great time	mes(m)	month
caramelo(m)	sweet	mí	me
casi	almost	nacional	national
cena(f)	dinner	nada	nothing
clásico	classical	nadar	to swim
compra(f)	shopping	nata(f)	cream
hacer la compra	to do the shopping	necesitar	to need
contar [ue]	to tell, relate	nevar [ie]	to snow
cuando	when	nevera(f)	refrigerator
chocolate(m)	chocolate	nunca	never
dar	to give	o	or
dar un paseo	to go for a walk	otoño(m)	autumn
depender	to depend	pasatiempo(m)	pastime
¿de veras?	really?	patata(f)	potato
educación(f)	education	patatas fritas(f.pl.)	chips
educación física	P.E.	plátano(m)	banana
entonces	then	playa(f)	beach
escuchar	to listen to	poder [ue]	to be able, can
esquiar	to ski	postre(m)	dessert, pudding
estudio(m)	studio, study	preguntar	to ask
estupendo	great, terrific	probar [ue]	to try, taste
física(f)	physics	profesora(f)	teacher
frío(m)	cold	quedarse	to stay, remain
hace frío	it's cold	querer [ie]	to want, wish, love
gaseosa(f)	'pop', fizzy drink	química(f)	chemistry
gustar	to please(like)	rato(m)	time, while
hambre(f)	hunger	ratos libres(m.pl.)	free time
tener hambre	to be hungry	receta(f)	recipe
hoy(m)	today	salsa(f)	sauce
hoy en día	nowadays	si	if
idioma(m)	language	siempre	always
infantil	infantile	sobre	on, above
ir de compras	to go shopping	sobre todo	above all
jamón(m)	ham	sol(m)	sun
llover [ue]	to rain	hace sol	it's sunny
malo	bad	tarde (adv.)	late
hace mal tiempo	the weather's bad	tener [ie] que	to have to
mamá(f)	Mum	tomar el sol	to sunbathe
manzana(f)	apple	traer	to bring
mañana(m)	tomorrow	vez(f)	time, occasion
mar(m)	sea	a veces	at times
		vino(m)	wine

Una excursión a la costa

► Aims ◄

1 Finding your way around a Spanish town
2 Giving and understanding directions
3 Buying food and drink for a picnic

Frases clave

1 ¿Hay una farmacia por aquí?

¿Hay una farmacia por aquí? Is there a chemist's around here?

Sí, hay una farmacia en la Plaza Mayor. Yes, there's a chemist in the Main Square.

¿Por dónde se va a la Plaza Mayor? How do I get to the Main Square?

Siga todo recto y tome la segunda calle a la derecha. Go straight ahead and take the second street on the right.

¿Está lejos? Is it far?

No, está bastante cerca, a unos doscientos metros. No, it's quite near; about two hundred metres away.

2 ¿Está cerca?

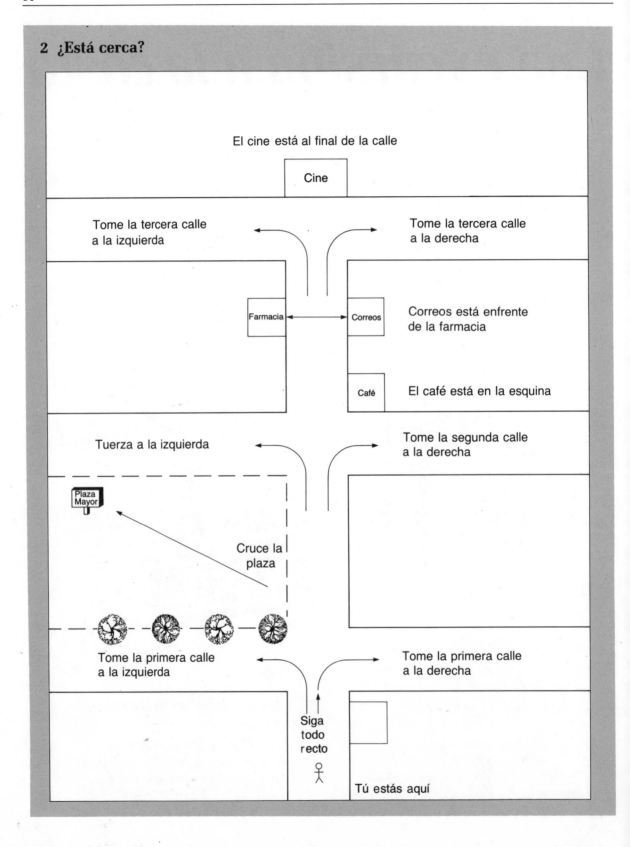

El cine está al final de la calle

Cine

Tome la tercera calle a la izquierda

Tome la tercera calle a la derecha

Farmacia

Correos

Correos está enfrente de la farmacia

Café

El café está en la esquina

Tuerza a la izquierda

Tome la segunda calle a la derecha

Plaza Mayor

Cruce la plaza

Tome la primera calle a la izquierda

Tome la primera calle a la derecha

Siga todo recto

Tú estás aquí

3 ¿Qué quiere usted?

Póngame dos kilos de plátanos. Give me two kilos of bananas.

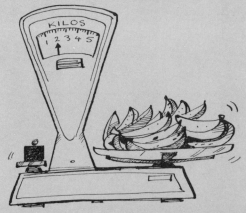

¿Cuánto vale el jamón? How much is the ham?

Vale seiscientas pesetas el kilo. It's six hundred pesetas a kilo.

¿Cuánto valen las peras? How much are the pears?

Valen ochenta pesetas el kilo. They are eighty pesetas a kilo.

Déme dos barras de pan y seis panecillos. Give me two loaves and six bread rolls.

Aquí tiene usted. Here you are.

¿Cómo son las manzanas hoy? What are the apples like today?

Son muy buenas. They're very good.

¿Tiene agua mineral con gas? Have you got fizzy mineral water?

Sí, vale treinta pesetas la botella. Yes, it costs thirty pesetas a bottle.

Conversaciones

1 En el pueblo de la costa

Transeúnte: Perdone, señora. ¿Hay una estación de servicio en el pueblo? Necesito gasolina.

Señora: Sí, hay una estación de servicio en la Calle de Bailén.

Transeúnte: Y, ¿por dónde se va a la Calle de Bailén?

Señora: Mire usted; siga todo recto por esta calle y tome la tercera calle a la derecha. Es una calle bastante ancha, y la estación de servicio está en esa calle al lado del Cine Sol.

Transeúnte: ¿Está lejos?

Señora: No, está bastante cerca, a unos cuatrocientos metros. ¿Va usted en coche?

Transeúnte: Sí.

Señora: ¿Dónde tiene su coche?

Transeúnte: Está ahí en el parking del supermercado.

Señora: Entonces va usted a tardar sólo unos dos o tres minutos en llegar a la estación de servicio.

Transeúnte: Muchas gracias, señora.

Señora: De nada.

2 Por la calle del pueblo

Chica: Perdone, señor. ¿Hay un banco por aquí? Necesito dinero.

Chico: Sí, señorita, hay un banco en la Plaza Mayor.

Chica: ¿Por dónde se va a la Plaza Mayor?

Chico: Vaya usted al final de esta calle y tuerza a la izquierda. Siga todo recto por esa calle y la Plaza Mayor está a unos trescientos metros a mano derecha. El banco está cerca del Ayuntamiento.

Chica: Y, ¿está abierto el banco ahora?

Chico: ¿Qué hora es?

Chica: Son las diez y cinco.

Chico: Entonces el banco está abierto. Los bancos aquí están abiertos desde las nueve de la mañana hasta las dos de la tarde.

Chica: Muchas gracias.

Chico: No hay de qué, señorita.

3 De compras en el pueblo

Tú estás en el pueblo con tu amiga española y quieres comprar comida para la merienda.

Tu amiga: ¿Tienes la lista?

Tú: Sí, la tengo aquí. Vamos a ver: jamón, queso, pan, fruta y una bebida. Eso es todo, ¿no?

Tu amiga: Sí. Pues ahí tienes el mercado.

Tú: ¿No vienes conmigo?

Tu amiga: No, no voy contigo porque tú quieres practicar tu español. Aquí tienes el dinero: dos mil pesetas. ¿Qué vas a comprar exactamente?

Tú: Un cuarto de kilo de jamón, un cuarto de kilo de queso, dos barras de pan, o panecillos si no tienen pan, fruta y una bebida. ¿Qué quieres para beber?

Tu amiga: Agua mineral sin gas. Una botella grande porque con el calor que hace, voy a tener mucha sed. ¿Vale?

Tú: Vale. Hasta pronto.

Tu amiga: Hasta pronto. Te espero aquí en la esquina.

4 En el mercado

Vendedora: Buenos días. ¿Qué desea usted?

Tú: Póngame un cuarto de kilo de jamón, por favor.

Vendedora: ¿Jamón serrano o jamón de York?

Tú: Jamón de York.

Vendedora: Aquí tiene usted. ¿Algo más?

Tú: Sí, un cuarto de kilo de ese queso manchego.

Vendedora: Muy bien. ¿Algo más?

Tú: No gracias. Nada más. ¿Cuánto es todo?

Vendedora: El jamón, ciento cincuenta pesetas, el queso, ochenta pesetas: son doscientas treinta pesetas.

Tú: Aquí tiene usted mil pesetas.

Vendedora: Doscientas treinta, trescientas, cuatrocientas, quinientas, más quinientas son mil.

Tú: Gracias.

Vendedora: A usted.

5 En la panadería

Panadero:	Buenos días. ¿En qué puedo servirle?
Tú:	Déme dos barras de pan, por favor.
Panadero:	¿Grandes o pequeñas?
Tú:	¿Cuánto valen?
Panadero:	Pues, las grandes valen sesenta y cinco pesetas, y las pequeñas valen treinta pesetas.
Tú:	Dos de las pequeñas, por favor.
Panadero:	Aquí tiene. Son sesenta pesetas.

6 En la frutería

Frutero:	Hola. ¿Qué quieres?
Tú:	¿Cuánto valen las peras?
Frutero:	Valen cincuenta pesetas el kilo.
Tú:	Póngame medio kilo.
Frutero:	Aquí tienes. ¿Alguna cosa más?
Tú:	¿Cuánto valen las uvas?
Frutero:	¿Las negras o las verdes?
Tú:	Las negras.
Frutero:	Valen ochenta pesetas el kilo.
Tú:	Póngame un kilo, por favor. ¿Cuánto es todo?
Frutero:	Son ciento treinta pesetas.
Tú:	Aquí tiene usted. Adiós.
Frutero:	Adiós.

7 En el puesto de bebidas

Tú:	¿Tiene agua mineral?
Vendedor:	Sí. ¿Con gas o sin gas?
Tú:	Sin gas, por favor. ¿Cuánto vale?
Vendedor:	La botella grande vale cuarenta pesetas, y la pequeña veinticinco. ¿Cuál quiere?
Tú:	La grande, por favor. Son cuarenta pesetas, ¿verdad?
Vendedor:	Eso es.
Tú:	Aquí tiene usted. Adiós.
Vendedor:	Adiós, y muy buenos días.

¿Comprendes?

Answer the following.

Primera conversación

1 What is the man looking for and why?
2 How does he get to it?
3 How far is it?
4 Where has he left his car?
5 How long will it take him by car?

Segunda conversación

1 What is the girl looking for and why?
2 Where is this building and how will she get there?
3 What else does she want to know about it?
4 What information is she given?

Tercera conversación

1 What is on the shopping list?
2 Why does your friend suggest you go shopping alone?
3 How much money does she give you?
4 What does she want to drink and why does she want a big bottle?
5 Where will she wait for you?

Cuarta conversación

What do you buy at this stall and what does it cost?

Quinta conversación

1 What are the prices of the two sorts of loaf?
2 Which do you select and what do they cost you?

Sexta conversación

What precisely do you buy at the fruit stall and what does it all cost?

Séptima conversación

1 What sorts of mineral water are available?
2 Which do you select and what do you pay for it?

 ## Vamos a hablar

Una merienda

Work with your partner and buy the following items for a picnic. Rewrite all the conversations so that they fit the picnic items and practise the results with your partner.

Cantidad	Comida o bebida
Medio kilo de	jamón de York.
Medio kilo de	queso manchego.
Cuatro	panecillos.
Medio kilo de	manzanas.
Un kilo de	plátanos.
Dos	coca colas.
Dos	Fantas de limón.

In each case:
— ask the price;
— ask what the total cost is;
— pay.

¿Qué quiere decir?

How much is the double ice-cream? With your partner, make up a dialogue to get a 'super giant'.

Cada oveja con su pareja (1)

¿Dónde vas a comprar la fruta?

Partner B: Turn to page 182.

Partner A: You and your partner both have pictures of a fruit stall. Your task is to find out which is the cheaper fruit stall by asking your partner for the prices of all the fruit given below and by giving the prices of the fruit on your stall. Decide which you think is the cheaper!

Decide who will ask the first question.

Your basic question will be:

¿Cuánto valen los/las...?
and your answer:
Valen...pesetas.

Cada oveja con su pareja (2)

¿Por dónde se va a...?

Partner B: Turn to page 183.

Partner A: Copy this map into your writing book.

By asking your partner the basic question:
¿Por dónde se va al/a la...?
find your way to the buildings listed below.
Then tell your partner how to get to the buildings you are asked about. **Do not write in the book**.
You want to find:

el cine 5
la farmacia 3
el mercado 4
la discoteca 2
la piscina 1

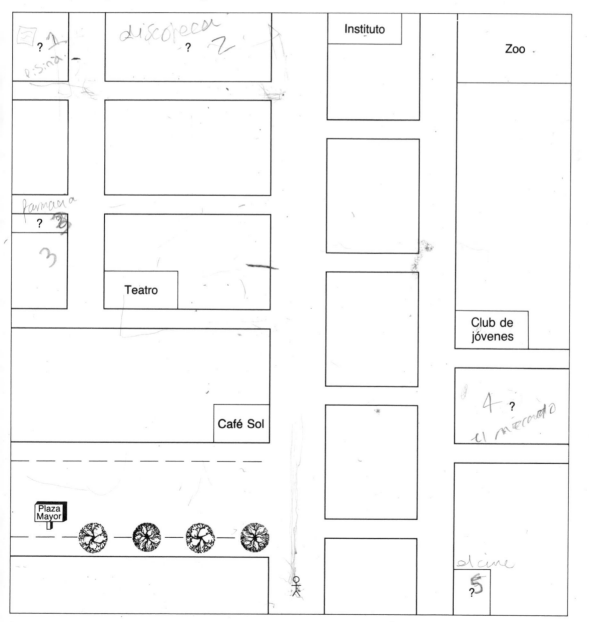

¿Qué se dice?

Work with your partner. One of you is A and the other B. Take it in turns to be A or B.

En la calle

A: (Ask if there is a bank in the village.)
B: *Sí, hay un banco en la Calle Mayor.*
A: (Ask how to get to the Calle Mayor.)
B: *Siga todo recto por esta calle y tome la primera calle a la derecha.*
A: (Ask if it is far.)
B: *No, está bastante cerca, a unos doscientos metros.*
A: (Ask if the bank is open now.)
B: *¿Qué hora es ahora?*
A: (Say it is 1.25.)
B: *Entonces, sí, está abierto.*
A: (Say thank you.)

¿Dónde está la farmacia, por favor?

A: *¿Dónde está la farmacia, por favor?*
B: (Say it is in the Main Square.)
A: *¿Por dónde se va a la Plaza Mayor?*
B: (Tell him/her to go straight ahead, take the second street on the right and the first on the left.)
A: *¿Está lejos?*
B: (Say it is quite near, about two hundred metres away.)
A: *Y, ¿está abierta ahora?*
B: (Ask what the time is.)
A: *Son las cuatro y cuarto.*
B: (Say the chemist's is open.)
A: *Gracias.*

En la frutería

A: (Ask what the bananas are like today.)
B: *Son muy buenos.*
A: (Ask the price per kilo.)
B: *Valen sesenta pesetas el kilo.*
A: (Ask for half a kilo.)
B: *¿Algo más?*
A: (Ask if he/she has any strawberries.)
B: *Claro que sí. Valen ciento cincuenta pesetas el kilo.*

A: (Ask for a kilo.)
B: *¿Alguna cosa más?*
A: (Say no thank you and ask for the total price.)
B: *Son ciento ochenta pesetas.*
A: (Give him/her one thousand pesetas.)

En la charcutería

A: (Ask for 100g of ham.)
B: *¿Jamón serrano o jamón de York?*
A: (Say you want York ham.)
B: *¿Algo más?*
A: (Ask the price of the Manchego cheese.)
B: *Vale doscientas pesetas el kilo.*
A: (Ask for half a kilo.)
B: *¿Eso es todo?*
A: (Say it is and ask the total price.)

Ejercicios

Ejercicio número uno

¿Cómo es tu colegio?

Say or write your answers in Spanish. You will find the following useful:

cerca de   lejos de   en el centro de   al final de   al lado de

1 *¿Dónde está tu colegio?*
2 *¿Cuántos alumnos hay en tu colegio?*
3 *¿Cuántos profesores hay?*
4 *¿Dónde está el despacho del director en tu colegio?*
5 *¿Hay una piscina en tu colegio?*
6 *¿Dónde está el laboratorio de química en tu colegio?*
7 *¿Dónde está el comedor?*
8 *¿Cuántos alumnos hay en tu clase?*
9 *¿Cuántas clases hay por semana?*
10 *¿Cuántos minutos duran las clases?*

Ejercicio número dos

En la tienda de segunda mano

Say or write the prices in Spanish.

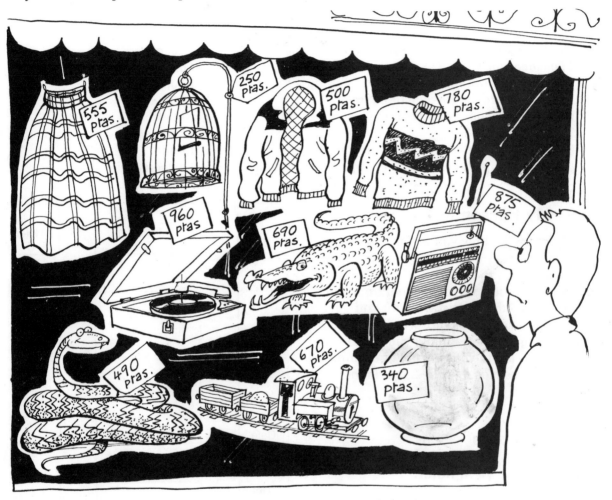

¿Cuánto vale...
...la radio?
...la falda?
...el tocadiscos?
...la jaula?
...el jersey?
...la serpiente?
...la chaqueta?
...el tren?
...el cocodrilo?
...la pecera?

Ejercicio número tres

Un pueblo español

Draw a quick sketch that shows you understand the following.

1 *La catedral está en el centro de la Plaza Mayor.*
2 *La piscina está al final de la calle.*
3 *El teatro está enfrente del mercado.*
4 *La discoteca está al lado del museo.*
5 *El Cine Montesol está cerca del club de jóvenes en una avenida muy ancha.*

Ejercicio número cuatro

¿Qué es esto?

Which item from Column B is described in
Column A? Match the number to the letter.

1 *Un líquido blanco que pones en el té o café.*
2 *La habitación en tu casa o en tu colegio donde comes.*
3 *Un deporte muy popular entre los norteamericanos.*
4 *Tiene doce meses.*
5 *Vas allí para estudiar y aprender.*
6 *La madre de tu madre o de tu padre.*
7 *Una fruta roja que comes con nata.*
8 *Trabaja en un colegio.*
9 *El líquido que está en una piscina o en un río.*
10 *La habitación en tu casa donde preparas la comida.*

a *Un profesor o una profesora.*
b *La fresa.*
c *La leche.*
d *La abuela.*
e *El colegio.*
f *El agua.*
g *El béisbol.*
h *El comedor.*
i *El año.*
j *La cocina.*

 ## My Personal Dossier

This lesson will allow you to add to your
Personal Dossier by writing instructions for
a Spanish friend to reach your house from
the railway station, or your school from your
house. You could also list what for you
would be a favourite picnic, giving foods,
drinks and quantities. Finally you could say
where things are in your town. For example:
*La discoteca está en la Calle....al lado
de...., etc.*

 ## Lectura

¿Por dónde se va al hotel?

A Spanish hotel sends you written
instructions on how to reach the hotel from
the bus station. Read the instructions and
then decide which hotel is the one you
want. Is it A, B or C?

Tuerza a la izquierda y tome la primera
calle a la derecha. Siga todo recto por esa
calle y tome la segunda calle a la
derecha. El hotel está por esa calle a unos
cien metros enfrente del Instituto Galdós.

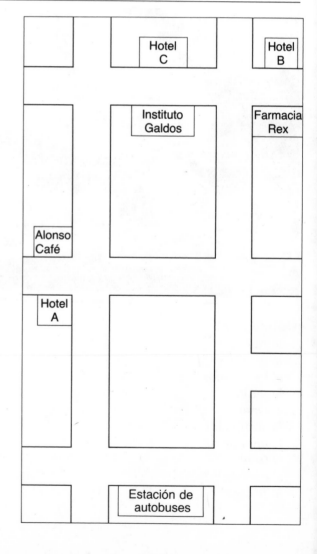

De compras

When staying with a Spanish family you offer to buy food and drink for a picnic in order to improve your Spanish. You are given the following list. What do you buy?

Lista de compras

Medio kilo de queso Manchego.
Un cuarto de kilo de jamón.
Dos barras grandes de pan.
Seis panecillos.
Medio kilo de plátanos.
Un kilo de manzanas.
Una botella grande de agua
   mineral con gas.
Cuatro coca colas.
Una botella de vino blanco.

 ## Vamos a escuchar

¿Por dónde se va a...?

Listen to the three conversations on the tape and write down for each one what the person is looking for and how he or she will get there.

¿Cuánto vale?

Now listen to the next five conversations on the tape and write down in English what the customer buys and what the cost is.

Explanations

Spanish money

Spanish money is very easy to understand because there is only one basic unit – the peseta. Spaniards do, however, also speak of *un duro* which is a five-peseta coin. So, if you hear *veinte duros*, you know the shopkeeper wants 100 pesetas. There are coins of 1, 2, 5, 10, 25, 50, 100 and 200 pesetas, and notes of 500, 1,000, 5,000 and 10,000 pesetas.

Spanish shops

You are likely to find many small, specialist shops in Spain, where the name of the shop is similar in many cases to the things sold in the shop.

For example:

Product sold	Shopkeeper	Shop
la fruta	el frutero la frutera	la frutería
la leche	el lechero la lechera	la lechería
el pescado	el pescadero la pescadera	la pescadería

Common exceptions to this simple rule are:

el pan	el panadero la panadera	la panadería
la carne (meat)	el carnicero la carnicera	la carnicería

Of course, you do not go into a shop because of the name above the door but because of what you see in the window. However, if you walk into a large department store, these names will be useful because many departments in stores have the same names as the shops.

You can do all your shopping in Spain in supermarkets if you wish and not utter a word of Spanish but, if you want to get to know the country and the people, you will do your shopping in small village shops where you can chat to the shopkeeper and improve your spoken Spanish.

Gramática

Numbers 50—1.000

The numbers 50—100 are as follows:

50	cincuenta
53	cincuenta y tres
60	sesenta
65	sesenta y cinco
70	setenta
71	setenta y uno
80	ochenta
87	ochenta y siete
90	noventa
99	noventa y nueve
100	ciento

When 100 is followed by a noun, it shortens to cien

100 pesetas   cien pesetas

If followed by another number, it goes back to ciento:

123   ciento veintitrés

The numbers 200—1,000 are as follows. Take care with the ones marked with an asterisk (*)!

200	doscientos
239	doscientos treinta y nueve
300	trescientos
400	cuatrocientos
500	quinientos*
600	seiscientos
700	setecientos*
800	ochocientos
900	novecientos*
1.000	mil

Mil does not change:
10.000   diez mil

These numbers behave like adjectives and agree with nouns:

Hay doscientas chicas en el colegio.   There are 200 girls in the school.
Hay trescientos chicos en el colegio.   There are 300 boys in the school.

Dates are expressed as follows:

1914   mil novecientos catorce
1988   mil novecientos ochenta y ocho

The numbers 'first' to 'tenth'

You will have noticed these at the beginning of each lesson:

1st	primero
2nd	segundo
3rd	tercero
4th	cuarto
5th	quinto
6th	sexto
7th	séptimo
8th	octavo
9th	noveno
10th	décimo

These numbers agree with nouns.
La primera lección.   The first lesson.

Primero and tercero shorten to primer and tercer before a masculine, singular noun.

El primer día de la semana.   The first day of the week.
El tercer hombre.   The third man.

These numbers are used:

In titles
Isabel segunda.   Elizabeth II.

In a series
La tercera casa a la derecha.   The third house on the right.

They are not used:

In dates (except for primero)
El primero de mayo.   May 1st. (El uno de mayo is also possible.)
El doce de abril.   April 12th.

They are not used beyond 10th as you will see when you reach Lección once.

La novena casa a la izquierda.   The ninth house on the left.
La lección doce.   Lesson 12.

Giving orders or instructions

This form of the verb is called the Imperative and is very easy to make if you follow this simple rule:

Tomar (to take)
You start with tomo (I take).
Remove the o and add e. Tom plus e = tome.
Tome la primera calle.   Take the first street.

Comer (to eat)
You start with *como* (I eat).
Remove the *o* and add *a*. Com plus *a* = *coma*.
Coma la manzana.   Eat the apple.

Escribir (to write)
Start with *escribo* (I write).
Remove the *o* and add *a*. Escrib plus *a* = *escriba*.
Escriba la carta.   Write the letter.

If the verb has an irregular form for the 1st person singular ('I'), then the Imperative is irregular.

Poner (to put)
Start with *pongo* (I put).
Remove the *o* and add *a*. Pong plus *a* = *ponga*.
Ponga la mesa en el   Put the table in the
  comedor.   dining-room.

Seguir (to continue, carry on)
Start with *sigo* (I carry on).
Remove the *o* and add *a*. Sig plus *a* = *siga*
Siga todo recto.   Carry on straight ahead.

Torcer (to turn, twist)
tuerzo (I turn).
Tuerza a la derecha.   Turn to the right.

Dar (to give)
doy (I give).
Déme un kilo.   Give me a kilo.

If you can remember this rule you will only to have to learn by heart one or two verbs. For example:

Ir (to go)
voy (I go)
BUT:
Vaya por esta calle.   Go along this street.

Pronouns are placed on the end of the Imperative.
Déme dos kilos.   Give me two kilos.
Escríbame pronto.   Write to me soon.

Another irregular verb: Venir (to come)

Vengo a pie.	I come on foot.
Vienes en autobús.	You come by bus.
Pedro viene en coche.	Peter comes by car.
Usted viene a las dos.	You come at two o'clock.
Venimos en tren.	We come by train.
Venís a las cinco.	You come at five o'clock.
Los chicos vienen en taxi.	The boys come by taxi.
Ustedes vienen a las diez.	You come at ten o'clock.

Saying 'O.K.'

You have been using the verb *valer* to ask prices.
¿Cuánto vale la leche?   How much is the milk?

You can also use it to say O.K.

A las dos en la plaza. ¿Vale?	At two o'clock in the square. O.K.?
Vale.	O.K.

Keeping it short

You can leave out the noun in Spanish sentences so long as the meaning is clear.

¿Cuánto valen las uvas?	How much are the grapes?
¿Las uvas negras o las uvas verdes?	The black grapes or the green grapes?
Las uvas verdes.	The green grapes.

This is far too long. Look how much neater this version is.

¿Cuánto valen las uvas?	How much are the grapes?
Las negras o las verdes?	The black ones or the green ones?
Las verdes.	The green ones.

Words to learn

abierto	open	limón(m)	lemon
¿algo más?	anything else?	líquido(m)	liquid
ancho	broad, wide	manchego	from la Mancha
Ayuntamiento(m)	Town Hall		(part of Spain)
banco(m)	bank	mano(f)	hand
barra(f)	loaf	mineral	mineral
coche(m)	car	minuto(m)	minute
conmigo	with me	panecillo(m)	bread roll
Correos	Post Office	parking(m)	car park
cuarto	a quarter	peseta(f)	peseta
derecho	right	plaza(f)	square
a la derecha	on the right	preparar	to prepare
desde	from	pronto	soon, quickly
desear	to wish, desire	recto	straight (ahead)
despacho(m)	office	sed(f)	thirst
dinero(m)	money	tener sed	to be thirsty
enfrente [de]	opposite	seguir	to follow, carry on
esquina(f)	street corner	señor(m)	sir
estación de autobuses(f)	bus station	señora(f)	madam
estación de servicio(f)	service station	señorita(f)	miss
final(m)	end	servir [i]	to serve
gas(m)	gas	sin	without
gasolina(f)	petrol	supermercado(m)	supermarket
hospital(m)	hospital	tardar	to take (of time)
izquierda	left	transeúnte	passerby
a la izquierda	on the left	venir [ie]	to come
kilo(m)	kilo	verde	green
laboratorio(m)	laboratory		

¿Qué tal lo pasaste?

1 Talking about what you did recently
2 Expressing how you feel at the moment
3 Buying postcards and stamps to write home

Frases clave

1 ¿Qué tal lo pasaste?

¿Qué tal lo pasaste en la costa?   Did
   you enjoy yourself on the coast?

Lo pasé muy bien.   I enjoyed myself
   very much.

¿Compraste tú la merienda?   Did you
   buy the picnic?

*Sí, compré una merienda estupenda en
   el mercado.*   Yes, I bought a
   smashing picnic in the market.

¿Hablaste inglés o español?   Did you
   speak English or Spanish?

Hablé español todo el día.   I spoke
   Spanish all day.

¿Te bañaste en el mar?   Did you bathe
   in the sea?

*Sí, me bañé en el mar y tomé el sol en la
   playa.*   Yes, I bathed in the sea and
   sunbathed on the beach.

*¿Comprendiste a los vendedores en el
   mercado?*   Did you understand the
   stallholders in the market?

Sí, les comprendí perfectamente.   Yes,
   I understood them perfectly.

2 ¿Qué tal estás hoy?

¿Estás cansado/cansada hoy?   Are you
   tired today?

No, estoy muy bien gracias.   No, I'm
   fine, thanks.

¿Tienes hambre?   Are you hungry?

Sí, tengo hambre.   Yes, I'm hungry.

¿Tienes sed?   Are you thirsty?

Sí, tengo sed.   Yes, I'm thirsty.

¿Dormiste bien anoche?   Did you sleep
   well last night?

Sí, dormí muy bien.   Yes, I slept very
   well.

*¿Te gustaría tomar un café con leche y
   un suizo?*   Would you like to have a
   coffee and a bun?

Sí, me gustaría mucho.   Yes, I'd like
   that very much.

3 ¿Tiene tarjetas postales de la ciudad?

*¿Tiene usted tarjetas postales de
   Ávila?*   Do you have postcards of
   Ávila?

Sí, ahí están al lado de las revistas. Yes, there they are beside the magazines.

¿Cuánto valen? How much are they?
Las grandes valen quince pesetas y las pequeñas diez. The large ones are fifteen pesetas and the small ones ten.

¿Tiene sellos para las tarjetas? Do you have stamps for the cards?

No, los sellos se venden en Correos. No, stamps are sold in the Post Office.

 ## Conversaciones

1 En la cocina de la casa de tu amiga española

El día después de tu visita a la costa con tu amiga española, estás en la cocina de su casa y su madre habla contigo.

La madre: ¿Lo pasaste bien en la costa ayer?
Tú: Sí, lo pasé muy bien.
La madre: ¿A qué hora llegaste a la costa?
Tú: Llegué a las diez menos cinco.
La madre: Y tú compraste la merienda, ¿verdad?

Tú: Eso es. Fui al mercado del pueblo con la lista que usted me dio y compré una merienda estupenda.
La madre: ¿Qué compraste exactamente?
Tú: ¡Huy! Muchas cosas. Pan, jamón, queso, fruta y bebidas.
La madre: Y, ¿comprendiste a los vendedores?
Tú: Sí, les comprendí bien porque todos me hablaron muy despacio.
La madre: ¿Dónde comiste la merienda?
Tú: En la playa. Luego me bañé en el mar y tomé el sol. Lo pasé muy bien. Es un pueblo encantador.
La madre: Me alegro.

2 ¿Cómo estás hoy?

La madre: Pero esta mañana estás cansada, ¿no?
Tú: No, no estoy cansada. Anoche dormí muy bien.

La madre:	Muy bien. Pero, ¿tienes hambre?	*Tú:*	¿Tiene tarjetas postales de la ciudad?
Tú:	Pues, sí, tengo hambre.	*Vendedor:*	Sí, ahí están al lado de la puerta.
La madre:	Y, ¿tienes sed?		

La madre: Muy bien. Pero, ¿tienes hambre?

Tú: Pues, sí, tengo hambre.

La madre: Y, ¿tienes sed?

Tú: Sí, tengo mucha sed. Hace mucho calor hoy, ¿verdad?

La madre: Siempre hace mucho calor aquí en el verano. Por eso vienen tantos turistas. ¿Te gustaría tomar algo? Vamos a ver. Un café con leche y un suizo. ¿De acuerdo?

Tú: Sí, me gustaría mucho. ¿Puedo hacer yo el café?

La madre: ¿Tú sabes hacer café?

Tú: Claro que sí.

La madre: Entonces yo voy a sentarme en mi butaca favorita en el salón y tú puedes hacer el café. Todo lo que necesitas está ahí en la cocina.

Tú: Vale.

La madre: ¡Qué bien hablas el español!

3 En la librería

Después de tomar el café, bajas a la calle porque quieres comprar unas tarjetas postales para mandar a tus padres y a tus parientes. Llegas a la librería, entras y preguntas al vendedor...

Tú: ¿Tiene tarjetas postales de la ciudad?

Vendedor: Sí, ahí están al lado de la puerta.

Tú: ¿Cuánto valen?

Vendedor: Las grandes valen veinte pesetas y las pequeñas valen quince.

Tú: Éstas tres grandes y éstas dos pequeñas, por favor.

Vendedor: Muy bien. Son noventa pesetas.

Tú: ¿Tiene usted sellos para las tarjetas?

Vendedor: No. Los sellos se venden en Correos.

Tú: ¿Dónde está Correos?

Vendedor: Está en esta misma calle. Unos doscientos metros más abajo y a mano derecha.

Tú: ¿Tiene cambio de mil pesetas?

Vendedor: Sí, claro. Noventa, cien, más cuatrocientas son quinientas, más quinientas son mil.

Tú: Gracias. Adiós.

Vendedor: Adiós.

4 En Correos

Tú: Aquí se venden los sellos, ¿verdad?

Empleado: Eso es. En la taquilla número cinco.

Vas a la taquilla.

Tú: Buenos días. ¿Cuánto vale mandar una tarjeta postal a Inglaterra?

Empleada: Vale treinta pesetas.

Tú: ¿Y una carta?

Empleada: Una carta vale treinta y ocho pesetas.

Tú: ¿Quiere darme seis sellos de treinta pesetas y dos de treinta y ocho pesetas?

Empleada: Aquí tiene. Doscientas cincuenta y seis pesetas en total.

Tú: Aquí tiene usted trescientas.

Empleada:	*Cuarenta y cuatro pesetas de vuelta.*
Tú:	*¿Dónde está el buzón, por favor?*
Empleada:	*Ahí está en el rincón.*
Tú:	*Gracias. ¿Puede decirme dónde se compran recuerdos en el pueblo?*
Empleada:	*Pues hay una buena tienda de recuerdos en la Calle de Guzmán. Por esta calle y la primera a la derecha. Ahí tienen de todo.*
Tú:	*Muchas gracias. Adiós.*
Empleada:	*Adiós, y muy buenos días.*

 ¿Comprendes?

Answer the following:

Primera conversación

Summarise in English what you did yesterday as if you are the person in the conversation.

Segunda conversación

1 What are the five questions put to you by your friend's mother?
2 What do you want to do?
3 What will the mother do whilst you are doing it?
4 What compliment does she pay you?

Tercera conversación

1 List exactly what you buy and what it all costs.
2 What cannot you buy in this shop, and where must you go?

Cuarta conversación

1 What do you find out about postal rates from Spain to England?
2 What do you buy exactly?
3 How much change do you get?
4 What other information do you get in the Post Office?

 Vamos a hablar

1 Practise the first conversation with your partner until you can do it well.

2 From the second conversation, find the Spanish phrases for:
   a I slept very well last night.
   b It's very hot today, isn't it?
   c Can I make the coffee?
   d Of course I can.
   e O.K.

3 Rewrite the third conversation with your partner, giving different prices to the postcards and buying a different number of each type. Practise the result with your partner.

Find out from your teacher if postal rates have changed recently and change the conversation to fit the most recent information. Practise the updated version with your partner.

Cada oveja con su pareja (1)

Un día en la costa

Partner B: Turn to page 184.

Partner A: Your partner will ask you questions on how you spent a day on the beach. Answer the questions, using the information contained in the pictures.

Then, ask your partner the following questions on what he/she did. Make a note of the replies you are given.

¿A qué hora llegaste a la costa?
¿Dónde compraste la merienda?
¿Qué compraste allí?

¿Dónde comiste la merienda?
¿Lo pasaste bien?

Cada oveja con su pareja (2)

¿Cuántos hay?

Partner B: Turn to page 184.

Partner A: Answer your partner's questions, using the information given below.

Then ask your partner the questions given here, and make a note of his/her answers.

¿Cuántos alumnos hay en tu colegio?	370
¿Cuántos profesores hay?	27
¿A qué distancia está tu colegio de Londres?	235 kilómetros
¿En qué año naciste?	1974

Now repeat the exercise but give genuine answers.

Cada oveja con su pareja (3)

¿A qué distancia está...?

¿A qué distancia está Valencia de Madrid?

Está a trescientos cincuenta y cuatro kilómetros.

Partner B: Turn to page 185.

Partner A: Your partner will ask you how far certain towns are from each other. Answer the questions, using the information on the chart.

Then, ask your partner how far the following towns are from each other. Make a note of the replies you are given.

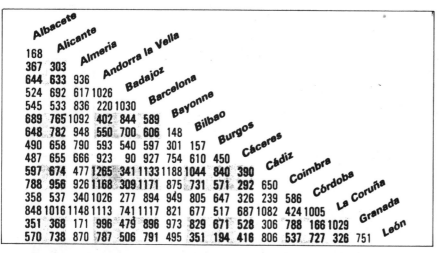

¿A qué distancia está...
Madrid de Vigo?
Oviedo de León?

Pamplona de Santander?
Málaga de Santander?
Murcia de Vigo?

¿Qué se dice?

Work with your partner. One of you is A and the other B. Take it in turns to be A or B.

¿Qué tal lo pasaste?

A: *¿Lo pasaste bien en la costa?*
B: (Say you thoroughly enjoyed yourself.)
A: *¿A qué hora llegaste allí?*
B: (Say at 11.15.)
A: *¿Compraste una merienda?*
B: (Say you bought a good picnic in the market.)
A: *¿Qué compraste exactamente?*
B: (Say you bought bread, cheese, fruit and a coca cola.)

En la costa

A: *¿Dónde comiste la merienda?*
B: (Say you had it on the beach.)
A: *Y luego te bañaste, ¿verdad?*
B: (Say you bathed in the sea and sunbathed on the beach.)
A: *¿Hablaste inglés o español con tu amiga?*
B: (Say you spoke Spanish all day.)
A: *Y ahora estás cansado/cansada, ¿no?*
B: (Say you are rather tired.)

En la tienda de recuerdos

A: (Ask the salesman if he has any postcards of Toledo.) *Tiene tarjetas postales de toledo?*
B: *Sí, ahí están.*
A: (Ask how much they cost.) *Cuanto valen?*
B: *Las grandes valen veinte pesetas y las pequeñas quince.*
A: (Select four large and two small and ask the total price.) *Estás cuatro grandes y estas dos pequeñas. Cuanto valen el todo en total*
B: *Son ciento diez pesetas.*
A: (Ask if he has stamps for the postcards.) *tiene usted sellos para las postales?*
B: *No. Los sellos se venden en Correos.*

En Correos

A: (Ask how much it costs to send a postcard to England.) *Cuanto vale mandar una tarjeta postal a inglaterra*

B: *Vale treinta pesetas.* *darme seis sellos de*
A: (Ask for six 30-peseta stamps.) *treinta pts.*
B: *Aquí tiene usted. Son ciento ochenta pesetas.*
A: (Ask if he has change for 1000 pesetas.)
B: *Claro que sí.* *tiene cambio de mil pts.*

Ejercicios

Ejercicio número uno

Ciudades de España

Look again at the distance charts on pages 115 and 185 and decode the names of these Spanish cities. For example:

RDUHKKZ = SEVILLA

1 AZQBDKÑMZ

2 YZQZFÑYZ

3 BNQCÑAZ

4 UZKDMBHZ

5 FQZMZCZ

6 ZKHBZMSD

Ejercicio número dos

¿Qué pasó?

For example:

¿Visitaste la discoteca?
No, visité la iglesia.

1 *¿Compraste pan y queso?*

2 ¿Escuchaste la radio?

3 ¿Nadaste en el mar?

4 ¿Tomaste el sol en el jardín?

5 ¿Estudiaste el inglés?

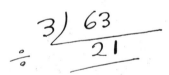

6 ¿Hablaste español?

7 ¿Trabajaste en casa?

8 ¿Cortaste la hierba?

9 ¿Jugaste al críquet?

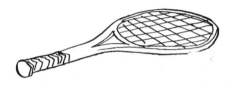

10 ¿Llegaste a las diez?

Ejercicio número tres

¿Qué te pasó?

For example:

¿Qué cogiste, el tren o el autobús?
Cogí el autobús.

1 ¿Qué bebiste, té o coca cola?

2 ¿Qué comiste, una manzana o un plátano?

3 ¿Qué escribiste, una carta o un artículo?

4 ¿Qué viste, una película o la televisión?

Ejercicio número cuatro

¿Qué puedes hacer en clase?

For example:

¿Puedes dormir en clase?
No, no puedo.

¿Puedes trabajar en clase?
Sí, puedo.

1 ¿Puedes bailar en clase?
2 ¿Puedes comer caramelos en clase?
3 ¿Puedes jugar al tenis en clase?
4 ¿Puedes estudiar en clase?
5 ¿Puedes esquiar en clase?

 My Personal Dossier

This lesson has taught you how to say what you did recently. You will now be able to describe what you did last weekend, answering questions such as:

¿Saliste o te quedaste en casa? ¿Con quién saliste? ¿Qué compraste el fin de semana pasado? ¿Escuchaste discos o la radio? ¿Qué estudiaste?, etc.

Try to write as full an account of the weekend as you can.

 Vamos a escuchar

¿Qué pasó?

Listen to the conversations on the tape and, after each one, write down in English what the person did.

¿En qué puedo servirle?

Now listen to the next conversation on the tape. Write down where it takes place, what the customer wants to do and what it costs.

 Lectura

Your Spanish friend has written to you describing what he did last weekend. Read the letter and then answer the questions in English.

1 Where did your friend go last weekend and whom did he visit?
2 How did he get there and how long did it take?
3 What did he have for lunch?
4 What did he do after lunch?
5 With whom did he speak on the beach?
6 What surprised him about this?
7 When did he leave Alicante?
8 What does he think you would like to do?

2

El fin de semana pasado visité a mi abuela que vive en Alicante. Cogí el tren a las ocho y cuarto de la mañana y llegué a Alicante a las doce menos cuarto. Como ya sabes, Alicante es una ciudad grande en la costa mediterránea cerca de Benidorm, adonde van tantos turistas ingleses en el verano. Comí en casa de la abuela y ella me preparó mi comida favorita, pescado frito con patatas fritas y fruta. Después de la comida me bañé en el mar y tomé el sol en la playa. Hablé inglés con una chica inglesa y creo que ella me comprendió.

Bastante raro ¿no?, porque ya sabes que no hablo el inglés muy bien.

A las siete y media cogí el tren otra vez y volví a Murcia. Lo pasé muy bien en Alicante y creo que te gustaría pasar unas vacaciones allí.

Escríbeme pronto y cuéntame como pasaste el último fin de semana.

Tu amigo español,

Manuel

Explanations

Spanish eating habits

The Spanish have a very light breakfast of coffee with bread and jam or thin, batter fritters called *churros*. They eat lunch later than we do and have dinner much later at around eight or nine o'clock. This means that at around five in the afternoon they are quite hungry and have a snack called *merienda*. For children this is often bread with chocolate and a soft drink and, for adults, cakes and coffee in a café. Some cafés specialise in this snack and put signs in their windows to say so. *Una merienda* is also a picnic and many Spanish hotels are happy to provide you with *una merienda* if you are going out for the day and will miss lunch at the hotel.

Spanish markets

Spanish markets are fascinating places to spend an hour or two when on holiday in Spain and very often are the cheapest place to buy food and souvenirs. Most towns and villages have a market, some out of doors in the square and some indoors in specialist buildings. The most famous market in Spain is the Rastro which is held in Madrid every Sunday morning in Ribera de Curtidores. In the Rastro you can buy virtually anything from a pet bird to a suit of armour and many of the shops and stalls specialise in antiques of every kind. But be careful — some of the 'antique' furniture may still smell of paint!

Gramática

Saying what you did

You use a tense called the Preterite which, for regular verbs, is as follows:

Comprar (to buy)

Compré pan.	I bought bread.
Compraste queso.	You bought cheese.
Juan compró fruta.	John bought fruit.
Compramos caramelos.	We bought sweets.
Comprasteis vino.	You bought wine.
Los chicos compraron manzanas.	The boys bought apples.

Remember the way you speak to adults or to people you do not know.

Usted compró una moto.	You bought a motorcycle.
Ustedes compraron pasteles.	You bought cakes.

Comer (to eat)

Comí bien.	I ate well.
Comiste mucho.	You ate a lot.
Comió en casa.	He ate at home.
Comimos fruta.	We ate fruit.
Comisteis mal.	You ate badly.
Comieron en la playa.	They ate on the beach.

Remember the way you speak to adults or to people you do not know.

Usted comió queso.	You ate cheese.
Ustedes comieron bien.	You ate well.

Escribir (to write)

Escribí una carta.	I wrote a letter.
Escribiste a tu madre.	You wrote to your mother.
Escribió a su padre.	He wrote to his father.
Escribimos mucho.	We wrote a lot.
Escribisteis bien.	You wrote well.
Escribieron un artículo.	They wrote an article.

Remember:

Usted escribió una carta.	You wrote a letter.
Ustedes no escribieron mucho.	You did not write very much.

Some verbs which end in -gar have a slightly different ending for the first person singular ('I'):

Llegué a las cinco.	I arrived at 5 o'clock.
Jugué al tenis.	I played tennis.

Some verbs are irregular and you will have to learn them carefully.

Ir (to go)

Fui a París.	I went to Paris.
Fuiste a Madrid.	You went to Madrid.
Juan fue al cine.	John went to the cinema.

(The plural is given in a later lesson.)

Dar (to give)

Di dinero a mi hermano.	I gave money to my brother.
Diste un pastel a tu madre.	You gave a cake to your mother.
Paco dio queso al ratón.	Paco gave cheese to the mouse.

(The plural is given in a later lesson.)

Using the Preterite

You use the Preterite to talk about something you did **once** in the past.

Visité Toledo.	I visited Toledo.
Llegó a Madrid.	He arrived in Madrid.
No comprendí la lección.	I did not understand the lesson.

There is another form of the verb for saying what you used to do or what you were doing and this you will learn later.

Saying how you are at the moment

The way you feel changes frequently and so, to describe how you feel, you use the verb estar which is used for temporary conditions or things that change.

¿Cómo estás?	How are you?
Estoy bien, gracias.	I'm fine, thanks. (You may feel rotten tomorrow.)
¿Estás cansada?	Are you tired?
Sí, estoy un poco cansada.	Yes, I'm a little tired. (You may feel fine later.)
Paco está aburrido.	Paco is bored. (Something may turn up to interest him.)

Saying you are hungry or thirsty

You use tener hambre to say you are hungry.

Tengo mucha hambre.	I'm very hungry.

You use *mucha* because *hambre* is a noun and you actually say:
'I have much hunger'.

¿Tienes sed?	Are you thirsty?
No, no tengo sed.	No, I'm not thirsty.

Saying what you would like

You use *gustaría* with the correct pronoun in front of it:

¿Te gustaría visitar España?	Would you like to visit Spain?
Sí, me gustaría mucho.	Yes, I would like to very much.
¿Te gustaría vivir en el campo?	Would you like to live in the country?
No, no me gustaría nada.	No, I wouldn't like it at all.

Asking where things are bought and sold

You use the normal verbs *comprar* and *vender* with se in front.

¿Dónde se vende la gasolina?	Where is petrol sold?
Se vende en la estación de servicio.	It's sold at the petrol station.
¿Dónde se venden los sellos?	Where are stamps sold?
En Correos.	At the Post Office.
¿Se compra el pan aquí?	Can you buy bread here? (Is bread bought here?)
No, se compra el pan en la panadería.	No, you buy bread at the baker's. (No, bread is bought at the baker's)
¿Dónde se compran las tarjetas postales?	Where can you get post-cards? (Where are post-cards bought?)
En la tienda de recuerdos.	In the souvenir shop.

Using pronouns

What are 'pronouns'? They are words used instead of using the noun. 'It', 'him', 'her', 'them' are all pronouns. In Spanish you put pronouns **in front of** the verb. (In English they come **after** the verb.) You will find Spanish pronouns easy to learn because you know the words already.

¿La bicicleta? La compré en Madrid.	The bike? I bought **it** in Madrid.
¿Los caramelos? Los comí ayer.	The sweets? I ate **them** yesterday.
¿Las chicas? No las veo.	The girls? I can't see **them**.

The pronouns in these examples are simply the same word as for 'the'. The examples have shown you three of these: therefore, you only need to learn one new word:

¿El chocolate? Lo comí.	The chocolate? I ate **it**.

The word for 'it' (when this replaces a singular, masculine noun) is *lo* − the new word to learn.

Being polite

As you saw in Lesson 9, you can tell someone to do something by using the form:

Póngame un kilo.	Give me a kilo.

If you want to be more polite, you say:

¿Quiere ponerme un kilo?	Will you give me a kilo?
¿Quiere darme tres sellos?	Will you give me three stamps?

Words to learn

abajo	down (as of a street)	*mismo*	same, self
acuerdo(m)	agreement	*nacer*	to be born
de acuerdo	O.K.	*número(m)*	number
ahí	there	*pariente(m/f)*	relation
alegrarse	to be glad	*pasado*	last, past
allí	there	*película(f)*	film
anoche	last night	*perfectamente*	perfectly
artículo(m)	article	*por eso*	therefore
ayer	yesterday	*puerta(f)*	door
bajar	to go down	*raro*	odd, curious
butaca(f)	armchair	*recuerdo(m)*	souvenir, regards
buzón(m)	post box	*revista(f)*	magazine
cambio(m)	change	*rincón(m)*	corner
cansado	tired	*sello(m)*	stamp
despacio	slowly	*sentarse [ie]*	to sit down
después(de)	after	*servir [i]*	to serve
distancia(f)	distance	*suizo(m)*	sugared bun
dormir [ue]	to sleep	*tanto*	so, so much, so many
ella	she, her	*taquilla(f)*	ticket office, ticket window
encantador	charming	*tarjeta postal(f)*	postcard
fin(m)	end	*teléfono(m)*	telephone
frito	fried	*total(m)*	total
guía(m)	guide	*vacaciones(f.pl.)*	holidays
hierba(f)	grass	*vendedor(m)*	salesman
invitar	to invite	*vender*	to sell
librería(f)	bookshop	*volver [ue]*	to return
lista(f)	list	*vuelta(f)*	change (money)

Otro buen repaso

► Aims ◄

1 Revision of Lessons 6–10 (See Checklist on page 132.)

 Primera parte: Vamos a escuchar

Un chico español habla de su vida diaria

Listen to the Spanish boy talking on the tape and then choose the correct answer from the ones given below.

1 He gets up at...
 a 7.00;
 b 7.15;
 c 7.30;
 d 7.45.
2 If the weather is fine he...
 a has breakfast in the garden;
 b plays with his dog in the garden;
 c goes for a walk;
 d takes his dog for a walk.
3 His dog is called...
 a Moro;
 b Mona;
 c Moto;
 d Ñono.
4 His breakfast is prepared by...
 a his sister;
 b his father;
 c himself;
 d his mother.
5 He normally drinks...
 a black coffee;
 b milk;
 c fruit juice;
 d white coffee.

6 He leaves for school at...
 a 8.00;
 b 8.15;
 c 8.30;
 d 8.45.
7 When he gets to school, he...
 a chats with his friends;
 b plays in the yard;
 c does his homework;
 d goes in.
8 On his daily timetable there are...
 a eight classes;
 b six classes;
 c five classes;
 d seven classes.
9 He leaves school at...
 a 4.10;
 b 4.15;
 c 4.35;
 d 4.45.
10 After doing his homework, he...
 a plays with his dog;
 b plays with his computer;
 c watches television;
 d goes to bed.

Una chica española habla de sus asignaturas

Listen to the Spanish girl on the tape discussing her school subjects. Write down in English what her favourite subject is and, in two columns, the subjects she likes and those she dislikes.

Un chico español habla de sus pasatiempos

Listen to the Spanish boy on the tape talking about his hobbies. Write down in English what he does on the various days of the week, when the weather is fine and when the weather is bad.

Por la calle

Listen to the Spaniards on the tape asking for directions. Write down after each short conversation the place each person is looking for and how he/she will get there.

En el mercado en España

Listen to the recordings of customers in a Spanish market. Write down what they buy and how much of it they buy. Also write down how much it costs them.

¿Adónde fuiste ayer?

Listen to the Spanish girl on the tape describing what she did yesterday. Write down in English where she went, with whom and what she did.

 ## Segunda parte: Vamos a hablar

¿Qué se dice?

Practise the following role-plays with your partner, taking it in turns to be A or B.

Mi vida diaria

A: ¿A qué hora te levantas por la mañana?
B: (Tell your partner at what time you get up.)
A: ¿Dónde tomas el desayuno?
B: (Tell your partner where you have breakfast.)
A: ¿Qué tomas para el desayuno?
B: (Tell your partner what you have for breakfast.)

A: ¿A qué hora sales de casa por la mañana?
B: (Tell your partner at what time you leave home.)
A: ¿Cómo vas al colegio?
B: (Tell your partner how you travel to school.)

Mi día en el colegio

A: ¿A qué hora llegas al colegio?
B: (Tell your partner at what time you arrive at school.)
A: ¿A qué hora empiezan las clases?
B: (Tell your partner when lessons start.)
A: ¿Cuántas clases tienes por día?
B: (Tell your partner how many lessons you have each day.)
A: ¿Cuál es tu asignatura favorita?
B: (Tell your partner your favourite subject.)
A: ¿Por qué?
B: (Give your partner a reason for your choice.)
A: ¿Qué asignatura no te gusta nada?
B: (Tell your partner the subject you dislike most.)
A: ¿Por qué?
B: (Give your partner a reason for your choice.)

¿Qué tiempo hace?

Make two copies of the map of Spain on page 6. On both mark the following cities and places:

Madrid   Los Pirineos   Málaga   Bilbao Sevilla

Decide what the weather is like in each place and draw a symbol for the weather. For example, a small umbrella could show it is raining. Do not show your partner what weather you have chosen for each place.

Then, question your partner about the weather shown on his/her map (putting the information on your blank map) and answer his/her questions about the weather on yours. When you have both found out about all five places, compare maps to see if you are right.

You will need the question:

¿Qué tiempo hace en...?

¿Qué te gusta hacer?

Find out from your partner what he/she likes to do, at certain times of the week and given certain weather conditions. Write down in English what the activity is and then check with your partner that you are right.

Then, answer his/her questions about what you like to do, at certain times of the week and given certain weather conditions. You can use the following questions, or make up some of your own.

¿Qué te gusta hacer...
...cuando hace buen tiempo?
...cuando hace mal tiempo?
...cuando hace mucho calor?
...los sábados por la mañana?
...los domingos por la tarde?
...los lunes por la tarde?
...durante las vacaciones?
...cuando no tienes deberes?

De compras en el mercado

Buy the following picnic food from your partner. A buys *Lista A* and B buys *Lista B*. You have to find out the following:

¿Tiene...?	Have you got...?
¿Cuánto vale/valen?	How much is it/are they?
Póngame...	Give me...
Déme.	Give me (bread, bottles of drink).
¿Cuánto es todo?	How much is it all together?
Aquí tiene.	Here you are.

Before you start, make up the prices you are going to charge per kilo, bottle, for the various items.

Lista A
A quarter of a kilo of ham.
Two large loaves.
A kilo of apples
Two bottles of fizzy mineral water.

Lista B
Half a kilo of cheese.
Six bread rolls.
Two kilos of pears.
Three bottles of white wine.

¿Dónde está?

Find your way to the various places.

1
A: (Ask if there is a chemist's nearby.)
B: *Sí, hay una farmacia en la Calle de Ronda.*
A: (Ask how you get to the Calle de Ronda.)
B: *Siga todo recto y tome la tercera calle a la derecha.*
A: (Ask if it is far.)
B: *No, está bastante cerca.*

2
A: (Ask if there is a bank in the village.)
B: *Sí, hay un banco en la Plaza Mayor.*
A: (Ask the way to the Plaza Mayor.)
B: *Vaya por esta calle y tome la tercera calle a la izquierda.*
A: (Ask if it is far.)
B: *No, está muy cerca.*
A: (Ask if the bank is open.)
B: *¿Qué hora es ahora?*
A: (Tell him/her it is 11.15.)
B: *Entonces está abierto.*

3
A: *¿Por dónde se va al Cine Sol?*
B: (Tell him/her to go straight ahead and the cinema is at the end of the street opposite the supermarket.)
A: *¿Está lejos?*
B: (Tell him/her it is quite a long way. About five hundred metres.)

4
A: *¿Hay un buen restaurante por aquí?*
B: (Tell him/her there is a good restaurant in the *Calle de Toledo*.)

A: *Y, ¿por dónde se va a la Calle de Toledo?*

B: (Tell him/her to cross the square and take the third street on the left. The restaurant is along that street on the right beside the Post Office.)

5

A: (Ask where bread is sold in the village.)

B: *El pan se vende en la panadería.*

A: (Ask where it is.)

B: *En la Plaza Mayor.*

A: (Ask how you get there.)

B: *Siga todo recto hasta el final de la calle y tuerza a la derecha.*

6

A: (Ask where you can buy records in the town.)

B: *En la tienda de discos.*

A: (Ask if there is a record shop nearby.)

B: *Sí, hay una tienda de discos muy buena en la Plaza de España.*

A: (Ask how you get there.)

B: *Vaya hasta el final de esta calle y tuerza a la izquierda.*

A: (Ask if the record shop is open now.)

B: *Sí, creo que sí.*

A: (Say thank you.)

B: *De nada.*

Cada oveja con su pareja

¿Qué tal lo pasaste?

Partner B: Turn to page 186.

Partner A: These pictures show where you went yesterday, how you travelled, what you did and what you bought. Study the pictures, and then answer the questions your partner will ask you.

Then, ask your partner the following questions to find out what he/she did yesterday: make a note of the replies you are given.

Preguntas

¿Adónde fuiste ayer?

¿Cómo fuiste?

¿A qué hora saliste?

¿A qué hora llegaste?

¿Visitaste algún museo?

¿Fuiste de compras?

¿Dónde comiste?

¿Compraste algo?

Tus vacaciones

Now think about your last holidays —
where you went, with whom, what you did,
etc. Ask each other questions to find out
what you both did.

¿Adónde fuiste de vacaciones?
¿Con quién fuiste?
¿Fuiste en tren?
¿Cuánto tiempo te quedaste allí?
¿Visitaste algún museo?

¿Te bañaste en el mar o en una piscina?
¿Jugaste al golf/al tenis?
¿Compraste algún recuerdo de tus
vacaciones?
¿Lo pasaste bien?

 ## Tercera parte: Vamos a leer

Your Spanish friend is on holiday and sends
you postcards from the places he has
visited. Can you read each one and write
down in English what he did?

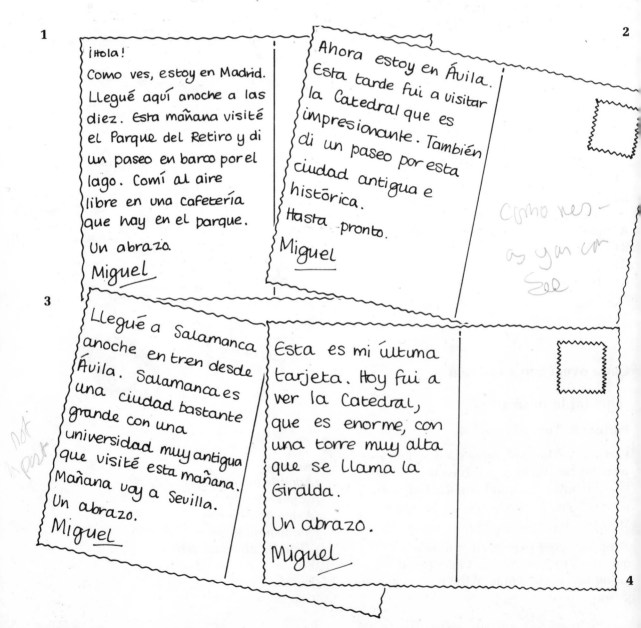

1

¡Hola!
Como ves, estoy en Madrid.
Llegué aquí anoche a las
diez. Esta mañana visité
el Parque del Retiro y di
un paseo en barco por el
lago. Comí al aire
libre en una cafetería
que hay en el parque.

Un abrazo
Miguel

2

Ahora estoy en Ávila.
Esta tarde fui a visitar
la Catedral que es
impresionante. También
di un paseo por esta
ciudad antigua e
histórica.
Hasta pronto.

Miguel

3

Llegué a Salamanca
anoche en tren desde
Ávila. Salamanca es
una ciudad bastante
grande con una
universidad muy antigua
que visité esta mañana.
Mañana voy a Sevilla.
Un abrazo.
Miguel

4

Esta es mi última
tarjeta. Hoy fui a
ver la Catedral,
que es enorme, con
una torre muy alta
que se llama la
Giralda.

Un abrazo.

Miguel

Una carta de España

Read this letter from your Spanish friend
and answer the questions in English.

Hola, amigo:

Hoy te voy a hablar de mis últimas vacaciones que pasé en San Sebastián en la costa del norte de España. Allí hace bastante calor en el verano, pero no hace el calor excesivo como en el sur. Fui a San Sebastián el veinte de agosto y pasé quince días en la costa. Me quedé en un hotel muy bueno muy cerca de la playa. Me bañé en el mar y tomé el sol en la playa. Comí mucho porque me gusta mucho comer bien y la comida en el hotel era estupenda. Visité el Museo de San Telmo que está al lado del Monte Urgull y es un antiguo monasterio del siglo dieciséis. La entrada vale cincuenta pesetas pero es un museo muy interesante. ¿Te gustan las cosas antiguas? A mí, sí. Un día fui al cine por la tarde y vi 'Cobra, el brazo fuerte de la ley' con un actor norteamericano muy fuerte (y bastante guapo) que se llama Sylvester Stallone. ¿Ponen esa película en los cines de Inglaterra? ¿Vas tú mucho al cine? Volví de San Sebastián la semana pasada y te puedo decir que lo pasé muy pero muy bien allí. ¿Por qué no me escribes una carta de tus últimas vacaciones?

Hasta muy pronto,
Un abrazo muy fuerte,
Angela

1 What is your friend going to write about?
2 Where did she go?
3 How is San Sebastián different from the south of Spain?
4 When did she go to San Sebastián?
5 How long did she spend there?
6 Where did she stay?
7 What did she do at the beach?
8 Why did the hotel please her particularly?
9 Where is the Museum of San Telmo and what is it?
10 Which film did she see and who was in it?
11 What does she ask you about this film?
12 When did she come back from San Sebastián?

Cuarta parte: Vamos a escribir

Preguntas y respuestas

These are the answers. Can you write the questions?

1 Me llamo Ángela.
2 Tengo quince años.
3 No me gustan las matemáticas.
4 Vale cien pesetas.
5 Me levanto a las ocho.
6 Las clases empiezan a las nueve y cinco.
7 Los sellos se venden en Correos.
8 Ayer fui al cine con mis amigos.
9 Llegué a casa a las once.
10 Siga todo recto y la Plaza Mayor está a mano derecha.

Una carta a tu amigo español

Read again the letter from your Spanish friend on page 129. Then write a similar letter describing your own holiday. Try to write about 80 words.

¿Por qué?

Match the questions with the correct answer, then copy them out.

1 ¿Por qué no comes la tarta de manzana?
2 ¿Por qué no estudias la informática?
3 ¿Por qué no bebes la coca cola?
4 ¿Por qué no juegas al golf?
5 ¿Por qué llegaste a las once?
6 ¿Por qué no ves la televisión?
7 ¿Por qué vas a Correos?
8 ¿Por qué no vas al banco?
9 ¿Por qué cogiste el autobús?
10 ¿Por qué no vienes conmigo a la piscina?

a Porque hace mal tiempo.
b Porque me levanté muy tarde.
c Porque no me gustan los programas.
d Porque necesito sellos.
e Porque no está abierto.
f Porque no sé nadar.
g Porque no tengo hambre.
h Porque no me gusta ir a pie.
i Porque es muy aburrida.
j Porque no tengo sed.

Quinta parte: Vamos a jugar

Sopa de letras: comida y bebidas

In this *sopa de letras* are hidden six things to eat and six to drink. The food is found horizontally and the drinks vertically. Find them and write them out. **Do not write in the book**.

Mensaje secreto

Can you crack the code?
3:15:7:9/21:14/20:1:24:9/25/6:21:9/1:12/
3:9:14:5/

A	P	R	O	T	K	T	B	O	X
Q	S	D	E	T	P	E	R	A	Y
C	N	A	R	A	N	J	A	M	L
W	Z	G	R	O	U	V	A	I	E
H	O	U	P	Q	T	I	C	E	C
N	M	A	N	Z	A	N	A	O	H
R	O	B	E	U	R	O	F	T	E
C	L	M	A	M	O	N	E	A	R
Q	U	E	S	O	K	E	L	O	V
E	P	A	N	O	Z	R	P	D	E

En el dormitorio

In this picture there are at least ten objects containing the letter *a* twice. Find them and write them out.

Diálogo: En la calle

Try to sort out this muddled up conversation and practise the result with your partner.

- Empiezan a las nueve y cuarto.
- ¿Cómo vas al Instituto?
- Salgo a las ocho y veinte.
- ¿A qué hora empiezan las clases?
- No me gustan mucho.
- Voy a pie porque no está lejos.
- ¿Te gustan las clases?
- ¿A qué hora sales de casa por la mañana?

Message for travellers

Start at the top left corner and find the message. Then write down the question to which it is the answer.

E	L			O	Y	M
	T	A	D	C		E
E	R	M	R	Ñ	I	D		A	R
N		A	I	D	C	I		T	D
L		A		A	S	A	L	A	E
L	E	G		L	A	D	E

Odd one out

Choose the odd one out and say why. For example:

Un ratón; un elefante; el perrò; una pera.
Es la pera porque no es un animal.

1 La biología; la química; el arte; la física.
2 El coche; el tenis; el fútbol; el críquet.
3 El té; el café; la cuchara; la leche.
4 La chaqueta; la manzana; la naranja; el limón.
5 El salón; la piscina; la cocina; el cuarto de baño.

Anagrams

Sort out the jumbled word and write out the sentence.
1 A las diez en la **zalpa**. ¿Vale?
2 Necesito dinero. Voy al **nboca**.
3 Si no hay plátanos en la frutería, puedo comprarlos en el **emrdaco**.
4 Esta tarde voy a bailar en la **itosecdac**.
5 En la estación de servicio se vende la **alagosin**.
6 Si hace buen tiempo, doy un paseo en **tecibalic**.

Checklist 2

As well as being able to do all the things found on Checklist 1 on page 65, you should now be able to do the following things in Spanish. Can you?

Copy out the list for your Personal Dossier. Tick the box if you can do these things and practise anything that you put a cross against.

- talk about what you do each day ☐
- tell the time and say at what time things happen ☐
- discuss your day at school with a Spanish friend ☐
- say what the weather is like and what you do given certain weather conditions ☐
- say which foods you like and dislike ☐
- say what you like doing in your spare time· ☑
- find your way around a Spanish town give and understand directions ☑
- buy food and drink for a picnic ☒
- talk about what you did recently ☑
- buy postcards and stamps in a souvenir shop and a Post Office ☐

gratis

Words to learn

actor(m)	actor
√ aire(m)	air
√ barco(m)	boat
√ brazo(m)	arm
cafetería(f)	cafeteria
√ conocer	to know (be familiar with)
√ cuadro(m)	picture
√ divertido	amusing
√ durante	during
√ enorme	enormous
entrevista(f)	interview
excesivo	excessive
folklórico	folk
hotel(m)	hotel
impresionante	impressive
√ lago(m)	lake
LR ley(f)	law
√ libre	free
mal	bad, badly
monasterio(m)	monastery
ni...ni...	neither...nor...
normal	normal
√ normalmente	normally
nuevo	new
LR panadería(f)	baker's
LR patio(m)	yard, playground
placer(m)	pleasure
restaurante(m)	restaurant
LR siglo(m)	century
LR torre(f)	tower
√ último	last
universidad(f)	university
vuestro	your (talking to friends)

¿Qué vamos a hacer?

1 Making plans
2 Making excuses and saying what you are doing now
3 Getting a snack in a café

Frases clave

1 ¿Qué quieres hacer?

¿Qué quieres hacer esta tarde? What do you want to do this evening?

¿Por qué no vamos al cine? Why don't we go to the pictures?

¿Qué ponen? What's on?

No sé. ¿Dónde está el periódico? I don't know. Where's the newspaper?

¿A qué hora empieza la sesión de la tarde? At what time does the evening performance begin?

A las siete. At seven o'clock.

¿Cuánto valen las entradas? How much are the tickets?

Trescientas pesetas. Three hundred pesetas.

¿Te gustaría ir a la discoteca? Would you like to go to a disco?

No, me gustaría más dar un paseo. No, I'd rather go for a walk.

2 ¿Puedes ayudarme?

¿Puedes ayudarme en la cocina?   Can you help me in the kitchen?

No, estoy haciendo los deberes.   No, I'm doing my homework.

¿Quieres bajar al supermercado?   Will you go down to the supermarket?

No puedo. Estoy arreglando mi bicicleta.   I can't. I'm repairing my bike.

¿Dónde está tu padre?   Where's your father?

Está leyendo el periódico en el cuarto de estar.   He's reading the paper in the sitting-room.

¿Qué está haciendo tu hermana?   What's your sister doing?

Creo que está escribiendo una carta.   I think she's writing a letter.

¿Vas a poner la mesa?   Are you going to lay the table?

No puedo. Estoy muy ocupado con este trabajo.   I can't. I'm very busy with this work.

3 ¿Qué quiere?

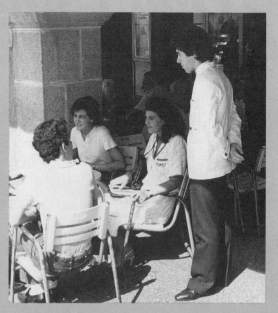

¿Qué va a tomar?   What are you going to have?

Un café con leche y una ración de churros.   A white coffee and a portion of 'churros'.

¿Qué le pongo?   What shall I serve you?

Una cerveza y una ración de patatas fritas.   A beer and a portion of crisps.

¿Algo para mojar?   Something to 'dunk'?

¿Tiene donuts?   Have you got any doughnuts?

¿Qué le debo?   What do I owe you?

Son trescientas pesetas.   That's three hundred pesetas.

¿Quiere cobrar?   Can I pay you?

Dos cervezas, dos naranjadas y una ración de tarta de manzana. Son trescientas veinticinco pesetas.   Two beers, two orangeades and a portion of apple tart. That's three hundred and twenty-five pesetas.

Conversaciones

1 ¿Qué te apetece hacer esta tarde?

Estás en el cuarto de estar de la casa de tu amigo español y estáis haciendo planes para la tarde.

Tu amigo: ¿Qué quieres hacer esta tarde?

Tú: ¿Por qué no vamos al cine?

Tu amigo: ¿Qué ponen?

Tú: No sé. ¿Hay una guía de espectáculos en el periódico?

Tu amigo: Sí. Me parece que está en la página once o doce.

Tú: Vamos a ver. Ah, sí, aquí está. Pues en el Cine Arlequín ponen 'Memorias de África'; en el Cine Avenida ponen 'Loca Academia de Policía 3' y en el Cine Aluche ponen 'Cobra, el brazo fuerte de la ley'. ¿Cuál te gusta más?

Tu amigo: Creo que me gusta más esa película de Robert Redford, 'Memorias de África'.

Tú: A mí también me gusta más esa película.

Tu amigo: ¿A qué hora empieza?

Tú: La sesión de la tarde empieza a las siete, y la sesión de la noche a las diez y cuarto. Vamos a la sesión de la tarde, ¿no?

Tu amigo: Claro que sí. ¿Cuánto valen las entradas?

Tú: Valen trescientas cincuenta pesetas.

Tu amigo: Bueno. Si salimos de aquí sobre las seis podemos ir andando hasta el cine y yo te puedo invitar a tomar algo antes de entrar. ¿Te parece bien? ¿Estás de acuerdo?

Tú: Me parece una idea magnífica. Estoy totalmente de acuerdo.

2 ¡Qué vagos sois!

Más tarde la madre de tu amigo entra y le dice:

La madre: Oye, ¿puedes ayudarme en la cocina?

Tu amigo: Lo siento, mamá, pero no puedo. Estoy haciendo los deberes del colegio.

La madre: ¿Qué estás haciendo exactamente?

Tu amigo: Pues estoy estudiando este capítulo de mi libro de historia para un examen mañana.

La madre:	¿Dónde está tu padre entonces?	*Tu amigo:*	Yo voy a tomar una Fanta de limón. ¿Qué tiene usted para mojar?
Tu amigo:	Creo que está leyendo el periódico en el jardín.	*Camarero:*	Pues hay suizos, ensaimadas, donuts, churros...
La madre:	¿Y tu hermana?	*Tu amigo:*	Para mí una ración de churros. ¿Qué quieres tú?
Tu amigo:	Me parece que ella está arreglando su bicicleta en el garaje. Dice que no anda muy bien.	*Tú:*	Voy a tomar un donut.
		Tu amigo:	Pues, una horchata, una Fanta de limón, una ración de churros y un donut, por favor.
La madre:	¡Qué vagos sois! ¿Qué hago entonces? Necesito aceite y no puedo dejar lo que estoy haciendo en la cocina.	*Camarero:*	En seguida.

La madre: ¿Dónde está tu padre entonces?
Tu amigo: Creo que está leyendo el periódico en el jardín.
La madre: ¿Y tu hermana?
Tu amigo: Me parece que ella está arreglando su bicicleta en el garaje. Dice que no anda muy bien.
La madre: ¡Qué vagos sois! ¿Qué hago entonces? Necesito aceite y no puedo dejar lo que estoy haciendo en la cocina.
Tú: Yo puedo bajar al supermercado, ¿no? ¿Cuánto aceite necesita?
La madre: ¡Qué bueno eres! Necesito un litro de aceite.
Tú: Voy en seguida.

3 ¿Qué vas a tomar?

Después de llegar a la Calle de San Bernardo donde está el Cine Arlequín, tu amigo te invita a tomar algo. Entráis los dos en un café y os sentáis en una mesa cerca de la puerta. Un camarero se acerca.

Camarero: ¿Qué van a tomar?
Tu amigo: ¿Qué te apetece?
Tú: ¿Hay horchata?
Camarero: Sí, hay horchata.
Tú: Para mí una horchata.

Tu amigo: Yo voy a tomar una Fanta de limón. ¿Qué tiene usted para mojar?
Camarero: Pues hay suizos, ensaimadas, donuts, churros...
Tu amigo: Para mí una ración de churros. ¿Qué quieres tú?
Tú: Voy a tomar un donut.
Tu amigo: Pues, una horchata, una Fanta de limón, una ración de churros y un donut, por favor.
Camarero: En seguida.

Llega el momento de pagar, y tu amigo llama al camarero.

Tu amigo: ¡Camarero! ¿Quiere venir un momento?
Camarero: Sí, señor.
Tu amigo: ¿Qué le debo?
Camarero: Una horchata, una Fanta de limón, una ración de churros y un donut.. Son doscientas veinticinco pesetas.
Tu amigo: Aquí tiene usted doscientas cincuenta. Quédese con la vuelta.
Camarero: Gracias, señor. Adiós, y muy buenas tardes.
Tu amigo: Adiós.

 ¿Comprendes?

Answer the following.

Primera conversación

1 What do you intend to do?
2 How do you find out what is on?
3 Which film do you choose?
4 When do the two performances begin?
5 Which performance do you decide to go to?
6 How much are the tickets?
7 What does your friend invite you to do before going to the cinema?

Segunda conversación

Select the correct answer:

1 Your friend is:
  a studying for a history test;
  b studying for a geography test;
  c writing a letter.
2 The father is:
  a working in the garden;
  b sleeping in the garden;
  c reading in the garden.
3 The sister is:
  a out on her bike;
  b fixing her bike;
  c cleaning her bike.
4 The mother needs:
  a oil;
  b milk;
  c fish.

Tercera conversación

List what you order for your snack, what it costs and how big a tip you give the waiter.

Vamos a hablar

Practise the first conversation with your partner until you can do it well. In the second conversation, change all the excuses given for other activities and then practise the new conversation with your partner.

For example, the first excuse: *Estoy haciendo los deberes del colegio* could become *Estoy escribiendo una carta a mi amigo de Sevilla.*

From the third conversation, find the words and phrases which mean:

1 What do you fancy?
2 I'm going to have a doughnut.
3 Can you come here for a moment?
4 What do I owe you?
5 Keep the change.

Cada oveja con su pareja (1)

Lo siento, pero no puedo.

Partner B: Turn to page 186.

Partner A: Look at the pictures and decide what you are doing. Then, when your partner asks you to help, give excuses for not being able to help him/her. Next ask if he/she can help and listen to his/her excuses for not helping you. Write down in English the various excuses given.

Your basic question is: *¿Puedes ayudarme?*

The beginning of each of your excuses is: *Lo siento, pero no puedo. Estoy...*

Cada oveja con su pareja (2)

¿Qué ponen?

Partner B: Turn to page 187.

Partner A: Your partner will ask you what is on at various cinemas. Use this page from a Madrid entertainments guide to answer his/her questions.

Then, ask your partner what is on at the following cinemas, at what time the performance starts and how much the tickets are. You will need the questions given below.

¿Qué ponen en el cine...?
¿A qué hora empieza?
¿Cuánto valen las entradas?

Los cines
Canciller
Capri
Cartago

LISBOA. (Aforo: 1.107.) Paseo de Extremadura, 152 (Carabanchel). Bus 31. Tel. 463 47 04. Cont. 16 h. 200 ptas. Miércoles laborables, 100 ptas.
LOS CAZAFANTASMAS.
DARYL (Tol.).

LOPE DE VEGA. (Aforo: 1.557.) Gran Vía, 55 (Centro). Metros Santo Domingo y Plaza de España. Tel. 247 20 11. Lab. y dom., 16,45, 19 y 22,15 h. 400 ptas.
COBRA, EL BRAZO FUERTE DE LA LEY.

LUCHANA. 3 Salas. Luchana, 38 (Chamberí). Metro Bilbao. Tel. 446 00 39. 400 ptas. Miércoles, excepto festivos y vísperas, 200 ptas. Laborables, excepto vísperas festivos, precio reducido mayores 65 años.
SALA 1. (Aforo: 722.) Cont. 17 h. Pases: 17, 18,55, 20,50 y 22,45 h.
COBRA, EL BRAZO FUERTE DE LA LEY.
SALA 2. (Aforo: 154.) Cont. 17,30 h. Pases: 17,45, 20 y 22,15 h.
LA JOYA DEL NILO (Tol.).
SALA 3. (Aforo: 154.) Cont. 17 h. Pases: 17,20, 19,40 y 22 h.
EL HONOR DE LOS PRIZZI (13).

LUNA. Luna, 2 (Centro). Metro Callao. Parking Tudescos. Tel. 222 47 52. 350 ptas. Miércoles, excepto festivos y vísperas, 225 ptas.
SALA 1. (Aforo: 322.) Lab. y dom., pases película: 18,15 y 22 h.
BARRY LINDON (Tol.).
SALA 2. (Aforo: 342.) Lab. y dom., pases película: 17,15 y 21,30 h.
LAWRENCE DE ARABIA (Tol.).

MADRID. Plaza del Carmen, 3 (Centro). Metro Sol. Tel. 221 56 94. 400 ptas. Lunes a sábado, excepto festivos, mayores 65 años y menores 14, 200 ptas. Miércoles laborables, 200 ptas.
SALA 1. (Aforo: 500.) Cont. 17,30 h. Pases: 17,40, 19,30, 21,20 y 23,10 h. Dom., 17,30, 20 y 22,30 h.
CHICO CELESTIAL.
SALA 2. (Aforo: 340.) Cont. 17,30 h. Pases: 17,50, 20,05 y 22,25 h. Dom., 17,30, 20 y 22,30 h.
LOS SUPERCAMORRISTAS (Tol.).
SALA 3. (Aforo: 500.) Cont. 17,30 h. Dom., 17,30, 20 y 22,30 h.
LOS ROMPECOCOS.
SALA 4. (Aforo: 180.) Cont. 17,30 h. Pases: 17,40, 19,20, 21 y 22,40 h. Dom., 17,30, 20 y 22,30 h.
LA ROSA PURPURA DE EL CAIRO (13).

Cada oveja con su pareja (3)

¿Dónde vamos a merendar?

Partner B: Turn to page 188.

Partner A: Tell your partner what things cost in your café, ask him/her what things cost in his/her café, and decide which is the cheaper. You must ask:
¿Cuánto vale…?

Give as your answer:
Vale…

 ## ¿Qué se dice?

Work with your partner. One of you is A and the other B.

En el café

Look again at the price list for the Café Universal above. You have 100 pesetas to spend and want something to drink and something to eat. Make your selection and answer the waiter's questions.

A: *Buenos días. ¿Qué va a tomar?*
B: (Select your drink.)
A: *¿Algo para mojar?*
B: (Select your food.)
A: *Aquí tiene usted.*
B: (Call the waiter and ask what you owe him.)
A: (Tell him/her.)

¿Puedes ayudarme?

Take your cues from the pictures to make excuses for not helping your partner.

A: *¿Puedes ayudarme?*
B:

A: *¿Y qué está haciendo papá?*
B:

A: *¿Y tu hermana? ¿Qué está haciendo ella?*
B:

A: *¿Y la abuela?*
B:

A: *Todos sois unos vagos.*

¿Qué hacemos?

A: *¿Qué quieres hacer esta tarde?*
B: (Suggest the pictures.)
A: *¿Qué ponen?*
B: (Say you do not know and ask where the newspaper is.)
A: *Ahí está, en la mesa.*
B: *(Say the Cine Rex has La ley de Murphy and the Cine Real has El retorno del Jedi and ask which your friend prefers.*
A: *Me gusta más 'El retorno del Jedi'. ¿Estás de acuerdo?*
B: (Agree.)
A: *¿A qué hora empieza?*
B: (Invent a time.)
A: *¿Cuánto valen las entradas?*
B: (Invent a price.)

¿Estás de acuerdo?

A: *¿Qué te apetece hacer esta tarde? ¿Vamos al cine?*
B: (Say you do not like the cinema. Ask why you do not go to the disco.)
A: *¡Huy, no! Hace mucho calor hoy. ¿Te gustaría dar un paseo?*
B: (Suggest that if it is hot, the swimming pool would be a good idea.)
A: *Vale. ¿Sabes nadar?*
B: (Say that of course you can. Ask how much it costs to get into the pool.)
A: *Creo que vale cien pesetas.*

Ejercicios

Ejercicio número uno

¿Dónde estás? ¿Qué estás haciendo allí?

Think of what you do at different times of the day and give genuine answers.

For example:
¿Dónde estás el lunes a las seis de la tarde?
Estoy en casa.
¿Qué estás haciendo allí?
Estoy viendo la televisión.

1 *¿Dónde estás el domingo a las cinco de la tarde? ¿Qué estás haciendo allí?*
2 *¿Dónde estás el martes a las ocho de la tarde? ¿Qué estás haciendo allí?*
3 *¿Dónde estás el sábado a las tres de la tarde? ¿Qué estás haciendo allí?*
4 *¿Dónde estás el miércoles a las once de la mañana? ¿Qué estás haciendo allí?*
5 *¿Dónde estás el jueves a las diez de la noche? ¿Qué estás haciendo allí?*

Ejercicio número dos

¡Qué raro!

Follow the lines and write what each person or animal is doing. Be careful! Some are a bit odd!

Ejercicio número tres

El camarero eres tú

Give the prices to your tourist customers. For example:

¿Qué le debo?   375 ptas.
Son trescientas setenta y cinco pesetas.

1 *¿Qué le debo?*   *550 ptas.*
2 *¿Quiere cobrar?*   *270 ptas.*
3 *¿Cuánto es todo?*   *485 ptas.*
4 *¿Qué le debo?*   *790 ptas.*
5 *¿Quiere cobrar?*   *900 ptas.*

Ejercicio número cuatro

Haciendo planes

Use each of the phrases once to invite your friend to go to the places listed here. (Remember that *a* plus *el* = *al*.)

¿Vamos a. . .?
¿Por qué no vamos a. . .?
¿Te apetece ir a. . .?
¿Te gustaría ir a. . .?
¿Te gusta más ir a. . .?
1 *El cine.*
2 *La discoteca.*
3 *La playa.*
4 *El campo.*
5 *El museo.*

Ejercicio número cinco

¿Qué te gusta más?

For example:
¿Qué te gusta más, el fútbol o el tenis?
Me gusta más el tenis.
¿Qué te gusta más, las matemáticas o los deportes?
Me gustan más los deportes.

1 *¿Qué te gusta más, el agua mineral o la coca cola?*
2 *¿Qué te gusta más, los días de colegio o las vacaciones?*
3 *¿Qué te gusta más, el español o la física?*
4 *¿Qué te gusta más, el frío o el calor?*

5 *¿Qué te gusta más, las naranjas o los plátanos?*
6 *¿Qué te gusta más, el verano o el invierno?*
7 *¿Qué te gusta más, los perros o los gatos?*
8 *¿Qué te gusta más, el tenis o el rugby?*
9 *¿Qué te gusta más, el café o el té?*
10 *¿Qué te gusta más, España o Inglaterra?*

singular

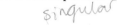 ## My Personal Dossier

You can now add a section to your Personal Dossier about the entertainment facilities in your town or village. You can say how many cinemas, discotheques, etc. there are, when the performance starts, how much the tickets cost.*

Another section could deal with exactly what happens in your house at a certain time of the day. This section could begin: *Son las ocho de la tarde en mi casa. Mi madre está. . . etc.*

*penny   penique(m)
 pound   libra(f)

 ## ¿Comprendes el español?

Mi familia y yo

Make a list in your writing book of the following names:

The father
The mother
The elder sister
The grandfather
The speaker

Listen to the tape and note down in English what each one of them is doing.

¿Qué le debo?

When in Spain you will have to be able to understand prices. Listen to the Spanish waiters and salespeople on the tape, and write down as figures how much they want.

 Lectura

Read this section of a Madrid entertainment guide and answer the questions in English.

PALAFOX. (Aforo: 1.424.) Luchana, 15 (Chamberí). Metros Bilbao y Quevedo. Tel. 446 18 87. Lab., 19 y 22,15 h. Sáb. y dom., 16, 19 y 22,15 h. 400 ptas. *MEMORIAS DE AFRICA* (Tol.).

PARIS. (Aforo: 1.883.) Carlos Martín Alvarez, 45 (Vallecas). Bus 24. Tel. 477 06 90. Cont. 16 h. 200 ptas. Miércoles laborables, 100 ptas. *LOS CAZAFANTASMAS.* *DARYL* (Tol.).

PAZ. (Aforo: 1.002.) Fuencarral, 125 (Chamberí). Metros Bilbao y Quevedo. Tel. 446 45 66. Lab., 19 y 22,15 h. Sáb. y dom., 16,30, 19 y 22,15 h. 400 ptas. Miércoles, excepto festivos y vísperas, 200 ptas. Laborables, excepto vísperas festivos, precio reducido mayores 65 años. *CRONICA SENTIMENTAL EN ROJO* (18).

PEÑALVER. (Aforo: 524.) Conde de Peñalver, 59 (Salamanca). Metro Diego de León. Tel. 402 89 18. Cont. 17 h. Pases: 17, 18,45, 20,30 y 22,15 h. 350 ptas. Miércoles laborables, 225 ptas. *LA JAULA* (18).

PLEYEL. (Aforo: 482.) Mayor, 6 (Centro). Metro Sol. Tel. 222 54 74. Cont. 10 h. 200 ptas. *LA CAMA ELECTRONICA.* *CARIÑO MIO, ¿QUE ME HAS HECHO?* (18).

POMPEYA. (Aforo: 420.) Gran Vía, 70 (Centro). Metro Plaza de España. Tel. 247 09 45. Lab. y dom., 17,10, 19,20 y 22 h. 400 ptas. *CONSUL HONORARIO* (18).

PRINCESA. (Aforo: 1.007.) Princesa, 63 (Moncloa). Metro Argüelles. Tel. 244 38 11. Lab. y dom., 16,30, 19 y 22 h. 350 ptas. *LA LEY DE MURPHY* (18).

PRINCIPE PIO. Cuesta de San Vicente, 16. Metro Plaza de España. Tel. 247 84 27. Cont. 16 h. 250 ptas. Miércoles laborables, 150 ptas. *LA AVENTURA COMIENZA.* *BUSCANDO A PERICO* (13).

PROYECCIONES (Cinerama). (Aforo: 1.087.) Fuencarral, 136 (Chamberí). Metros Bilbao y Quevedo. Tel. 448 27 82. Cont. 17 h. Pases: 17, 18,50, 20,40 y 22,25 h. 400 ptas. Miércoles, excepto festivos y vísperas, 200 ptas. Laborables, excepto vísperas festivos, precio reducido mayores 65 años. *MY CHAUFFEUR* (13).

REAL CINEMA (Cinerama). (Aforo: 1.367.) Plaza de Isabel II, 7 (Centro). Metro Opera. Tel. 248 59 18. Lab. y dom., 16,15, 19 y 22 h. 400 ptas. Miércoles, excepto festivos y vísperas, 200 ptas. laborables, excepto vísperas festivos, precio reducido mayores 65 años. *EL RETORNO DEL JEDI* (Tol.).

RENOIR. Martín de los Heros, 12 (Centro). Metro Plaza España. Tel. 248 57 60. 350 ptas. Lun. a vier., excepto festivos, primera sesión, estudiantes y mayores de 65 años, 250 ptas.

SALA 1. (Aforo: 90.) *YESTERDAY.* V. o. polaco (sesiones: 16,45, 18,50, 20,50 y 23 h.). *HISTORIAS EXTRAORDINARIAS.* V. o. francés (vier. y sáb., sesión madrugada, 1 h.).

SALA 2. (Aforo: 145.) *HISTORIAS EXTRAORDINARIAS.* V. o. francés (sesiones: 16,45, 19,30 y 22,40 h.). Jueves 14, estreno: *STREAMERS* (16,30, 18,30, 20,30 y 22,45 h.). *EL BAZAR DE LAS SORPRESAS.* V. o. inglés (vier. y sáb., sesión madrugada, 1 h.).

SALA 3. (Aforo: 150.) *STRANGER'S KISS.* V. o. inglés (sesiones: 16,30, 18,30, 20,40 y 22,45 h.). *DERSU UZALA* (vier. y sáb., sesión madrugada, 0,45 h.).

SALA 4. (Aforo: 80.) *LA DIAGONALE DU FOU.* V. o. francés (sesiones: 16,15, 18,30, 20,45 y 23 h.). *TO BE OR NOT TO BE.* V. o. inglés (vier. y sáb., sesión madrugada, 1 h.).

1 When are there performances at 4 p.m., 7 p.m. and 10.15 p.m. at the Cine Palafox?

2 When does it cost only 100 pesetas to go into the Paris Cinema?

3 Give the English title of the film at the Peñalver Cinema.

4 What does it cost to see 'Murphy's Law'?

5 Who gets reduced prices at the Real Cinema?

6 What other group of people also get reduced prices at the Renoir Cinema?

This section of the guide deals with
restaurants. Try to find out the following:

Seleccionados **MARISCOS**

PESCADOS DE PRIMERA CALIDAD
AMBIENTE DISTINGUIDO
SERVICIO GUARDA COCHES

RESTAURANTE _____
NARVAEZ, 68 • **Tels. 273 10 87 y 273 82 98**

FADO. Plaza de San Martín, 2 (Centro-Callao). (231 89 24.)
Coc. portuguesa e internacional. (2).

LA FARFALLA. Santa María, 17 (Huertas). Pizzería y carnes
argentinas. Sólo cenas.

FASS. Concha Espina, 34 (Chamartín). (457 00 24 y
457 22 02.) **Coc. alemana.** Diner's, Visa, American, Euro-
card. **(2).**

FIGON DE SANTIAGO. Santiago, 9 (Mayor). (241 32 99.)
Comedor privado. **Coc. casera.** Cerrado domingos. **(5).**

FLORIDA PARK. Parque del Retiro (entrada avenida Menéndez Pelayo, frente calle Ibiza). (273 78 04 y 273 78 05.)
Todos los días, gran espectáculo internacional. Abierto desde las 9,30 de la noche hasta las 3,30 de la madrugada, con
cena o consumición para espectáculo o baile. Restaurante
Pombo Comedor, con terraza al aire libre, abierto mediodía
y noche. Servico aparcacoches. Cerrado domingos.

EL FOGON DE SAN MATEO. San Mateo, 6. (231 84 81.)
Coc. internacional. Espec.: fondues, suprema de merluza.
Cerrado domingos y lunes mediodía. Admite tarjetas. **(2).**

LA FOLIE. Hermosilla, 7. (431 10 72.) **Cocina francesa
creativa.** Cerrado domingos. Tarjetas, todas. **(1).**

LA FONDA. Lagasca, 11 (Salamanca). (403 83 07.) **Coc. cata-
lana. (3).**

LA FONDA. Príncipe de Vergara, 211. (250 61 47.) **Coc. cata-
lana. (3).**

1 Where would you go to eat
  American-style food?
2 Which restaurants are closed on
  Sundays?
3 Where can you get Argentinian food?
4 Which restaurant promises you a great
  international show?
5 Which restaurant allows you to pay with
  all types of credit cards?

Explanations

Cafés

Spanish cafés serve alcoholic drinks and they are generally open all day. Many have terraces and you can have a drink sitting outside watching the people pass by – this is a favourite Spanish pastime. Cafés and bars also have two prices for everything they sell. If you stand up at the bar, the price is slightly lower than if you sit down at a table and are served.

Decide what you want to do, but do not get a drink at the bar and then sit down at a table, because this might annoy the waiters or waitresses.

Prices do vary a lot from café to café and you must not be surprised if you find that you are charged more in one than in another. Find the cheapest and stick to it! By law, all cafés have to display their full price list and so, if you are in any doubt, look for this list which is normally found behind the bar. If you are served by a waiter or waitress, you should leave a tip and 10% of the bill is usually thought to be about right.

Gramática

Saying what you are doing at the moment

This form of the verb is similar to the English form.

Estoy trabajando en el jardín.	I am working in the garden. (I am working in the garden **now**.)

All −ar verbs end in −ando:

Estás jugando al golf.	You are playing golf.

Nearly all -er and -ir verbs end in -iendo:

El ratón está comiendo el queso.	The mouse is eating the cheese.

A few verbs end in -yendo:

Papá está leyendo el periódico.	Dad is reading the newspaper.

Saying what you are going to do very shortly

This form of the verb is also similar to the English form.

Voy a visitar Madrid.	I am going to visit Madrid.
¿Qué vas a tomar?	What are you going to have?
Vamos a tomar una cerveza.	We are going to have a beer.

Saying what you prefer

You simply add *más* after the verb *gusta* or *gustan.*

Me gusta la leche.	I like milk.
Me gusta más la leche.	I prefer milk.
Me gustaría más ser futbolista.	I would prefer to be a footballer.
Me gustan más los deportes.	I prefer sports.

Saying what you fancy

You use *apetecer* which behaves like *gustar* and has two forms.

Me apetece un café con leche.	I fancy a white coffee.
No me apetece salir esta tarde.	I don't fancy going out this evening.
¿Te apetecen unas uvas?	Do you fancy some grapes?

Expressing opinions

You use *parecer* which is like *gustar* and has two forms.

Me parece muy grande.	I think it's very big. (It seems very big to me.)
Me parecen bastante caros.	I think they're rather dear. (They seem rather dear to me.)
¿Qué te parece?	What do you think?
Me parece muy bien.	It seems fine to me.
Me parece que no está en casa.	I think he's not at home. (It seems to me that he's not at home.)

Expressing other opinions

Short phrases are very useful to express opinions.

Claro.	Of course.
Claro que sí.	Obviously.
Claro que no.	Of course not.
Creo que sí.	I think so.
Creo que no.	I don't think so.
Creo que salió.	I think he left.

Saying you agree

You use *de acuerdo* by itself or with the verb *estar.*

A las tres en la plaza.	At three in the square.
De acuerdo.	O.K.
¿Estás de acuerdo?	Do you agree?
No, no estoy de acuerdo.	No, I don't agree.

Giving different meanings to verbs

Poner (to put)

Pongo el dinero en la caja.	I put the money in the box.

Only the first person is odd in the Present Tense.

Juan pone el coche en el garaje.	John puts the car in the garage.

Other meanings

Pongo la mesa.	I lay the table.
¿Qué ponen?	What's on? (What are they putting on?)
¿Qué le pongo?	What shall I serve you? (What shall I put on the bar for you?)

Andar (to walk)

Ando por la plaza.	I walk round the square.

Other meanings

La bicicleta anda bien.   The bike goes well. (All mechanical things can be described using *andar*.)

¿Cómo anda tu vida?   How are you getting along? (How is your life going?)

Words to learn

academia(f)	academy	*idea(f)*	idea
aceite(m)	oil	*libro(m)*	book
antes (de)	before	*litro(m)*	litre
apetecer	to fancy	*loco*	mad, crazy
arreglar	to fix, repair	*magnífico*	magnificent
ayudar	to help	*memoria(f)*	memory
camarero(m)	waiter	*mojar*	to 'dunk', make wet
capítulo(m)	chapter	*naranjada(f)*	orangeade
cero	zero	*ocupado*	busy, occupied
cerveza(f)	beer	*pagar*	to pay
cobrar	to earn, get paid	*página(f)*	page
cocinar	to cook	*papá(m)*	dad
contra	against	*parecer*	to seem, appear
cuarto de estar(m)	sitting-room	*periódico(m)*	newspaper
dejar	to leave, let, allow	*plan(m)*	plan
donut(m)	doughnut	*policía(m)*	policeman
ensaimada(f)	type of round bun	*policía(f)*	police
entrar	to enter, go in	*ración(f)*	portion
espectáculo(m)	entertainment	*seguida*	
examen(m)	examination	*en seguida*	immediately, straight away
ganar	to win, earn	*sesión(f)*	performance
gol(m)	goal	*totalmente*	totally
horchata(f)	non-alcoholic drink made with nuts	*vago*	idle, lazy

De compras en España

Frases clave

1 ¿Qué deseaba?

Chicas

Quisiera ver algunas blusas de verano, por favor.   I'd like to see some summer blouses, please.

¿Qué talla, por favor?   What size, please?

Creo que llevo un treinta y ocho.   I think I wear a thirty-eight.

¿De qué es? ¿De seda?   What's it made of? Silk?

No, es de algodón.   No, it's made of cotton.

Es un poco cara. ¿No tiene usted otra más barata que ésta?   It's a little expensive. Don't you have a cheaper one than this?

¿Quiere probársela? El probador está por aquí.   Do you want to try it on? The fitting-room is over here.

Le va muy bien, ¿no?   It suits you very well.

Sí, me la quedo.   Yes, I'll take it.

Chicos

Quisiera ver algunas camisas de verano, por favor.   I'd like to see some summer shirts, please.

¿Sabe usted la medida del cuello?   Do you know the collar size?

Sí, llevo un treinta y siete.   Yes, I take a thirty-seven.

¿Con manga larga o con manga corta?   With long sleeves or short sleeves?

Con manga corta.   With short sleeves.

¿Le gusta ésta?   Do you like this one?

No está mal, pero ¿no tiene usted otra más oscura?   It's not bad, but don't you have one in a darker colour?

2 En la joyería

¿Quiere mostrarme algunos collares, por favor?   Will you show me some necklaces, please?

Había unos en el escaparate que me gustaban mucho.   There were some in the window which I liked a lot.

¿Dónde estaban exactamente?   Where were they exactly?

Estaban a la derecha y valían seis mil pesetas.   They were on the right and cost six thousand pesetas.

¿Éstos, quizás?   These, perhaps?

¿De qué son?   What are they made of?

Son de oro.   They are made of gold.

Éste, por favor.   This one please.

¿Se lo envuelvo?   Shall I wrap it?

Sí por favor, es un regalo para mi madre.   Yes, please, it's a present for my mother.

3 ¿Cómo era su vida?

¿Dónde vivías?   Where did you use to live?

Vivía en Ávila.   I used to live in Ávila.

¿Trabajabas mucho en la escuela?   Did you work hard at school?

No, no trabajaba mucho.   No, I didn't work hard.

¿Qué te gustaba hacer en tus ratos libres?   What did you like doing in your free time?

Me gustaba ver dibujos animados en la televisión.   I liked watching cartoons on television.

¿Comías mucho?   Did you eat a lot?

Sí, comía mucho, y estaba bastante gordo/gorda.   Yes, I used to eat a lot and I was rather fat.

¿Ibas a la piscina?   Did you go to the swimming pool?

No, no iba a la piscina porque no sabía nadar.   No, I didn't go to the swimming pool because I didn't know how to swim.

 ## Conversaciones

1 En la tienda de ropa

Karen está en España y hace mucho calor. Decide que necesita ropa de verano y va a la tienda.

Dependiente: Buenas tardes. ¿Qué deseaba?

Karen: Quisiera ver algunas blusas de verano.

Dependiente: Muy bien. ¿Qué talla, por favor?

Karen: Creo que llevo un treinta y ocho.

Dependiente: Y, ¿de qué color quería la blusa?

Karen: Azul, creo, o quizás verde. Había una en el escaparate ayer que me gustaba mucho.

Dependiente: ¿Dónde estaba exactamente?

Karen: Estaba a la izquierda del escaparate al lado de un vestido rojo y valía cuatro mil quinientas pesetas.

Dependiente: A ver si me acuerdo. Era ésta, ¿no?

Karen: Sí, creo que sí. ¿De qué es? ¿De algodón?

Dependiente: No, es de políester. ¿Le gusta? ¿Quiere probársela?

Karen: Sí, por favor.

Dependiente: Muy bien. El probador está por aquí.

Unos momentos después.

Dependiente: Le va muy bien.

Karen: ¿No le parece que es un poco grande? ¿No tiene usted otra un poco más pequeña?

Dependiente: Un momento, por favor. Sí, aquí tiene usted un treinta y seis.

Karen: ¿Me la puedo probar?

Dependiente: Claro que sí.

Unos momentos más tarde.

Karen: Sí, ésta es mucho mejor. Me gusta mucho. Me la quedo.

Dependiente: Muy bien. ¿Quiere pagar en caja? Está por aquí.

2 En la tienda de bisutería

Después de comprar la blusa, Karen se da cuenta de que necesita un regalo para su madre y va a la bisutería.

Dependienta: Buenas tardes. ¿En qué puedo servirle?

Karen: ¿Quiere mostrarme algunos pendientes, por favor? Vi unos en el escaparate esta mañana que eran muy bonitos, pero ahora no están allí.

Dependienta: ¿Dónde estaban en el escaparate?

Karen: A la derecha, cerca de las sortijas.

Dependienta: Entonces eran éstos.

Karen: Son muy grandes, ¿no? ¿No tiene usted otros más pequeños?

Dependienta: Más pequeños. ¿Éstos, entonces?

Karen: Sí, ésos son mejores. ¿De qué son?

Dependienta: Son de oro macizo, y valen cinco mil pesetas. ¿Son para usted? Puede probárselos si quiere.

Karen: No, son para mi madre. Son muy bonitos, ¿verdad? Sí, éstos. Me los quedo.

Dependienta: Muy bien. Los voy a poner en una caja muy bonita. Estoy segura de que le van a gustar mucho a su madre.

Karen: Espero que sí. Valen cinco mil pesetas, ¿verdad?

Dependienta: Eso es. ¿Quiere pagar en caja?

Estás en casa de tu amigo español y empiezas a hablar de su vida cuando vivía en otra región de España.

Tú: ¿Dónde vivías antes de venir aquí a Ávila?

Tu amigo: Vivía en Madrid.

Tú:	¿Trabajabas mucho en la escuela?
Tu amigo:	Sí, trabajaba mucho porque me gustaban todas las asignaturas.
Tú:	¿Qué hacías en tus ratos libres? ¿Ibas a la piscina?
Tu amigo:	No, no iba a la piscina porque no había piscina cerca de mi casa, pero iba mucho a la discoteca.
Tú:	¿Cómo era tu casa en Madrid?
Tu amigo:	No era una casa, sino un piso. Era bastante grande, pero no me gustaba porque no había jardín. Aquí tenemos un jardín muy grande, como ya sabes, y puedo jugar con mi perro en el jardín. Mi vida es mucho mejor aquí y mucho más divertida.
Tú:	Ya lo creo.

¿Comprendes?

Answer the following.

Primera conversación

Describe exactly what the girl bought, why she wanted a different size and how much she paid.

Segunda conversación

Select the correct answer.

1 Karen wants to see...
   a ear rings;
   b necklaces;
   c rings;
   d bracelets.
2 The ones she liked were...
   a on the left near the rings;
   b on the right near the necklaces;
   c at the front next to the bracelets;
   d on the right near the rings.

3 She asks to see some that are...
   a dearer;
   b cheaper;
   c smaller;
   d bigger.
4 They cost...
   a   5,000 pesetas;
   b   3,000 pesetas;
   c 10,000 pesetas;
   d   6,000 pesetas.
5 The present is for...
   a herself;
   b her sister;
   c her aunt;
   d her mother.
6 The shop assistant puts the present into...
   a a pretty bag;
   b a pretty box;
   c her hand;
   d pretty wrapping paper.

Tercera conversación

Write down in English what your friend used to do before moving to live in Ávila.

 ## Vamos a hablar

1

Girls
Rewrite the first conversation and buy a green, woollen skirt (*falda de lana*), choosing the correct size from page 154. Practise the result with a partner.

Boys
Rewrite the first conversation and buy a white, cotton shirt (*camisa de algodón*), choosing the correct size from page 154. Practise the result with a partner.

Boys and girls
a Work with your partner and change the second conversation so that you buy a silver necklace (*collar de plata*). Practise the result with your partner.

b Change the third conversation to fit yourself. (If you have not moved house, ignore the first part.) Practise the result with your partner.

2

Imagine you are in the shop shown in the photograph on page 147. Decide which garment you wish to buy and make up the necessary dialogue to be able to buy it. You might want to buy one of the following:

un jersey	una camisa
unos pantalones	un polo
unos pantalones vaqueros	un vestido (de verano)
una blusa	etc.

Work with your partner on this dialogue, taking turns to be the shop assistant.

3

Look at the photograph on page 148. Imagine you are in the shop and write the dialogue which will let you buy one of the following:

una sortija	un reloj
un collar	una pulsera
unos pendientes	etc.

Again, work with your partner on this dialogue, taking turns to be the shop assistant.

 ## Cada oveja con su pareja (I)

A los diez años

Partner B: Turn to page 188

Partner A: Use the information given in the pictures to answer your partner's questions. Then ask the questions given below, write down your partner's answers in English and check that you have got everything correct. Then do the exercise again, but this time giving genuine answers.

¿Dónde vivías cuando tenías diez años?

¿Vivías en una casa o en un piso?

¿Trabajabas mucho en la escuela?

¿Dormías en clase?

¿Qué hacías en tus ratos libres?

¿Tenías algún animal en casa?

¿Dónde pasabas las vacaciones?

Cada oveja con su pareja (2)

Partner A and Partner B: Each of you imagines you are a famous person from history. Your partner will try to find out who you were, but you can only answer: *sí* or *no*. So, questions such as:

¿Cómo te llamabas? and *¿Vivías en Inglaterra o en Francia?* are **not** allowed.

You must ask questions like these:
¿Eras bueno/buena?
¿Eras malo/mala?
¿Vivías en Inglaterra/Francia/España/ Alemania/América/ Escocia/Irlanda?
¿Escribías libros/novelas/poesía/comedias?
¿Eras un rey/reina?
¿Vivías en el siglo doce/trece/catorce/ quince/dieciséis/diecisiete/dieciocho/ diecinueve/veinte?

¿Qué se dice?

Work with your partner with one of you taking the part of the shop assistant and the other that of the customer.

En la tienda de ropa

Buy either:

a a size 40, blue, silk summer dress (*vestido de verano*)

or:

b a size 37, yellow, cotton shirt (*camisa*).

Make sure you get exactly what you want and ask to see cheaper, bigger or smaller garments.

En la joyería

Work with your partner. One of you is A and the other B.

A: (Ask to see some necklaces. Say there are some in the window you like.)

B: *¿Dónde están exactamente?*

A: (Say they are on the left and cost 2,000 pesetas.)

B: *Entonces son éstos, ¿verdad?*

A: (Ask what they are made of.)

B: *Son de plata.*

A: (Select one.)

B: *¿Se lo envuelvo?*

A: (Say yes please, and say it is a present for your sister.)

B: *Entonces se lo voy a poner en una caja bonita.*

A: (Say thank you.)

Cada oveja con su pareja (3)

¿Qué tiempo hacía ayer en España?

Partner B: Turn to page 189.

Partner A: Use the following phrases to question your partner about the weather yesterday.

¿Hacía mal tiempo en Madrid?
¿Hacía sol en Vigo?
¿Llovía en Badajoz?
¿Dónde nevaba?
¿Qué tiempo hacía en Barcelona?

Ejercicios

Ejercicio número uno

Un elefante es más grande que un ratón.

Compare the following subjects following the model above:

1 *El inglés – el español*   útil
2 *El arte – la historia*   interesante
3 *Los deportes – las matemáticas*   aburrido
4 *La biología – la física*   difícil

Ejercicio número dos

El zumo de fruta es mejor que la coca cola

Which is better? What's your opinion?

1 *El zumo de fruta – la coca cola.*
2 *La cerveza – el vino.*
3 *El críquet – el baloncesto.*
4 *Una bicicleta – una motocicleta.*
5 *El té – el café.*

Ejercicio número tres

¿Qué hacían?

Draw the following and add the sentences as captions. Display the results in the classroom.

1 *El elefante escribía una carta con su trompa.*
2 *El cocodrilo tomaba una merienda de café con churros.*
3 *El ratón blanco veía la televisión en su casa pequeña.*
4 *La serpiente hablaba con el profesor.*

Ejercicio número cuatro

¿Qué hacías tú a los once años?

1 *¿Qué deporte practicabas?*

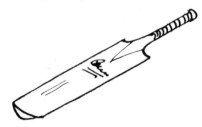

2 *¿Qué bebías con la cena?*

3 *¿A qué hora te ibas a la cama?*

4 *¿Qué comprabas con tu dinero?*

5 *¿Qué escuchabas en tu dormitorio?*

My Personal Dossier

You can now add a section to your Dossier about what you were like some years ago, saying where you lived, which classes you preferred, which sports you played, which pets you had, etc. Old photographs of yourself, your house and animals would make the written information look attractive.

Vamos a escuchar

En la tienda de modas

Listen to this recording of a woman in a shop and write down in English exactly what she buys and what she pays for the goods.

¡Salud!

Nowadays, many people are very concerned about their health, and have changed their lifestyle, in order to live more healthily. How have these people changed their lives?

Lectura

Read the story and work out what the twist is at the end.

La ventana y la pared

El hombre viejo vivía en el hospital porque era pobre y no tenía bastante dinero para tener su propia casa. Su habitación estaba en el segundo piso y el hombre viejo pasaba todo el día en la cama porque estaba muy enfermo. En la habitación había otro hombre y su cama estaba cerca de la única ventana que había en la habitación. Desde esa ventana el otro hombre podía mirar lo que pasaba abajo en la calle y contaba a su amigo todo lo que veía.

– Mira – decía –, ya son las ocho y cuarto de la mañana, y todos los chicos empiezan a salir de sus casas para ir al colegio. Aquí viene un grupo de jóvenes con los libros en la mano. Parecen preocupados. Quizás van a tener un examen hoy. ¿A ti te gustaban los exámenes cuando estabas en el colegio? A mí, sí, porque siempre sacaba buenas notas y mis padres me daban caramelos.

El hombre viejo no contestaba nunca a las preguntas de su compañero porque él quería tener la cama cerca de la ventana para poder mirar la calle.

– Y ahora – continuaba el otro hombre –, viene el cartero con todas las cartas para las casas del barrio. ¡Qué horror! ¡Ese cartero va por la calle leyendo las tarjetas postales! No hay derecho a hacer eso.

Una noche el hombre que tenía la cama cerca de la ventana se murió. Por la mañana entró el médico y dijo al hombre viejo que su compañero estaba muerto.

– ¿Puedo tener la cama cerca de la ventana? – preguntó el hombre viejo.

– Claro que sí – contestó el médico. Un poco más tarde dos empleados colocaron la cama al lado de la ventana.

– ¡Qué contento estoy! –, pensó el hombre viejo – Ahora puedo ver lo que pasa en la calle debajo de esta ventana.

Miró por la ventana. Enfrente de él había una pared alta y gris; una pared y...nada más.

Explanations

Shopping

Most shops in Spain are open from 9 a.m. until 1.30 p.m. and again from 4 p.m. until 7.30 p.m. or 8 p.m. Large department stores, like *Galerías Preciados* or *El Corte Inglés*, are open from 10 a.m. until 8 p.m. and do not close for lunch. Banks are usually open from 9 a.m. until 2 p.m.

If you want to go shopping for clothes in Spain, you will need to know Spanish sizes:

Clothes

Britain	8	10	12	14	16	18
Spain	36	38	40	42	44	46

Shirts

Britain	13 13.5 14 14.5 15 15.5 16
Spain	33 34 35/6 37 38 39 40

Shoes

Britain	3 4 5 6 7 8 9 10 11 12
Spain	36 37 38 39 40 41 42 43 44 45

The questions you need to be able to answer are:

a For clothes: ¿Qué talla lleva usted?
b For shirts: ¿Qué medida de cuello lleva usted?
c For shoes: ¿Qué número gasta usted?

Gramática

Asking to see things in shops

You use the simple phrases: *Quisiera ver algunos/algunas...* plus the name of the thing.

Quisiera ver algunos guantes de piel.	I would like to see some leather gloves.
Quisiera ver algunas faldas de lana.	I would like to see some woollen skirts.

Comparing one thing with another

You use *más...que* in the following ways:

With adjectives
Soy más grande que usted.	I am taller than you.

With nouns
Tengo más dinero que tú.	I've got more money than you.

With verbs
Trabajo más que tú.	I work more than you.

If a number is involved, *que* changes to *de*.

Tiene más de treinta años.	He is over thirty years old. (More than thirty years old)

Saying 'this one', 'that one', 'these' and 'those'

You simply leave out the noun.

Este jersey es más bonito que ese jersey.	This jersey is nicer than that jersey.
Éste es más bonito que ése.	This one is nicer than that one.
Estas faldas son más caras que esas faldas.	These skirts are more expensive than those skirts.
Éstas son más caras que ésas.	These are more expensive than those.

Expressing what you used to do — the Imperfect tense

This is an easy form of the verb to learn and use correctly.

'-ar' verbs like 'trabajar' (to work)
Trabajaba en Madrid.	I used to work in Madrid.
Trabajabas mucho.	You used to work a lot.
Manuel trabajaba en el jardín.	Manuel used to work in the garden.
Usted trabajaba en la tienda.	You used to work in the shop.

'-er' verbs like 'comer' (to eat)
Comía en el colegio.	I used to eat at school.
Comías mucho.	You used to eat a lot.
Juan comía en casa.	John used to eat at home.
Usted comía muy bien.	You used to eat very well.

'ir' verbs like 'vivir' (to live)
Vivía en Londres.	I used to live in London.
Vivías en Edimburgo.	You used to live in Edinburgh.
Pepa vivía en la costa.	Pepa used to live on the coast.
Usted vivía cerca de su trabajo.	You used to live near your work.

(Notice that -er and -ir verbs have the same form in the Imperfect.)

Irregular verbs

Only two verbs are irregular in the Imperfect:

Ir (to go)
Iba a la piscina.	I used to go to the swimming pool.
Ibas a la discoteca.	You used to go to the discotheque.
María iba a la iglesia.	Mary used to go to church.
Usted iba al mercado.	You used to go to the market.

Ser (to be)
Era un buen alumno.	I was a good pupil.
Eras muy tonto.	You used to be very stupid.
Paco era muy inteligente.	Paco used to be very intelligent.
Usted era mi profesor.	You used to be my teacher.

(You must remember that the verb *ver* (to see), keeps the e in the Imperfect:
Veía la televisión. I used to watch television.)

Saying you realise something

You use *darse cuenta de*, and it looks like this:

Me doy cuenta de que tú me quieres.	I realise that you love me.
¿Te das cuenta de que María es tonta?	Do you realise that Mary is stupid?
Juan se da cuenta de que no tiene dinero.	John realises that he has no money.

Saying that something suits you

You simply use parts of the verb *ir*.

Ese vestido te va muy bien.	That dress suits you very well.
Esas gafas de sol me van bien.	These sunglasses suit me.

Concluding a sale

When you have chosen what you want in a shop, you use a set phrase with a small difference depending on whether the noun is singular, plural, masculine or feminine.

El polo: Me lo quedo.	I'll take it.
La falda: Me la quedo.	I'll take it.
Los guantes: Me los quedo.	I'll take them.
Las gafas: Me las quedo.	I'll take them.

'Sino' for 'pero'

The word for 'but' is usually *pero*. However, after a negative, it is *sino*:

No soy inglés sino galés.	I'm not English but Welsh.
No quiero peras sino fresas.	I don't want pears but strawberries.

Words to learn

acordarse [ue]	to remember	*escaparate(m)*	shop window
algodón(m)	cotton	*escuela(f)*	primary school
barato	cheap	*footing(m)*	jogging
barrio(m)	district, part of a town	*fumar*	to smoke
bisutería(f)	cheap jeweller's	*horror(m)*	horror
blusa(f)	blouse	*joyería(f)*	expensive jeweller's
caja(f)	box, till in shop, cash-desk	*lana(f)*	wool
		macizo	solid
camisa(f)	shirt	*manga(f)*	sleeve
caro	dear, expensive	*médico(m)*	doctor
cartero(m)	postman	*medida(f)*	size, measure
cigarrillo(m)	cigarette	*mejor*	better
colocar	to place	*morir [ue]*	to die
collar(m)	necklace	*mostrar [ue]*	to show
comedia(f)	play (in theatre)	*muerto*	dead
compañero(m)	companion	*nota(f)*	note, mark (at school)
contestar	to answer	*novela(f)*	novel
continuar	to continue	*oro(m)*	gold
cuello(m)	neck	*oscuro*	dark (of colour)
darse cuenta	to realise	*paquete(m)*	packet
decidir	to decide	*pendiente(m)*	ear-ring
dependienta(f)	shop assistant (female)	*pensar [ie]*	to think
dependiente(m)	shop assistant (male)	*pesar*	to weigh
dibujo animado(m)	cartoon	*pobre*	poor
diferente	different	*poesía(f)*	poetry
enfermo	ill, sick	*poliéster(m)*	polyester (man-made fibre)
envolver [ue]	to wrap up a parcel, etc.		

portero(m)	porter	sacar	to get, obtain
pregunta(f)	question	salud(f)	health
probador(m)	fitting-room	sano	healthy
probarse [ue]	to try on clothes	seda(f)	silk
quizás	perhaps	seguro	sure, certain
regalo(m)	gift, present	sino	but (after negative)
región(f)	region	sortija(f)	ring
reina(f)	queen	talla(f)	size
rey(m)	king		

¿Cómo te sientes?

Frases clave

1 ¿Cómo estás?

¿Qué te pasa?   What is the matter with you?

Estoy enfermo/enferma.   I'm ill.

¿Cómo te sientes?   How do you feel?

Me siento bien.   I feel well.

¿Cómo se siente usted?   How do you feel?

Me siento mal.   I feel ill.

¿Te sientes mejor?   Do you feel better?

Sí, me siento mejor.   Yes, I feel better.

¿Qué te duele?   What's the matter? (What's hurting you?)

Me duele el estómago.   I've got a stomach-ache.

Me duele la cabeza.   I've got a headache.

Me duele el brazo.   My arm hurts.

Me duele la pierna.   My leg hurts.

¿Dónde te duele?   Where does it hurt?

Me duelen los ojos.   My eyes hurt.

Me duelen los pies.   My feet hurt.

¿Qué te pasa?   What's the matter with you?

Tengo dolor de cabeza.   I've got a headache.

Tengo fiebre.   I've got a fever.

Tengo un resfriado.   I've got a cold.

2 ¿Tiene algo para el dolor de cabeza?

¿Tiene algo para el dolor de cabeza?   Have you got something for a headache?

OKAL es muy bueno.   OKAL is very good.

Necesito algo para la tos. I need something for a cough.

¿Tiene algo para el dolor de estómago?   Have you got something for a stomach-ache?

Necesito algo para la diarrea.   I need something for diarrhoea.

¿Qué recomienda usted para el dolor de ojos?   What do you recommend for sore eyes?

¿Qué recomienda para las quemaduras del sol?   What do you recommend for sunburn?

3 ¿Qué hiciste ayer?

¿Qué comiste ayer?   What did you eat yesterday?

Comí merluza y fruta.   I ate hake and fruit.

¿Era fresca la merluza?   Was the hake fresh?

Sí, creo que sí.   Yes, I think so.

¿Lavaste la fruta antes de comerla?   Did you wash the fruit before you ate it?

No, no sabía que era necesario.   No, I didn't know it was necessary.

¿Cuánto tiempo pasaste en la playa?   How long did you spend on the beach?

Dos o tres horas.   Two or three hours.

¿Hacía mucho calor?   Was it very hot?

Sí, hacía mucho calor.   Yes, it was very hot.

¿Es grave, doctor?   Is it serious, doctor?

No te preocupes. No es nada.   No, don't worry. It's nothing.

Quédate en la cama y toma esta medicina.   Stay in bed and take this medicine.

 Conversaciones

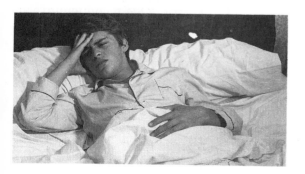

Tu amigo:	¡Vamos, Peter, levántate! Son las ocho y media y salimos para la costa a las nueve.
Tú:	¡Ay, Juan! No me siento bien.
Tu amigo:	¿Qué te pasa?
Tú:	Me duele la cabeza y creo que tengo fiebre.
Tu amigo:	Sí, estás muy pálido. ¿Te duele algo más?
Tú:	Sí, me duele un poco el estómago.
Tu amigo:	¡Mamá! ¿Quieres venir un momento?

La madre: ¿Qué pasa?

Tu amigo: Es Peter. No se siente bien. Le duele la cabeza y le duele el estómago.

La madre: ¿De veras? ¿Qué comiste ayer en el pueblo?

Tú: Pues comí una hamburguesa cuando fui al pueblo con Juan.

La madre: ¿Dónde la compraste?

Tú: En aquel quiosco que hay en la Plaza Mayor.

La madre: ¡Qué horror! Todo el mundo sabe que ese quiosco vende cosas de muy mala calidad. Mira, tú te quedas ahí en la cama y yo voy a llamar al médico.

2 Viene el médico

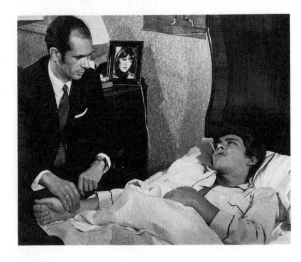

El médico: Pues dice la señora que no te encuentras bien y que comiste una de esas hamburguesas horribles que venden ahí en el pueblo.

Tú: Eso es, doctor, pero yo no sabía que ese quiosco vendía cosas de mala calidad. ¿Es grave, doctor?

El médico: No, no es nada. Quédate en la cama hasta mañana y toma esta medicina. Voy a venir a verte mañana por la tarde.

Tú: ¿Tengo que pagar la medicina, doctor? Soy inglés, ¿sabe?

El médico: No te preocupes, Peter. Esto lo voy a arreglar con la señora. Adiós.

3 En la farmacia

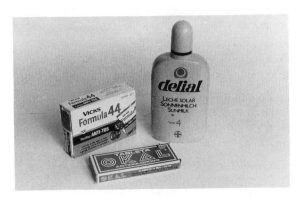

Farmacéutico: Buenos días. ¿En qué puedo servirle?

Mujer: ¿Tiene algo para la tos?

Farmacéutico: Sí, señora. Esto es excelente. Vicks Fórmula cuarenta y cuatro. Ciento cincuenta pesetas. ¿Algo más?

Mujer: Sí. Necesito algo para el dolor de cabeza. ¿Qué recomienda usted?

Farmacéutico: OKAL es muy bueno, señora. Cien pesetas el paquete.

Mujer: Déme un paquete de OKAL, entonces.

Farmacéutico: ¿Eso es todo?

Mujer: No. También necesito algo para las quemaduras del sol. ¿Qué recomienda?

Farmacéutico: ¿Para las quemaduras del sol? Pues, vamos a ver. Hay esta crema que es muy buena, señora, o este aceite que es nuevo.

Mujer: ¿Cuánto vale la crema?

Farmacéutico: Doscientas ochenta pesetas.

Mujer: ¿Y el aceite?

Farmacéutico:	*Quinientas pesetas.*
Mujer:	*Déme un tubo de la crema, por favor.*
Farmacéutico:	*¿Alguna cosa más?*
Mujer:	*No, gracias, nada más. ¿Cuánto es todo?*
Farmacéutico:	*Ciento cincuenta pesetas, más cien, más doscientas ochenta...son quinientas treinta pesetas, señora.*
Mujer:	*Aquí tiene usted. Adiós.*
Farmacéutico:	*Adiós, señora, y muy buenos días.*

¿Comprendes?

Answer the following.

Primera conversación

List in English your symptoms, the probable cause of your illness and what you have to do.

Segunda conversación

1 What do you now know about the hamburgers?
2 What does the doctor tell you to do?
3 What worries you about having called in a doctor?

Tercera conversación

Make a list in three columns giving the following information.

Problem   Medicine   Cost

Vamos a hablar

1 Using the *Frases clave*, rewrite the conversation to fit the following facts:
   a you have a severe stomach-ache and a slight headache.
   b you bought and ate a kilo of strawberries yesterday in the village.
   c you bought the strawberries from a small fruitshop in the Main Square.

2 Practise the second conversation with your partner and record it if you can.
3 Decide with your partner what three health problems you have, invent names for the medicines if necessary, rewrite the conversation and give different prices to those found.

Cada oveja con su pareja (1)

¿Qué te pasa?

Partner B: Turn to page 189

Partner A: Draw a matchstick sketch of your partner.
Your partner will try to find out what your symptoms are by asking you various questions. Your symptoms are given below. Then, find out your partner's symptoms by asking, for example:

¿Te duele la cabeza?
¿Te duelen los pies? etc

Mark your partner's symptoms on the sketch you have drawn.

Cada oveja con su pareja (2)

En la consulta del médico

Partner B: Turn to page 190.

P.190

'i' form

Partner A: Your partner will ask you questions, in order to diagnose your illness. Use the pictures below to answer his/her questions.
Then ask him/her the questions below in order to diagnose his/her illness.

mosto

merluza

¿Adónde fuiste ayer?
¿Cuánto tiempo pasaste allí?
¿Hacía calor?
¿Comiste algo?
¿Dónde la compraste?

¿Qué se dice?

Work with your partner. One of you is A and the other B.

¿Cómo te sientes?

A: *¿Estás bien?*
B: (Say you are ill.)
A: *¿Qué te duele?*
B: (Stomach-ache.)
A: *¿Qué comiste ayer?*
B: (Hake and chips.)
A: *¿Era fresca la merluza?*
B: (Say you do not know.)
A: *Siempre hay problemas con el pescado, ¿sabes?*

¿Te duele algo?

A: *¿Qué te pasa?*
B: (Your feet hurt.)
A: *¿Qué hiciste ayer?*
B: (Say you went for a walk in the country.)
A: *¿Anduviste mucho?*
B: (Say about 15 kilometres.)
A: *Pues esto me parece mucho.*
B: (Say you do not feel well and are going to bed.)

En la farmacia

A: (Ask what he/she recommends for a cough.)
B: *Esto es muy bueno.*
A: (Ask the price.)
B: *Doscientas pesetas el paquete.*
A: (Ask him/her to give you a packet.)
B: *¿Algo más?*
A: (Ask him/her if he/she has got anything for sunburn.)
B: *Esta crema es muy buena.*
A: (Ask if it is expensive.)
B: *No, sólo ciento ochenta pesetas el tubo.*
A: (Ask for a tube.)
B: *¿Alguna cosa más?*
A: (Say nothing more thanks and ask for the total price.)

En la consulta del médico

1

You and your partner must both think up three things that are wrong with you. Each of you has to try to find out what is wrong with the other, but you can only answer, *sí* or *no*.

Use questions such as:

¿Te duele...?
¿Te duelen...?
2
¿Tienes...?
¿Te sientes...?

Ejercicios

Ejercicio número uno

Unscramble the word and write out the sentence.

3

1 *Me duelen los **sipe**.*
2 *Tengo dolor de **zaceba**.*
3 *¿Qué te **leedu?***
4 *Me duele la **inrepa**.*
5 *Creo que tengo **beerif**.*

Ejercicio número dos

You are the person in the picture. Write what is wrong with you.

4

For example:

5

Me duele el pie.

Ejercicio número tres

Match up the question with the correct answer.

1 ¿Por qué te duele la cabeza?

a Por esta calle y la primera a la derecha.

2 ¿A qué hora salió el tren para Madrid?

b El sábado pasado.

3 ¿Dónde está Correos?

c Sí, lo pasé muy bien.

4 ¿Cuánto valen las peras?

d Un café con leche y una ensaimada.

5 ¿Cuánto llegaste a Madrid?

e Porque necesito dinero.

6 ¿Lo pasaste bien en Madrid?

f Porque bebí mucho vino ayer.

7 ¿Qué va a tomar?

g ¡Qué va! Es muy fácil.

8 ¿Es difícil el español?

h Ya lo creo.

9 ¿Por qué quieres ir al banco?

i Ochenta pesetas el kilo.

10 ¿Te gusta Madrid?

j A las ocho y cuarto.

 ## My Personal Dossier

In this final section of your Dossier write down how you feel at the moment, answering questions such as:

¿Cómo te sientes?
¿Estás enfermo/enferma?
¿Qué te duele?
¿Dónde compras medicinas en tu pueblo/ciudad?

 ## ¿Comprendes el español?

En la consulta del médico

Draw five stickpeople, and number them. Listen to the conversations on the tape and mark on the stickpeople which part of their body is causing the trouble.

En la farmacia

Listen to the recordings of people talking to the chemist, and write down in English what is wrong with each of them and how much they pay for their medicine.

 ## Lectura

Una chica española escribe a su madre

Read the letter carefully and answer the questions at the end.

1 Where is Marta today?
2 How does she feel?
3 What does the doctor say?
4 Where did Marta go yesterday?
5 What did she buy there?
6 Where did she eat it?
7 What are her symptoms today?
8 Why did the doctor say she was rather odd?
9 What is her medicine like?
10 How does she end her letter?

Villajoyosa . 20 de julio.

Querida mamá:

Hoy estoy en casa y también estoy en la cama porque no me siento bien. Pero, no te preocupes, porque el médico dice que no es grave y que dentro de dos o tres días voy a estar bien otra vez. Ya sabes que me gusta mucho la fruta. Pues ayer fui con mi amiga Carolina a Alicante, donde hay un mercado de fruta muy bueno. Entré en el mercado y me compré un kilo de fresas porque eran muy buenas y bastante baratas. Fui a la playa con Carolina, me senté al sol y me comí casi medio kilo de fresas en una hora.

Ahora me duele el estómago y me duele la cabeza y también tengo fiebre. Dice el médico que soy una chica bastante rara porque no sabía que hay que lavar la fruta antes de comerla.

Me dio una medicina que es horrible y no me gusta nada, pero la tengo que tomar porque no tengo más remedio. Pero ya te digo, mamá, que no te preocupes porque no es nada y voy a estar bien dentro de muy poco.

Un abrazo de tu hija que te quiere mucho.

Marta x

Explanations

What to do if you are ill

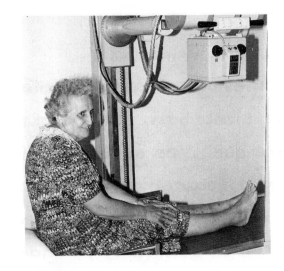

When you go to Spain you should take with you any medicines you need.

The best way to stay healthy in Spain is to avoid excesses of sun, sudden changes in diet or eating too much of anything – chips, fruit, etc. If you are ill you can often find what you want at the chemist's, because chemists in Spain are particularly good at diagnosing and prescribing for many minor illnesses and can often save you the trouble and possible expense of a visit to a doctor. If you need a chemist urgently when the chemist's is closed, you should look for a notice displayed outside all chemist's shops which tells you which ones are open late – the *farmacia de guardia*.

Doctors in Spain display their surgery hours (*horas de consulta*) outside their surgeries.

Most hotels have a doctor on call and, should you need one, you should ask at the reception desk. In addition to the normal doctor's services, there are emergency departments (*centros de urgencia*) in most hospitals and roadside first-aid posts (*puestos de Socorro* or *primeros puestos auxiliares*) manned by doctors or other medically qualified staff.

Ambulances are less common in Spain than in other countries and it is often a taxi that takes a patient or road-accident victim to hospital. When they are doing this, they blow their horn and wave a white handkerchief out of the window to warn other road users.

Gramática

Saying how you feel

You use the verb *sentirse*, which changes the *e* of the first part into *ie* in the first, second and third persons, as follows:

Me siento bien.	I feel well.
¿Cómo te sientes?	How do you feel?
Mi madre se siente mejor.	My mother feels better.

You can also use *estar*, as follows:

Estoy peor.	I'm worse.
¿Estás mal?	Are you ill?
Mi padre está mejor.	My father is better.

Saying what hurts

You use the verb *doler* which changes the *o* to *ue*. It is like *gustar* and so you only use two persons, the third person singular and the third person plural.

Me duele el brazo.	My arms hurts. (My arm hurts me)
Me duele la cabeza.	I've got a headache. (My head hurts me)
¿Te duele el estómago?	Have you got a stomach-ache?
Le duele el pie.	His/her foot is hurting.

If what hurts is plural, the form changes to *duelen*:

Me duelen los ojos.	My eyes hurt.
Me duelen los pies.	My feet hurt.

Asking what hurts

If you are talking to a friend you ask:

¿Qué te duele?   What's hurting you?

If you are talking to a stranger, you ask:

¿Qué le duele?   What's hurting you?

Another way of saying what hurts

You can also use *tener* to say what is hurting.

Tengo dolor de cabeza.	I've got a headache.
Tengo dolor de estómago.	I've got a stomach-ache.
Tengo fiebre.	I've got a fever.
Tengo un resfriado.	I've got a cold.

Asking for things at the chemist's

You can also use *tener* to ask for things at the chemists.

¿Tiene algo para el dolor de cabeza?	Have you got something for a headache?
¿Tiene algo para la diarrea?	Have you got something for diarrhoea?

Or you can use the verb *necesitar*:

Necesito algo para la tos.	I need something for a cough.
Necesito algo para las quemaduras del sol.	I need something for sunburn.

If you wish to ask the chemist's advice, you use *recomendar*:

¿Qué recomienda usted para el dolor de cabeza?	What do you recommend for headache?

Asking what the matter is

You use part of the verb *pasar*:

¿Qué pasa?	What's happening? (What's the matter?)
¿Qué te pasa?	What's the matter with you? (When talking to friends)
¿Qué le pasa?	What's the matter with you? (When talking to strangers)

Giving orders

This is how you tell a friend, member of your family, etc. what to do. You use the third person singular of the Present tense.

Toma la medicina.	Take the medicine.
Come la hamburguesa.	Eat the hamburger.
Escribe a tu madre.	Write to your mother.

Pronouns go on the end of this form of the verb (but not on the end of the negative).

Come la sopa. Cómela.	Eat the soup. Eat it.
Toma la medicina. Tómala.	Take the medicine. Take it.
Escribe la carta. Escríbela.	Write the letter. Write it.

Words to learn

ahora	now	necesario	necessary
auxiliar	auxiliary	ojo(m)	eye
cabeza(f)	head	pálido	pale
calidad(f)	quality	pastilla(f)	tablet, pill
crema(f)	cream	pierna(f)	leg
dentro (de)	within	preocuparse	to worry
diarrea(f)	diarrhoea	problema(m)	problem
doctor(m)	doctor	puesto(m)	stall (in market)
doler [ue]	to hurt	quemaduras del sol(f.pl.)	sunburn
dolor(m)	pain	quiosco(m)	kiosk
esto	this	recomendar [ie]	to recommend
estómago(m)	stomach	remedio(m)	remedy
excelente	excellent	no tener más remedio	to have no other choice
fiebre(f)	fever	resfriado(m)	cold
fresco	fresh	socorro(m)	help
grave	grave, serious	tos(f)	cough
hamburguesa(f)	hamburger	tubo(m)	tube
lavar	to wash	urgencia(f)	urgency, emergency
medicina(f)	medicine		
mundo(m)	world		
todo el mundo	everybody		

El último repaso

 ## Primera parte: Vamos a escuchar

Haciendo planes

Listen to the recordings of Spanish people talking and then write down in English what they plan to do, where they agree to meet and at what time.

¡Qué familia!

Listen to the tape, on which the various members of a family give excuses for not helping the mother. Write down in English the excuse given by each person.

En el café

Listen to the recordings of customers in a café in Spain, and write down in English what each one orders.

De compras en España: En la tienda de modas

Listen to the recording of a girl in a dress shop in Spain. Write down what she buys, giving the colour, size and price.

De compras en España: En la tienda de recuerdos

What does the boy on the tape buy for his sister? Write down what he buys, what it costs and what it is made of.

Ahora no

Listen to the Spanish young people on the tape, and write down what they used to do but do not do now.

En la consulta del médico

Listen to the recordings of patients in a doctor's surgery, and write down in English what is wrong with them and what may have caused the trouble.

Segunda parte: Vamos a hablar

¿Qué se dice?

Practise the following role-plays with your partner, taking it in turns to be A or B as appropriate.

Haciendo planes

You wish to invite your partner to go and see *Amor libre* at the cinema this evening at 7 p.m. Find out if he/she is free and arrange to meet in the small café in the Main Square. Practise the conversation with your partner.

Lo siento pero no puedo

Make up excuses for not doing whatever your partner asks you to do. You can begin:

Lo siento pero no puedo...
and then give your excuse.

1 *¿Puedes ayudarme a arreglar mi bicicleta?*
2 *¿Quieres ir a la discoteca conmigo esta tarde?*
3 *¿Puedes ir al supermercado? Necesito pan.*
4 *¿Por qué no tomamos un café?*

Tengo hambre

Work out for yourself a snack you might want to buy in Spain — something to eat and something to drink. Then work out with your partner what you would have to say to get it. Practise the conversation with your partner, taking turns to be the customer.

¿Vamos de compras?

Chicas
Work out the conversation with your partner which would allow you to buy the following: A green, silk blouse size 38. Practise the result with your partner.

Chicos
Work out the conversation with your partner which would allow you to buy the following: A white, cotton shirt size 40. Practise the result with your partner.

¿Qué regalo voy a comprar?

Look at this photograph of presents you might buy in Spain for your mother, sister, aunt, etc. Select a present and write a conversation with your partner that would help you to buy it. Find out:

a if the shop has what you want;
b what it is made of;

¿Cómo eras?

Think back to your days in junior school and answer your partner's questions honestly.

A: *¿A qué hora llegabas a la escuela por la mañana?*
B: (Tell him/her.)
A: *¿Trabajabas mucho en la escuela?*
B: (Tell him/her.)
A: *¿Cómo se llamaba tu profesor favorito?*
B: (Tell him/her.)
A: *¿Comías en la escuela o en casa?*
B: (Tell him/her.)
A: *¿A qué hora salías de la escuela por la tarde?*
B: (Tell him/her.)

¿Cómo te sientes?

Imagine an illness and see if your partner can diagnose it. You can only answer *sí* or *no*. Your partner cannot say: *¿Qué te duele?* but must ask? *¿Te duele. . .?* or *¿Te duelen. . .?* (Make it is as difficult for your partner as possible.)

¿Qué necesitas?

Go to a chemist's in Spain and buy medicines, etc. for headache, sunburn and a stomach-ache. Find out what the chemist recommends and the various prices. A is the chemist and B is the customer.

 ## Tercera parte: Vamos a leer

Recados

The following notes have been left for you by Spanish friends. Can you write down in English what each one is trying to tell you?

No puedo ir a la discoteca contigo esta tarde porque mi madre está enferma y yo tengo que quedarme en casa para hacer la cena.
Juan.

Manolo y yo vamos a la costa mañana. Vamos a salir a las nueve de la mañana. Si estás libre y quieres venir, ven a la casa de Manolo a las nueve menos cuarto.
Pepita

Lo siento mucho, pero no puedo venir a tu casa esta tarde para ayudarte a hacer los deberes de matemáticas. Estoy muy ocupada porque tengo un examen mañana
Isabel.

Si estás libre me gustaría mucho ir al cine contigo mañana por la tarde. Hay una película estupenda en el Cine Sol. Empieza a las siete de la tarde. Si estás libre y quieres venir, ven al cine un poco antes de las siete.
Roberto

Una carta de tu amigo español

Read this letter from your Spanish friend
and answer the questions in English.

2

Este año fui de vacaciones a la costa con mis padres.
Lo pasé muy bien porque me gusta mucho bañarme
y tomar el sol y la playa de Villajoyosa es estupenda.
Pasé quince días en Villajoyosa en un hotel muy
bueno donde la comida era magnífica. Ahora estoy
bastante gordo porque comí mucho. Durante dos días
estuve un poco enfermo porque comí muchas
hamburguesas que compré en un quisco que había
en la playa y no eran de buena calidad. También
pasé muchas horas en la playa tomando el sol.
Ahora me siento mucho mejor.
¿Adónde fuiste tú de vacaciones? ¿Lo pasaste
bien? ¿Te quedaste en un hotel o en casa
de amigos? Escríbeme pronto y cuéntame lo
que hiciste durante las vacaciones.
Un abrazo muy fuerte.

Pablo

1 Where did your friend go and with whom? 2
2 Why did he enjoy himself?
3 What was good about the hotel?
4 Why did your friend put on weight?
5 Why was he ill for a time? 3
6 How is he now?
7 What does he want you to write about?

Cuarta parte: Vamos a escribir

1

Look again at the notes on page 171. Write similar ones to Spanish friends to give the following messages:

a You cannot go to the swimming pool this morning because you have to do your school homework.

b You and your friend Peter are going to the pictures tomorrow evening. Tell your friend that if he/she is free and wants to go with you, he should come to your house at 6.45.

c You are very sorry but you cannot help your friend to repair his/her bike. You have to stay at home and help your dad in the garden.

d You would very much like to invite your friend to go to the disco with you tomorrow evening. The disco starts at 8 p.m. and, if your friend is free, he should come to the disco a bit before 8 p.m.

2

Read again the letter on page 172. Then write a similar letter to your Spanish friend saying what you did on your holidays.

Quinta parte: Vamos a jugar

Sopa de letras

In this *sopa de letras* fourteen words to do with shopping for clothes and jewellery are hidden. They are found horizontally or vertically. Ten of them will fill the gaps in the sentences below. Which ten are they? **Do not write in the book.**

P	L	A	T	A	M	A	N	G	A
O	Q	C	A	M	I	S	A	S	P
L	E	N	L	A	N	A	J	O	Z
I	R	B	L	U	S	A	L	R	J
E	S	C	A	P	A	R	A	T	E
S	C	F	A	L	D	A	P	I	R
T	O	N	S	A	B	O	P	J	S
E	C	O	L	L	A	R	D	A	E
R	S	E	D	A	E	O	L	K	Y
O	P	R	O	B	A	D	O	R	A

1 *Me gustaría mucho comprarme una...de seda pura.*

2 *¿Es de lana la...? No, es de algodón.*

3 *No voy a llevar mis pantalones para ir a la discoteca. Me gusta más llevar una....*

4 *Ese...de lana gris me gusta mucho.*

5 *Hay unos en el...que me gustan mucho.*

6 *¿Es de algodón? No, es de....*

7 *¿Quiere la camisa con...larga o con...corta?*

8 *¿Es de oro? No, es de....*

9 *¿Quiere probárselo? El... está por aquí.*

10 *¿Qué...por favor?*

Mensaje secreto

Start with the ringed letter and go from letter to letter find the message. You might say this to a friend.

I	B	R	E
L	(E)	S	E
S	A	T	S
D	R	A	T

E?

¿Qué palabra?

Which word from Column B best completes the phrase started in Column A

Columna A	Columna B
Una taza de	vino/café/peras.
Un litro de	aceite/plátanos/camisas.
Un paquete de	café/gasolina/seda.
Una blusa de	seda/pescado/agua.
Medio kilo de	tenis/tocadiscos/uvas.

¡Qué raro!

This person knows little about Spanish! Can you correct the errors?

1 Necesito dinero. Voy al teatro.
2 La gasolina se vende en la frutería.
3 Si tienes sed, ¿por qué no tomas una naranja?
4 Voy a comprar sellos en la estación de servicio.
5 ¿Por qué no tomamos el sol en la planta?

Checklist 3

As well as being able to do all the things found on Checklists 1 and 2 on pages 65 and 132, you should now be able to do the following things in Spanish. Can you? Copy out the list and if you can, tick the boxes. If you cannot, put a cross in the box and ask your teacher for some more practice.

- make plans and arrange to meet ☐
- make excuses ☐
- say what you are doing now ☐
- get a snack in a café ☐
- buy clothes ☐
- buy presents for family and friends ☑
- say what you used to do ☑
- say you feel ill ☑
- buy medicines at a chemist's ☑
- say what you think caused the illness ☑

And now you can go on learning more Spanish and more about Spain. ¡Suerte!

Pair-work Partner B

Segunda lección

Partner A should be looking at page 15.

Partner B: Ask your partner the questions in the left-hand column, and make a note of his/her answers. Then, answer the questions your partner will put to you, as if you were the girl in the photograph. Use the information given here to answer the questions.

¿Cómo te llamas?	Susan.
¿Cuántos años tienes?	14.
¿De dónde eres?	Londres. (London)
¿Eres inglés o español?	Inglesa.

When you have finished, do the exercise again but this time give genuine answers.

Tercera lección

(1) Mi familia

Partner A should be looking at page 26.

Partner B: Ask your partner the questions in the left-hand column, and make a note of his/her replies. Then, answer the questions your partner will ask you, using the information given in the right-hand column.

¿Tienes hermanos?	3
¿Son chicos o chicas?	1 hermano, 2 hermanas
¿Cómo se llaman?	Rafael, Anita y Pepa
¿Cuántos años tiene tu hermano?	11
¿Y cuántos años tiene tu hermana?	14 y 23

When you have finished, do the exercise again but this time give answers for your own situation, ignoring any questions which do not apply.

(2) ¿Cómo es?

Partner A should be looking at page 26.

Partner B: Ask your partner the questions in the left-hand column, and make a note of his/her replies. Then, answer the questions your partner will ask you, using the pictures given on the next page for your replies.

¿Cómo es tu madre?

Y tu hermano, ¿cómo es?

Y, ¿cómo es el bebé de la familia?

When you have finished, do the exercise again but this time give answers for your own family and do not answer any questions which do not apply to you. For example, there may not be a baby in your family.

Cuarta lección

Partner A should be looking at pages 34 and 35.

Partner B: Before you start this pair-work, copy the map on the opposite page into your writing book, writing down all the information it contains.

Ask your partner where the towns and cities mentioned below are, and write them onto your copy of the map. Then, your partner will ask you where various towns and cities in Spain are. Use the information found on the map to answer the questions put to you.

¿Dónde está Toledo?
¿Dónde está Bilbao?
¿Dónde está Valencia?
¿Dónde está Sevilla?
¿Dónde está Badajoz?

¿Está cerca o lejos?
Check with your partner that your two maps are accurate, and then use them to ask each other these questions, taking turns to ask and answer.

¿Está Toledo cerca de Madrid?
¿Está Valencia cerca de San Sebastián?
¿Está Bilbao lejos de Málaga?
¿Está San Sebastián lejos de Bilbao?
¿Está Madrid lejos de Alicante?
¿Está Sevilla cerca o lejos de Cáceres?

Quinta lección

(1) ¿Cómo es tu dormitorio?

Partner A should be looking at page 45.

Partner B: Ask your partner the following questions about his/her bedroom, and make a note of his/her answers. Then, answer the questions your partner will ask you about the bedroom in the picture on the opposite page: answer as if it were your bedroom, using the information in the picture.

¿Es grande tu dormitorio?
¿Cuántas camas hay en tu dormitorio?
¿Tienes un armario?
¿Cuántas sillas hay?
¿Tienes una mesa?
¿Tienes un ordenador?
¿Qué hay en la pared?
When you have finished, make a plan of
your own bedroom at home and then answer
the same questions again, but this time
giving genuine answers.

(2) ¿Tienes algún animal en casa?

Partner A should be looking at page 46.

Partner B: Ask your partner the following questions about his/her pet animal, and make a note of his/her answers. Your partner will then ask you questions about your pet animal: use the information contained in the picture below to answer the questions.

¿Tienes algún animal en casa?
¿Cómo se llama?
¿Es grande o pequeño?
¿De qué color es?
¿Qué come?

Séptima lección

(1) ¿Cómo se dice?

Partner A should be looking at page 70.

Partner B: Ask your partner how to say the words in the left-hand column, in Spanish. For example:
¿Cómo se dice knife en español?

Then, your partner will ask you how to say the five words in the right-hand column, for which you have a Spanish translation. Tell him/her how to say these.

1 knife
2 spoon

3 milk
4 plate
5 bread

1	sugar	*el azúcar*
2	marmalade	*la mermelada de naranjas*
3	butter	*la mantequilla*
4	cup	*la taza*
5	black coffee	*el café solo*

When you have finished, work through the questions again but answer them about your own pet, if you have one. If you do not have a pet, invent one.

(2) ¿A qué hora?

Partner A should be looking at page 71.

Partner B: Find out at what time your partner does various things by asking the questions in the left-hand column; make a note of the answer you receive.

Then your partner will ask you at what time you do various things: the times are given in the right-hand column.

Give short answers, for example:

A las diez.

When you have finished, do the activity again, but this time give genuine answers as they apply to you.

2 *¿A qué hora sales de casa?*

3 *¿A qué hora empiezan las clases?*

¿A qué hora sales del Instituto?

¿A qué hora ves la televisión?

¿A qué hora te vas a la cama?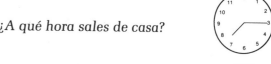

(3) ¿En qué clase estás?

Partner A should be looking at page 71.

Partner B: Copy the timetable below into your writing book. Then fill in the gaps by asking your partner:
¿En qué clase estás el (day of week) a las (time)?

When your partner has given you this information, he/she will then ask you the same questions to fill in the gaps on his/her timetable.

Your answer will be
Estoy en la clase de...

Hora	Lunes	Martes	Miércoles	Jueves	Viernes
9.00		Informática	Matemáticas	Trabajos manuales	
10.00	Francés		Geografía	Matemáticas	Ciencias
11.00	Español	Corte	Ciencias	Francés	Español
2.00	Arte	Historia		Historia	Deportes
3.00	Matemáticas	Inglés	Español		Deportes

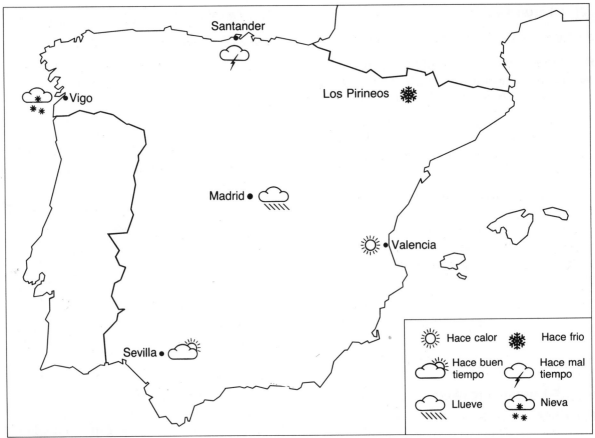

Octava lección

(1) ¿Qué tiempo hace en España?

Partner A should be looking at page 83.

Partner B: Copy this map of Spain into your writing book. Mark on it the towns and places given here, but **not** the symbols for the weather.

Ask your partner what the weather is like at all the places named on the map. Make a note of the weather, using symbols, on the map you have copied into your writing book.

Your partner will then ask you what the weather is like in Spain. Use the information from the map given here to answer the questions.

(2) ¿Te gusta o no?

Partner A should be looking at page 84.

Partner B: Find out whether your partner likes a number of different things. Record the answers, using the following symbols.

Your partner will then ask you whether you like these things: give answers according to the ticks and crosses found after each question.

✓ = me gusta (Remember gustan for plurals.)
✓✓ = me gusta mucho
✗ = no me gusta
✗✗ = no me gusta nada

Write down the numbers 1–10 so that you can record the answers. Ask your partner whether he/she likes the following things. Record the answers, using the symbols given above. When you have finished, check that you have got the correct results.

Your partner will then ask you whether you like these things: give answers according to the ticks and crosses after each question below. Then do the exercise again, but this time give genuine answers.

1 ¿Te gusta el inglés? ✓
2 ¿Te gustan los ratones? ✗✗
3 ¿Te gusta nadar en el mar? ✓✓
4 ¿Te gustan las chicas estúpidas? ✗✗
5 ¿Te gusta el francés? ✓
6 ¿Te gusta ver la televisión? ✗
7 ¿Te gustan los caramelos? ✓
8 ¿Te gusta visitar museos? ✗
9 ¿Te gustan las matemáticas? ✓✓
10 ¿Te gustan los discos de música pop? ✗✗

(3) ¿Te gusta el colegio?

Partner A should be looking at page 84.

Partner B: Choose the school subject that you like best from the following list.

Try to find out which subject your partner has chosen.

Then answer your partner's questions until he/she discovers which subject you have chosen.

Remember to use the correct question, when asking your partner. For example:

Los deportes = ¿Te gustan los deportes?
La música = ¿Te gusta la música?

1 El español.
2 El inglés.
3 Las matemáticas.
4 Las ciencias.
5 El arte.
6 La educación física.

Novena lección

(1) ¿Dónde vas a comprar la fruta?

Partner A should be looking at page 100.

Partner B: You and your partner both have pictures of a fruit stall. Your task is to find out which is the cheaper fruit stall by asking your partner for the prices of all the fruits given below and by giving the prices of the fruit on your stall. Decide which you think is the cheaper!

Decide who will ask the first question.

Your basic question will be:

¿Cuánto valen los/las...?
and your answer:
Valen...pesetas.

(2) ¿Por dónde se va a....?

Partner A should be looking at page 101.

Partner B: Copy this map into your writing book.

Tell your partner how to get to the buildings you are asked about.

Then, by asking your partner the basic question:

¿Por dónde se va al/a la...?
Find your way to the following buildings:

el Café Sol
el club de jóvenes
el Instituto
el zoo
el teatro

Décima lección

(1) Un día en la costa

Partner A should be looking at page 114.

Partner B: Ask your partner the following questions on how he/she spent a day on the beach. Make a note of the replies you are given.

Then, your partner will ask you questions on what you did. Answer the questions, using the information contained in the pictures.

¿Cómo viajaste a la costa?
¿Dónde te bañaste?
¿Dónde comiste?
¿Tomaste el sol?
¿Lo pasaste bien?

(2) ¿Cuántos hay?

Partner A should be looking at page 114.

Partner B: Ask your partner the following questions, and make a note of his/her replies. Then, answer your partner's questions, using the information given below.

¿Cuántas chicas hay en tu colegio?	785
¿Cuántas profesoras hay?	47
¿A qué distancia está tu colegio de Cardiff?	125 kilómetros
¿En qué año nació tu hermano?	1972

Now repeat the exercise but give genuine answers.

(3) ¿A qué distancia está...?

¿A qué distancia está Valencia de Madrid?
Está a trescientos cincuenta y cuatro kilómetros.

Partner A should be looking at page 115.

Partner B: Ask your partner how far the following towns are from each other, and make a note of the replies you are given.

Then, your partner will ask you how far certain other towns are from each other. Answer the questions, using the information on the chart.

¿A qué distancia está...
Badajoz de Bilbao?
Almería de Cádiz?
Granada de Barcelona?
Cáceres de Badajoz?
Alicante de Córdoba?

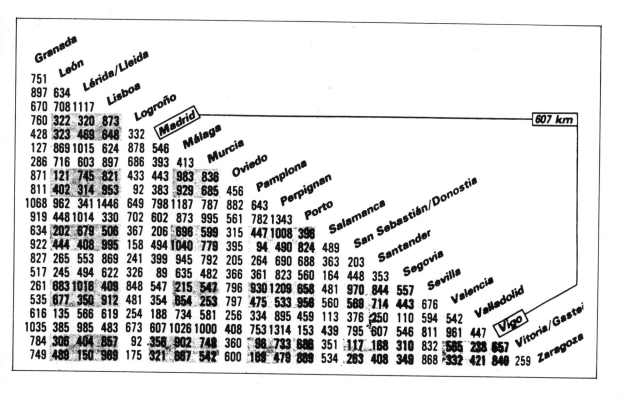

```
Granada
751   León
897   634   Lérida/Lleida
670   708  1117   Lisboa
760   322   320   873   Logroño
428   323   469   848   332   Madrid
127   869  1015   624   878   546   Málaga
286   716   603   897   686   393   413   Murcia
871   121   745   821   433   443   983   836   Oviedo
811   402   314   953    92   383   929   685   456   Pamplona
1068  962   341  1446   649   798  1187   787   882   643   Perpignan
919   448  1014   330   702   602   873   995   561   782  1343   Porto
634   202   679   506   367   206   696   599   315   447  1008   398   Salamanca
922   444   408   995   158   494  1040   779   395    94   490   824   489   San Sebastián/Donostia
827   265   553   869   241   399   945   792   205   264   690   688   363   203   Santander
517   245   494   622   326    89   635   482   366   361   823   560   164   448   353   Segovia
261   683  1018   408   848   547   215   547   796   930  1209   858   481   970   844   557   Sevilla
535   677   350   912   481   354   854   253   797   475   533   956   560   569   714   443   676   Valencia
616   135   566   619   254   188   734   581   256   334   895   459   113   376   250   110   594   542   Valladolid
1035  385   985   483   673   607  1026  1000   408   753  1314   153   439   795   607   546   811   961   447   Vigo
784   306   404   857    92   356   902   748   360    96   733   688   351   117   168   310   832   585   238   657   Vitoria/Gasteiz
749   489   150   969   175   321   807   542   600   169   479   889   534   263   408   349   868   332   421   840   259   Zaragoza
```

607 km   [Madrid]   [Vigo]

Lección once

¿Qué tal lo pasaste?

in = i

ras = re

Partner A should be looking at page 127.

Partner B: These pictures show where you went yesterday, how you travelled, what you did and what you bought. Study them.

Ask your partner the following questions to find out what he/she did yesterday: make a note of the replies you are given.

Then, answer the questions your partner will ask you about what you did yesterday.

Preguntas
¿Adónde fuiste ayer?
¿Cómo fuiste?
¿A qué hora saliste?
¿A qué hora llegaste?
¿Te bañaste en el mar?
¿Tomaste el sol en la playa?
¿Dónde comiste?
¿Compraste algo?

Lección doce

(1) Lo siento, pero no puedo

Partner A should be looking at page 137.

Partner B: Look at the pictures and decide what you are doing.

Then, ask your partner if he/she can help you. Listen to his/her excuses for not helping you and write down in English the various excuses given. Then, when your partner asks you if you can help, give excuses for not being able to do so.

Your basic question is: ¿Puedes ayudarme?

The beginning of each of your excuses is: Lo siento, pero no puedo. Estoy....

(2) ¿Qué ponen?

Partner A should be looking at page 138.

Partner B: Ask your partner what is on at the following cinemas, at what time the performance starts and how much the tickets are. You will need the following questions.

Then use this page from a Madrid entertainments guide to answer his/her questions.

	Los cines
¿Qué ponen en el cine...?	Lisboa
¿A qué hora empieza?	Magallanes
¿Cuánto valen las entradas?	Lope de Vega

BULEVAR. (Aforo: 1.180.) Alberto Aguilera, 56 (Centro). Metro Argüelles. Tel. 247 28 60. Lab. y dom., 17, 19,15 y 22 h. 350 ptas. Miércoles laborables, 225 ptas.
EL AMOR BRUJO (Tol.).

CALIFORNIA. (Aforo: 533.) Andrés Mellado, 47 (Moncloa). Metro Moncloa. Tel. 244 00 58. Lab. y dom., 16,30, 19,15 y 22,15 h. 300 ptas. Miércoles, excepto festivos y vísperas, 200 ptas.
PLENTY (13).

CALLAO. (Aforo: 1.147.) Plaza Callao, 3 (Centro). Tel. 222 58 01. Lab. y dom., 16,30, 19 y 22 h. 400 ptas.
DRAGON RAPIDE (Tol.).

CANCILLER. (Aforo: 1.216.) Alcalde López Casero, 15 (Ciudad Lineal). Metro Carmen. Tel. 404 34 71. Cont. 16,30 h. 250 ptas.
SIN ALIENTO.
TEEN WOLF (13).

CANDILEJAS. (Aforo: 1.486.) Plaza Luca de Tena, 7 (Arganzuela). Metro Palos de Moguer. Tel. 228 74 92. Cont. 17 h. Pases: 17, 18,55, 20,50 y 22,45 h. 325 ptas. Miércoles, excepto festivos y vísperas, 200 ptas. Laborables, excepto vísperas festivos, precio reducido mayores 65 años.
COBRA, EL BRAZO FUERTE DE LA LEY.

CAPITOL. (Aforo: 1.848.) Gran Vía, 41 (Centro). Metro Callao. Tel. 222 22 29. Cont. 16 h. 400 ptas. Miércoles, excepto festivos y vísperas, 200 ptas. Laborables, excepto vísperas festivos, precio reducido mayores 65 años.
TRES SOLTEROS Y UN BIBERON (Tol.).

CAPRI. (Aforo: 1.146.) Narciso Serra, 14 (Retiro). Metro Menéndez Pelayo. Tel. 252 35 28. Cont. 16,30 h. 225 a 275 ptas.
CRAKERS.
MIEDO AZUL (18).

CARLOS III. (Aforo: 1.390.) Goya, 5 (Salamanca). Metro Serrano. Tel. 276 36 81. Lab. y dom., 16,30, 19 y 22 h. 400 ptas.
DRAGON RAPIDE (Tol.).
Jueves 14, estreno: Horario sin determinar.
KARATE KID II.

CARLTON. (Aforo: 984.) Ayala, 95 (Salamanca). Metro Manuel Becerra. Tel. 401 41 27. Cont. 17 h. Pases: 17, 18,50, 20,40 y 22,25 h. 375 ptas. Miércoles, excepto festivos y vísperas, 200 ptas. Laborables, excepto vísperas festivos, precio reducido mayores 65 años.
MY CHAUFFEUR (13).

CARRETAS. (Aforo: 1.467.) Carretas, 13 (Centro). Metro Sol. Tel. 221 98 08. Cont. 10 h. 175 ptas.
Lunes a miércoles:
SEXUALIDAD PELIGROSA.
TIERNAS PRIMAS (18).
Jueves a domingo:
EN BUSCA DEL POLVO PERDIDO.
LA PARTE MAS APETITOSA DEL HOMBRE (S).

CARTAGO. (Aforo: 996.) Bravo Murillo, 28 (Chamberí). Metro Quevedo. Tel. 447 39 30. Cont. 17 h. 300 ptas. Miércoles, excepto festivos y vísperas, 200 ptas.
EL SECRETO DE JOEY (13).

CID CAMPEADOR. (Aforo: 974.) Príncipe de Vergara, 26 (Salamanca). Metro Velázquez. Tel. 276 21 61. Lab. y dom., 16,45, 19 y 22,15 h. 375 ptas.
EL SECRETO DE JOEY (13).

(3) ¿Dónde vamos a merendar?

Partner A should be looking at page 139.

Partner B: Ask your partner what things cost in his/her café, tell him/her what things cost in yours, and decide which is cheaper. You must ask:
¿Cuánto vale...?

Give as your answer:
Vale...

Lección trece

(1) A los diez años

Partner A should be looking at page 151.

Partner B: Use the information given here to answer your partner's questions. Ask your partner the following questions, write down his/her answers in English, and check that you have got everything correct.

Then, use the information given below to answer your partner's questions.

Then do the exercise again, but this time give genuine answers.

¿Dónde vivías cuando tenías diez años?

¿Qué te gustaba comer?

¿Cuál era tu asignatura favorita?

¿Cómo se llamaba tu mejor amigo?

¿Adónde ibas en tus ratos libres?

¿Tenías algún animal en casa?

¿Qué cogías para ir a la escuela?

(3) ¿Qué tiempo hacía ayer en España?

Partner A should be looking at page 152.

Partner B: Look at the map to answer your partner's questions.

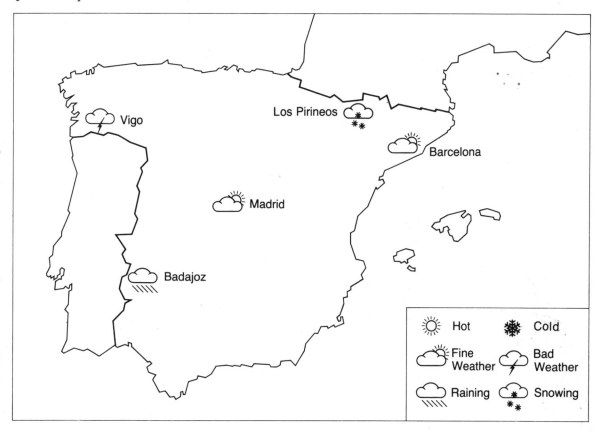

Lección catorce

(1) ¿Qué te pasa?

Partner A should be looking at page 161.

Partner B: Draw a matchstick sketch of your partner. Find out what your partner's symptoms are by asking, for example:

¿Te duele la cabeza?
¿Te duelen los pies? etc.

Mark your partner's symptoms on the sketch you have drawn.

Then, your partner will try to find out your symptoms: these are given on the right.

(2) En la consulta del médico

Partner A should be looking at page 162.

Partner B: Diagnose your partner's illness, by asking the following questions. Your partner will then ask you questions to diagnose your illness. Use the pictures below to answer his/her questions.

¿Adónde fuiste ayer?
¿Compraste algo allí?
¿Lavaste la fruta antes de comerla?
¿Comiste muchas manzanas?
¿Cómo te sientes ahora?

Index to grammar reference

Grammar reference

Verb tables

Here are three examples of regular verbs:

Infinitive	Present	Preterite	Imperfect	Imperative (tú; vosotros)	Imperative (usted; ustedes)
hablar (to speak)	hablo	hablé	hablaba	habla	hable (usted)
	hablas	hablaste	hablabas	hablad	hablen (ustedes)
	habla	habló	hablaba		
	hablamos	hablamos	hablábamos		
	habláis	hablasteis	hablabais		
	hablan	hablaron	hablaban		
comer (to eat)	como	comí	comía	come	coma (usted)
	comes	comiste	comías	comed	coman (ustedes)
	come	comió	comía		
	comemos	comimos	comíamos		
	coméis	comisteis	comíais		
	comen	comieron	comían		
vivir (to live)	vivo	viví	vivía	vive	viva (usted)
	vives	viviste	vivías	vivid	vivan (ustedes)
	vive	vivió	vivía		
	vivimos	vivimos	vivíamos		
	vivís	vivisteis	vivíais		
	viven	vivieron	vivían		

Irregular verbs — Present Tense

The following are verbs where the First Person Singular is irregular:

1 Verbs ending in '-ar'

dar	doy	I give
estar	estoy	I am

2 Verbs ending in '-er'

coger	cojo	I catch, take, pick up
conocer	conozco	I know, am familiar with
hacer	hago	I do, make
parecer	parezco	I seem, appear
poner	pongo	I put, place
saber	sé	I know (a fact, how to do)

tener	tengo	I have (also Radical-changing — see page 194)
traer	traigo	I bring
ver	veo	I see (watch television)

3 Verbs ending in '-ir'

decir	digo	I say, tell (also Radical-changing — see page 194)
salir	salgo	I leave, go out
venir	vengo	I come (also Radical-changing — see page 194)

Radical-changing verbs – Present Tense

These verbs have a change in the stem* in the Present Tense. However, the endings are the same as regular verbs. The changes are of three types:

1 –e– to –ie–
2 –o– or –u– to –ue–
3 –e– to –i– (Verbs ending in –ir only)

Here are examples of each of these three types:

1 Empezar (to begin)

empiezo	empezamos
empiezas	empezáis
empieza	empiezan

2 Dormir (to sleep)

duermo	dormimos
duermes	dormís
duerme	duermen

3 Servir (to serve)

sirvo	servimos
sirves	servís
sirve	sirven

All the Singular forms and the 3rd Person Plural of these verbs are affected. In the Word List these verbs are shown as follows: *Jugar [ue]* to play.

Two common Irregular Verbs

Ir (to go)		**ser (to be: permanent characteristics)**	
voy	vamos	soy	somos
vas	vais	eres	sois
va	van	es	son

Irregular verbs – Preterite Tense

Spelling changes in the First Person Singular

Verbs ending in '-ar'

Those which end -gar add a u to the stem* before the Preterite ending is added.
Llegúe a las nueve.   I arrived at 9 o'clock.

Those which end -car change the c to qu:
Saqué las entradas.   I got the tickets.

Those which end -zar change the z to a c:
Crucé la calle.   I crossed the street.

*The stem is the Infinitive of the verb without the -ar, -ir, -er endings.

Spelling changes in the Third Person Singular and Plural

The i found between two vowels changes to a y:

Leer (to read)
Leyó el libro.   He read the book.
Leyeron la carta.   They read the letter.

Creer (to believe)
This has a similar form to *leer*.

Spelling changes in the Third Person Singular and Plural of Radical-changing Verbs

All these verbs belong to the -ir group. Some change o to u and others e to i.

Morir (to die)
Murió.   He died.
Murieron.   They died.

Servir (to serve)
Sirvió vino.   He served wine.
Sirvieron cerveza.   They served beer.

Verbs with irregular stems

These verbs have irregular stems, but endings are common to them all. Notice that there are no accents.

Poner (to put)

puse	pusimos
pusiste	pusisteis
puso	pusieron

Verbs found in this book which have a similar form:

Infinitive	Preterite
andar (to walk)	anduve
decir (to say)	dije (3rd Person Plural is dijeron)
estar (to be)	estuve
hacer (to do, make)	hice (3rd Singular is hizo)
poder (to be able)	pude
poner (to put)	puse
saber (to know)	supe
querer (to want, wish)	quise
traer (to bring)	traje (3rd Person Plural is trajeron)
venir (to come)	vine

Ir, ser, dar

These have completely irregular Preterite forms and must be learned carefully.

Ir (to go)   **Ser (to be)**

fui	fuimos	fui	fuimos
fuiste	fuisteis	fuiste	fuisteis
fue	fueron	fue	fueron

These two verbs are identical in the Preterite form, but you can usually work out what is meant.

Ayer fui al mercado.   Yesterday I went to the market.

¿Qué fue eso?   What was that?

Dar (to give)

di	dimos
diste	disteis
dio	dieron

Irregular verbs – Imperfect Tense

Only three verbs are irregular in the Imperfect.

Ser (to be)

era	éramos
eras	erais
era	eran

Ir (to go)

iba	íbamos
ibas	ibais
iba	iban

Ver (to see)

veía	veíamos
veías	veíais
veía	veían

There is a stress mark on *éramos* and *íbamos* when the word does not start with a capital letter.

Reflexive verbs

These verbs have a Reflexive Pronoun before the verb as follows:

Lavarse (to wash oneself)

me lavo	I wash (myself)
te lavas	you wash (yourself)
se lava	he/she washes (himself/ herself)
nos lavamos	we wash (ourselves)
os laváis	you wash (yourselves)
se lavan	they wash (themselves)

In the Word List these verbs end in se.

The Third Person Singular and Plural of Reflexive Verbs are used to express the idea of 'is made, are made', etc.

El vino se hace con uvas.   Wine is made with grapes.

Se arreglan coches.   Cars are repaired.

The use of 'gustar'

You use the Third Person Singular or Plural of gustar with pronouns.

Me gusta el vino.	I like wine.
Te gusta el vino.	You like wine.
Le gusta el vino.	He/She likes wine.

If what you like is plural, you use gustan:

Me gustan las uvas.	I like grapes.
Te gustan las fresas.	You like strawberries.
Le gustan las peras.	He/She likes pears.

If what you like is an activity, you use gusta:

Me gusta bailar.   I like to dance.

The full range of tenses can be used:

¿Te gustó la película?   Did you like the film?
Me gustaría vivir en París.   I would like to live in Paris.

To say what you prefer, add más after the verb:

Me gusta más el fútbol.   I prefer football. (Football pleases me more.)

'Ser' and 'estar'

These are the two verbs translated 'to be' in English. You use these verbs as follows:

Ser

a when followed by a noun or pronoun:

Mi padre es profesor.   My father is a teacher.
Soy yo.   It's me.

b with adjectives when these describe something that is more or less permanent:

Mi hermano es muy inteligente.	My brother is very intelligent.

Estar

a to say where something or somebody is:

Bilbao está en el norte.	Bilbao is in the north.
Estoy en la cocina.	I'm in the kitchen.

b to express temporary conditions:

¿Cómo estás?	How are you?
Estoy bien.	I'm fine. (You may feel rotten tomorrow.)
Estoy enfermo.	I'm ill. (But I'll be OK soon.)

c to describe a condition which results from an action:

Murió.	He died.
Está muerto.	He is dead. (Condition he is now in after dying.)

Nouns

Gender

Nouns are either Masculine or Feminine. Generally speaking, nouns which end in *o* are Masculine — common exceptions: *la mano* (hand), *la radio* (radio) — and those which end in *a* are Feminine.

Articles

The Definite Article in English is 'the' and in Spanish there are four forms for this: *el, la, los, las.*

El vino	(Masculine Singular)
La cerveza	(Feminine Singular)
Los chicos	(Masculine Plural)
Las chicas	(Feminine Plural)

The Indefinite Article in English is 'a', 'an' and in Spanish there are four forms for this: *un, una, unos, unas.*

Un perro	(Masculine Singular)
Una cerveza	(Feminine Singular)
Unos hombres	(Masculine Plural)
Unas mujeres	(Feminine Plural)

The Plural forms, *unos* and *unas* are not used much. They mean 'some'.

Plurals

To make a noun plural you add *s* to a vowel and *es* to a consonant.

El libro	*Los libros*
El profesor	*Los profesores*

Words borrowed from English just add *s*:

El póster	*Los pósters*

Adjectives

Endings

Adjectives have different endings depending on the noun they are describing. An adjective ending in *o* (like *rojo*, for example) has four forms:

El libro es rojo.	*Los libros son rojos.*
La falda es roja.	*Las faldas son rojas.*

Those which end in anything else have two forms, Singular and Plural:

El libro es grande.	*Los libros son grandes.*
La casa es grande.	*Las casas son grandes.*

Adjectives of nationality

Those that end in *o* behave like *rojo* above.
Those that end in a consonant have four forms:

El chico es inglés.	*Los chicos son ingleses.*
La chica es inglesa.	*Los chicas son inglesas.*

To change the meaning of adjectives you use the word in bold:

Es tonto.	He's stupid.
*Es **bastante** tonto.*	He's rather stupid.
*Es **muy** tonto.*	He's very stupid.
*Es **demasiado** tonto.*	He's too stupid.
*Es **algo** tonto.*	He's a bit stupid.
*Es **tontísimo**.*	He's very, very stupid.

Position of Adjectives

Adjectives are usually placed after the noun.

Quiero el libro verde.   I want the green book.

Comparisons

To compare one thing with another, you use *más...que*:

Un perro es más grande que un ratón.   A dog is bigger than a mouse.

To say something is better, you use *mejor*:

El zumo de fruta es mejor que la coca cola.   Fruit juice is better than Coca Cola.

Demonstrative adjectives

This
'This' has four forms in Spanish:

Este libro es muy bueno.	This book is very good.
Esta revista es muy interesante.	This magazine is very interesting.
Estos chicos son mis hermanos.	These boys are my brothers.
Estas uvas son muy caras.	These grapes are very dear.

That
'That' also has four forms:

Ese chico se llama Pedro.	That boy is called Peter.
Esa casa es muy grande.	That house is very big.
Esos vestidos son muy bonitos.	Those dresses are very nice.
Esas chicas son mis hermanas.	Those girls are my sisters.

Possessive adjectives

This is how you say what belongs to you or to someone else.

My	Your (To a friend)	His, her , your* their *(older person or stranger)
mi amigo	*tu amigo*	*su amigo*
mi amiga	*tu amiga*	*su amiga*
mis padres	*tus padres*	*sus padres*

There are only two forms, a Singular and a Plural.

Our	Your (To friends)
nuestro profesor	*vuestro profesor*
nuestra amiga	*vuestra amiga*
nuestros padres	*vuestros padres*
nuestras amigas	*vuestras amigas*

Pronouns

These usually replace nouns in the sentence.

Subject Pronouns

yo	I
tú	you (to a friend, member of family, child, animal)
él	he
ella	she
usted	you (to a stranger, person in authority, older person)
nosotros/nosotras	we
vosotros/vosotras	you (to friends, family, etc.)
ellos	they (male)
ellas	they (female)
ustedes	you

Only *usted* and *ustedes* are regularly used; the others are only really used to give emphasis or clarity.

Yo hablo inglés pero tú hablas español.   **I** speak English but **you** speak Spanish.

Direct Object Pronouns

These replace nouns which are the Direct Object of the verb.

*Cojo la manzana y **la** como.*   I pick up the apple and eat **it**.

The pronouns are as follows:

me	*Me escucha.*	He listens to me.
te	*Te veo.*	I see you.
lo	*Lo quiero.*	I want it. (Masculine Singular)

la	La quiero.	I want it. (Feminine Singular)
le	Le veo.	I see him.
la	La veo.	I see her.
le	Le veo.	I see you. (You usted and Masculine)
la	La veo.	I see you. (You usted and Feminine)
nos	Nos ven.	They see us.
os	Os veo.	I see you.
los	Los compro.	I buy them. (Masculine Plural)
las	Las como.	I eat them. (Feminine Plural)
las	Las veo.	I see them. (Feminine Plural – people)
les	Les conozco.	I know them. (Masculine Plural – people)
les	Les veo.	I see you. (Masculine Plural – ustedes – you)
las	Las veo.	I see you. (Feminine Plural – ustedes – you)

Pronouns are usually put before the verb, but come on the end of an order.

| ¡Come la sopa! | Eat the soup! |
| ¡Cómela! | Eat it! |

They can be placed on the end of the Infinitive:

| ¿El trabajo? Voy a hacerlo ahora. | The work? I'm going to do it now. |

They can also be placed at the end of the Present Participle:

| ¿El trabajo? Estoy haciéndolo. | The work? I'm doing it. |

Indirect Object Pronouns

These replace people that are the Indirect Object of the verb.

| Coge la manzana y **me** la da. | He picks up the apple and gives it to me. |

They are the same as the Direct Object Pronouns except for the Third Person, when only le is used.

| Le doy dinero. | I give money to him. (to her, to you) |
| Les doy dinero. | I give money to them. (to you) |

Demonstrative Pronouns

This is how you say 'this one', 'that one', etc. Use the same words as for 'This' and 'That' and miss out the noun. Put an accent where the stress normally falls.

| ¿Quieres este libro o ese libro? | Do you want this book or that book? |
| ¿Quieres éste o ése? | Do you want this one or that one? |

Negatives

To say you do not do something, you put no before the verb.

| Hablo francés. | I speak French. |
| No hablo francés. | I don't speak French. |

Other negatives are as follows:

Nunca (never)

| ¿Fumas? No fumo **nunca.** | Do you smoke? I never smoke. |

Nada (nothing)

| ¿Qué tienes en la mano? No tengo **nada.** | What have you got in your hand? I've got nothing. |

Ordinal numbers: 1st – 10th

Only 1st – 10th are used regularly and are as follows:

primero	first	sexto	sixth
segundo	second	séptimo	seventh
tercero	third	octavo	eighth
cuarto	fourth	noveno	ninth
quinto	fifth	décimo	tenth

Primero and tercero shorten to primer and tercer before a Masculine Singular noun.

These numbers are used:

a in a series

| La segunda calle a la derecha. | The second street on the right. |

b for titles

| Isabel Segunda | Elizabeth the Second. |

c for the 1st of the month (but only the 1st)

| El primero de abril. | April 1st. (El uno de abril can also be used.) |
| El tres de enero. | January 3rd. |

Vocabulary list

a   at to
abajo   down
abierto   open
abrazo(m)   embrace
abuela(f)   grandmother
aburrido   boring
academia(f)   academy
accidente(m)   accident
aceite(m)   oil
acercarse   to approach
acordarse [ue]   to remember
actor(m)   actor
acuerdo(m)   agreement
   de acuerdo   O.K.
adiós   goodbye
¿adónde?   where...to?
África(f)   Africa
agua(f)   water
ahí   there
ahora   now
aire(m)   air
alegrarse   to be glad
algo   something
   ¿algo más?   anything else?
algodón(m)   cotton
alguno   some
alto   tall
alumno(m)   pupil
allí   there
amarillo   yellow
amiga(f)   friend
amigo(m)   friend
ancho   wide, broad
andar   to walk, go (of machines)
animal(m)   animal
anoche   last night
antes (de)   before
antiguo   old, ancient
antipático   unpleasant
año(m)   year
apetecer   to fancy
aprender   to learn
aquí   here
   por aquí   around here
árbol(m)   tree
Argentina(f)   Argentine
argentino   Argentinian
armario(m)   wardrobe, cupboard

arquitecto(m)   architect
arreglar   to fix, repair
arriba   up, upstairs
arte(m)   art
artículo(m)   article
así   so, thus
asignatura(f)   school subject
atletismo(m)   athletics
autobús(m)   bus
auxiliar   auxiliary
avenida(f)   avenue
ayer   yesterday
ayudar   to help
Ayuntamiento(m)   Town Hall
azúcar(m)   sugar
azul   blue

bailar   to dance
bajar   to go down
bajo   short, small
baloncesto(m)   basketball
bañarse   to bathe
banco(m)   bank
barato   cheap
barco(m)   boat
barra(f)   loaf of bread
barrio(m)   district, part of town
bastante   fairly, rather
bebé(m)   baby
beber   to drink
bebida(f)   drink
béisbol(m)   baseball
bicicleta(f)   bike
bien   well
bienvenido   welcome
biología(f)   biology
bisutería(f)   jeweller's
blanco   white
blusa(f)   blouse
bomba(f)   bomb, pump
   pasarlo 'bomba'   to have a great time
bonito   nice, pleasant
botella(f)   bottle
brazo(m)   arm
bueno   good
butaca(f)   armchair
buzón(m)   post box

cabeza(f) head
café(m) coffee, café
  café solo black coffee
  café con leche white coffee
cafetería(f) cafeteria
caja(f) box, till, cash-desk
calidad(f) quality
calor(m) heat
calle(f) street
cama(f) bed
camarero(m) waiter
cambio(m) change
camisa(f) shirt
campo(m) field, countryside
cansado tired
cantante(m/f) singer
capital(f) capital
capítulo(m) chapter (in book)
caramelo(m) sweet
cariñoso affectionate
caro dear, expensive
carta(f) letter
cartero(m) postman
casa(f) house
casi almost
catedral(f) cathedral
cena(f) dinner
centímetro(m) centimetre
centro(m) centre
cerca (de) near to
cero(m) zero
cerrar [ie] to close, shut
cerveza(f) beer
ciencia(f) science
cigarrillo(m) cigarette
cine(m) cinema
ciudad(f) town, city
claro clear, clearly
clase(f) class
clásico classical
club(m) club
  club de jóvenes youth club
cobrar to earn, get paid
coca cola(f) coca cola
cocina(f) kitchen
cocinar to cook
cocodrilo(m) crocodile
coche(m) car
coger to catch, pick up
colección(f) collection
colegio(m) secondary school
colocar to place, put

color(m) colour
collar(m) necklace
comedia(f) play (in theatre)
comedor(m) dining-room
comer to eat, have lunch
comercial commercial
comida(f) food, meal, lunch
como as, how like
¿ cómo? how?
cómodo comfortable
compañero(m) companion
compra(f) shopping
comprar to buy
comprender to understand
con with
conmigo with me
conocer to know, be familiar with
contar [ue] to tell, relate
contento happy, pleased
contestar to answer, reply
contigo with you
continuar to continue
contra against
copo(m) flake
Correos Post Office
cortar to cut
corte(m) dressmaking
corto short
cosa(f) thing
costa(f) coast
creer to think, believe
crema(f) cream
críquet(m) cricket
cuadro(m) picture
¿ cuál? which, which one?
cuando when
¿ cuánto? how much?
¿ cuántos? how many?
cuarto(m) quarter
cuarto(m) room
  cuarto de baño bathroom
  cuarto de estar sitting-room
cuchara(f) spoon
cuchillo(m) knife
cuello(m) neck

chaqueta(f) jacket
chica(f) girl
chico(m) boy
chocolate(m) chocolate
churro(m) batter fritter

dar   to give
  dar un paseo   to go for a walk
  darse cuenta   to realise
debajo (de)   underneath
deber(m)   duty
  deberes(m.pl.)   homework
decidir   to decide
decir [i]   to say, tell
dejar   to leave, let, allow
dentista(m/f)   dentist
dentro (de)   inside, within
depender   to depend
dependienta(f)   shop assistant (female)
dependiente(m)   shop assistant (male)
deporte(m)   sport
deprisa   quickly, fast
derecho   right
  a la derecha   on the right
desayuno(m)   breakfast
descripción(f)   description
desde   from
desear   to wish, want
despacio   slowly
despacho(m)   office
después (de)   after
detrás (de)   behind
¿de dónde?   where from?
¿de veras?   really?
día(m)   day
  todos los días   every day
diario   daily
diarrea(f)   diarrhoea
dibujo(m)   sketch
  dibujos animados   cartoon
diccionario(m)   dictionary
diferente   different
difícil   difficult
dinero(m)   money
director(m)   headteacher, manager
disco(m)   record
discoteca(f)   discotheque
distancia(f)   distance
divertido   amusing, funny
doctor(m)   doctor
doler [ue]   to hurt
dolor(m)   pain
¿dónde?   where?
donut(m)   doughnut
dormir [ue]   to sleep
dormitorio(m)   bedroom
durante   during
durar   to last
duro(m)   5—peseta coin

educación(f)   education
  educación física   P.E.
ella   she her
empezar [ie]   to begin
encantador   charming
enemigo(m)   enemy
enfermo   ill
enfrente [de]   opposite
enorme   enormous
ensaimada(f)   type of round bun
entonces   then
entrada(f)   entrance, ticket
entrar   to go in, enter
entre   between
entrevista(f)   interview
envolver [ue]   to wrap up
equipo(m)   team
eres (from ser)   you are
escaparate(m)   shop window
escocés   Scottish
escribir   to write
escuchar   to listen to
escuela(f)   primary school
eso es   that's so
España(f)   Spain
español   Spanish
espectáculo(m)   entertainment
esperar   to wait for, hope
esquiar   to ski
esquina(f)   corner (of street)
estación   station, season
estación de
  autobuses(f)   bus station
estación de
  servicio(f)   service station
Estados Unidos (m.pl.)   U.S.A.
ésta   this one
estar   to be (position)
este(m)   east
este   this
éste   this one
esto   this
estómago(m)   stomach
estudiante(m/f)   student
estudiar   to study
estudio(m)   study
estupendo   great, stupendous
estúpido   stupid
Europa   Europe
exactamente   exactly
examen(m)   examination
excelente   excellent
excesivo   excessive
excursión(f)   outing, excursion

fácil   easy
falda(f)   skirt
familia(f)   family
farmacia(f)   chemist's
fatal   fatal, horrible
favor(m)   favour
  por favor   please
favorito   favourite
fenomenal   great, tremendous
fiebre(f)   fever
fin(m)   end
final(m)   end
física(f)   physics
flor(f)   flower
folklórico   folk
footing(m)   jogging
fotografía(f)   photograph
fotógrafo(m)   photographer
francamente   frankly
francés   French
Francia(f)   France
fresa(f)   strawberry
fresco   fresh
frío(m)   cold
frito   fried
fruta(f)   fruit
frutería(f)   fruit-shop
fuerte   strong
fumar   to smoke
fútbol(m)   football

galés   Welsh
ganar   to win, earn
garaje(m)   garage
gas(m)   gas
gaseosa(f)   fizzy drink
gasolina(f)   petrol
gato(m)   cat
gaucho(m)   S. American cowboy
general   general
  por lo general   generally
geografía(f)   geography
gol(m)   goal
gordo   fat
gracias   thank you
grande   big
grave   grave, serious
gris   grey
grupo(m)   group
guapo   pretty, handsome
guardar   to keep, store
guau   woof, woof!

guía(m/f)   guide, guide-book
gustar   to please (like)
gusto(m)   pleasure
  mucho gusto   pleased to meet you

habitación(m)   room
hablar   to speak, talk
hacer   to do, make
hambre(f)   hunger
hamburguesa(f)   hamburger
hámster(m)   hamster
hasta   until
  hasta luego   see you later
hay   there is, there are
hermana(f)   sister
hermano(m)   brother
hermoso   beautiful
hierba(f)   grass
hija(f)   daughter
hijo(m)   son
historia(f)   history
histórico   historical
hola   hello
hombre(m)   man
hora(f)   hour, time
horchata(f)   nutty drink
horrible   horrible
horror(m)   horror
hospital(m)   hospital
hotel(m)   hotel
hoy   today
  hoy en día   nowadays

idea(f)   idea
idioma(m)   language
iglesia(f)   church
importante   important
impresionante   impressive
India(f)   India
industrial   industrial
infantil   infantile
informática(f)   computer studies
Inglaterra(f)   England
inglés   English
Instituto(m)   secondary school
inteligente   intelligent
interés(m)   interest
interesante   interesting
internacional   international
invierno(m)   winter
invitar   to invite

ir   to go
  ir de compras   to go shopping
izquierda(f)   left
  a la izquierda   on the left

jamón(m)   ham
jardín(m)   garden
jaula(f)   cage
jersey(m)   jersey
joven(m/f)   young
joyería(f)   jeweller's
jugar [ue]   to play (sports)

kilo(m)   kilo
kilómetro(m)   kilometre

laboratorio(m)   laboratory
lado(m)   side
  al lado de   beside
lago(m)   lake
lámpara(f)   lamp
lana(f)   wool
largo   long
lástima(f)   shame, pity
lavar   to wash
lección(f)   lesson
lectura(f)   reading
leche(f)   milk
leer   to read
lejos (de)   far from
levantarse   to get up
ley(f)   law
libra(f)   pound (weight, money)
libre   free
librería(f)   bookshop
libro(m)   book
limón(m)   lemon
líquido(m)   liquid
lista(f)   list
litro(m)   litre
loco   mad, crazy
luego   then

llamarse   to be called
llegar   to arrive
llover [ue]   to rain

macizo   massive, solid
madre(f)   mother
magnífico   magnificent
maíz(m)   maize
mal   badly
malo   bad

mamá(f)   Mum
manchego   from la Mancha
mandar   to send
manga(f)   sleeve
mano(f)   hand
mantequilla(f)   butter
manzana(f)   apple
mañana(f)   morning
  por la mañana   in the morning
mañana   tomorrow
mar(m)   sea
marrón   brown
más   more
matemáticas(f.pl.)   mathematics
mayor   bigger, elder
medicina(f)   medicine
médico(m)   doctor
medida(f)   size, measure
medio   half
mediterráneo   mediterranean
mejillón(m)   mussel
mejor   better
memoria(f)   memory
menor   younger, smaller
menos   less
mentiroso   lying, deceitful
mercado(m)   market
merienda(f)   snack, picnic
merluza(f)   hake
mermelada(f)   jam
mes(m)   month
mesa(f)   table
metro(m)   metre
mi   my
mí   me
miau   miaow
mil(m)   a thousand
mineral   mineral
minuto(m)   minute
mío   mine
mirar   to look at
mismo   same, self
moderno   modern
mojar   to wet, dampen, 'dunk'
momento(m)   moment
monasterio(m)   monastery
morir [ue]   to die
mostrar [ue]   to show
motocicleta(f)   motorbike
mucho   much, a lot
muerto   dead
mujer(f)   woman

mundo(m)   world
  todo el mundo   everybody
museo(m)   museum
música(f)   music
muy   very

nacer   to be born
nacional   national
nada   nothing
nadar   to swim
naranja(f)   orange
naranjada(f)   orangeade
nata(f)   cream (from milk)
naturalmente   naturally
necesario   necessary
necesitar   to need
negro   black
nevar [ie]   to snow
nevera(f)   refrigerator
ni...ni...   neither...nor...
ninguno   none, not any
niño(m)   little boy
nombre(m)   name
normal   normal
normalmente   normally
norte(m)   north
norteamericano   North American
nota(f)   note, mark (at school)
novela(f)   novel
nuestro   our
nuevo   new
número(m)   number
nunca   never

o   or
ocupado   busy
oeste(m)   west
oficina(f)   office
ojo(m)   eye
olvidar   to forget
ordenador(m)   computer
oro(m)   gold
oscuro   dark (of colour)
otoño(m)   autumn
otro   other, another
oveja(f)   sheep
oyente(m/f)   listener

padre(m)   father
  padres (m.pl.)   parents
pagar   to pay
página(f)   page

pálido   pale
pan(m)   bread
panadería(f)   baker
panadero(m)   bread roll
panecillo(m)   bread roll
papá(m)   Dad
paquete(m)   packet
para   for, destined for
parecer   to seem, appear
pared(f)   wall
pariente(m/f)   relative, relation
parking(m)   car park
parque(m)   park
pasado   last, past
pasar   to happen, occur, spend (of time)
pasatiempo(m)   pastime
paseo(m)   walk
  dar un paseo   to go for a walk
pastel(m)   cake
pastilla(f)   tablet, pill
patata(f)   potato
  patatas fritas   chips, crisps
patio(m)   yard, patio
pecera(f)   fish-bowl
película(f)   film
pelo(m)   hair
pendiente(m)   ear-ring
pensar [ie]   to think
pequeño   small, little
perfectamente   perfectly
periódico(m)   newspaper
pero   but
perro(m)   dog
persona(f)   person
pesar   to weigh
pescado(m)   fish
peseta(f)   peseta
pez(m)   fish (in water)
pie(m)   foot
  a pie   on foot
pierna(f)   leg
piscina(f)   swimming-pool
piso(m)   floor, storey, flat
placer(m)   pleasure
plan(m)   plan
planta(f)   floor (of building)
plata(f)   silver
plátano(m)   banana
plato(m)   dish, course (of meal)
playa(f)   beach
plaza(f)   square
pobre   poor

poco   little, a little
poder [ue]   to be able, can
poesía(f)   poetry
policía(f)   police
policía(m)   policeman
políester(m)   polyester (man-made fibre)
poner   to put, place
ponerse   to put on (clothing)
popular   popular
por eso   therefore
porque   because
¿por qué?   why?
portero(m)   porter
póster(m)   poster
postre(m)   dessert, pudding
pozo(m)   well (for water)
práctica(f)   practice
practicar   to play (games)
pregunta(f)   question
preguntar   to ask •
preocupado   worried
preocuparse   to worry
preparar   to prepare
presentar   to introduce (people to each other)
primero   first
probador(m)   fitting-room
probar [ue]   to try, taste
probarse [ue]   to try on (clothes)
problema(m)   problem
profesor(m)   teacher
profesora(f)   teacher
programa(m)   programme
prohibido   forbidden
pronto   soon, quickly
propio   own
pueblo(m)   village
puerta(f)   door
pues   then, well
puesto(m)   stall (in market)
punto(m)   point
  en punto   sharp (of time)

que   who, which, etc.
¿qué?   what? which?
quedarse   to stay, remain
quemaduras del sol (f.pl.)   sunburn
querer [ie]   to wish, want, love
queso(m)   cheese
¿qué tal?   how are you?
¿quién?   who?
química(f)   chemistry

quiosco(m)   kiosk
quizás   perhaps

ración(f)   portion
radio(f)   radio
raro   odd, curious
rato(m)   a while, space of time
ratos libres(m.pl.)   free time
ratón(m)   mouse
receta(f)   recipe
recomendar [ie]   to recommend
recto   straight ahead
recuerdo(m)   souvenir, memory
regalo(m)   gift, present
región(f)   region
regular   O.K., not bad
revista(f)   magazine
reina(f)   queen
remedio(m)   remedy
resfriado(m)   cold (illness)
restaurante(m)   restaurant
revista(f)   magazine
rey(m)   king
rincón(m)   corner (of room)
río(m)   river
rojo   red
romano   Roman
ropa(f)   clothing
rugby(m)   rugby
ruina(f)   ruin

saber   to know, know how to
sacar   to get out, take, obtain
salir   to go out, leave
salmón (m)   salmon
salón (m)   sitting-room
salsa(f)   sauce
salud(f)   health
salvo   safe
sano   healthy
secretaria(f)   secretary
sed(f)   thirst
seda(f)   silk
seguida
  en seguida   immediately
seguir [i]   to follow, carry on
segundo   second
seguro   sure, certain
sello(m)   postage stamp
semana(f)   week
sentarse [ie]   to sit down
sentirse [ie]   to feel

señor (m) Mr, gentleman
señora(f) Mrs, lady
señorita(f) Miss, young lady
séptimo seventh
ser to be
serio serious
 en serio seriously
serpiente(f) snake
serrano from the mountains
servir [i] to serve
sesión(f) performance
si if
sí yes
siempre always
siglo(m) century
silla(f) chair
simpático nice, pleasant
sin without
sino but (after negative)
sitio(m) place, room
sobre on, above
 sobre todo above all
socorro(m) help
sol(m) sun
sólo only
sortija(f) ring
soy (from ser) I am
suerte(f) good luck
suéter(m) sweater
suizo(m) sugared bun
supermercado(m) supermarket
sur(m) south

talla(f) size (for clothing)
también also
tanto so, so much, so many
taquilla(f) ticket office
tardar to take (of time)
tarde(f) afternoon, evening
 por la tarde in the afternoon
tarde late
tarjeta postal(f) postcard
tarta(f) tart
taza(f) cup
té(m) tea
teatro(m) theatre
teléfono(m) telephone
televisión(f) television
tener to have
 tener que to have to
tenis(m) tennis
ti you

tiempo(m) weather, time
tienda(f) shop
tocadiscos(m) record player
todo all
tomar to take, have (food & drink)
 tomar el sol to sunbathe
tonto foolish, stupid
torcer [ue] to turn, twist
torre(f) tower
tos(f) cough
total(m) total
totalmente totally
trabajar work
trabajo(m) work
 trabajos manuales (m.pl.) craft
traer to bring
transeúnte(m/f) passerby
tren(m) train
trompa(f) trunk (of animal)
tú you
tu your
tubo(m) tube
turismo(m) tourism
turista(m/f) tourist

último last
único only (as only child)
universidad(f) university
urgencia(f) urgency
útil useful
uva(f) grape

vacaciones(f.pl.) holidays
vago lazy, idle
valenciano from Valencia
valer to cost, be worth
vale O.K.
vendedor(m) salesman
vender to sell
venir [ie] to come
ventana(f) window
ver to see
verano(m) summer
verdad(f) truth, true
verde green
vestido(m) dress
vez(f) time, occasion
 a veces at times
vida(f) life
viejo old
vino(m) wine
visita(f) visit

visitar to visit
vivir to live
volver [ue] to return
vuelta(f) change (money)
vuestro your

y (e) and

ya now, already
yo I

zoo(m) zoo
zumo(m) juice